WANTED

WANTED

by
Yaacov Eliav

Translated and Adapted from the Hebrew
by Mordecai Schreiber

SHENGOLD PUBLISHERS, INC.
New York

To my wife Hannah
and our children

ISBN 0-88400-107-5
Library of Congress Catalog Card Number: 84-50676
Copyright © 1984 by Yaacov Eliav

Published by Shengold Publishers, Inc.
New York, N.Y.

Printed in the United States of America

Contents

Introduction

This book is the story of my fight to free my homeland from a foreign occupier. My friends and I in the Land of Israel fought the British Empire not only for national liberation, but also for physical survival. We fought in the thirties, when millions of our brothers and sisters in Europe could have been saved from Nazi barbarism, had the British allowed them to enter their historical homeland. We fought in the forties, when those millions were being murdered, so that the surviving remnants could have a home to go to.

Throughout the ages our people have known two kinds of heroes. The first kind, exemplified by the Maccabees, chose active resistance against the foreign occupier. The second kind, dauntless souls like Hannah and her seven sons, chose martyrdom instead of apostasy. We Jews have survived because of both the active and the passive heroes. Yet who can deny the fact that in our time we would have been overrun by our enemies if that ancient spirit of the Maccabees had not been rekindled in us? The courage of martyrs is sacred. But the courage of active fighters has brought us national redemption.

All nations glorify their liberators. All admire those who, like William Tell, or Joan of Arc, or George Washington, brought freedom to their people. We who fought the British in order to bring about Israel's independence had written on our banner:

> There is no sacrifice except blood,
> The price of freedom is life.
> There is no national victory, except at the price of one's life.

7

We live in a cynical world. Today's United Nations, by majority vote, calls freedom fighters "racists," while terrorists are referred to by that same institution as "freedom fighters." Before I begin my own story, I find it necessary to answer a question asked by many around the world today: what is the difference between a national liberation movement and a terrorist organization?

In order to answer this question, one should examine both the aims and the methods of such groups. The aim of a genuine national liberation movement is to free its people from oppression and/or its historical homeland from foreign occupation, by fighting the armed and security forces as well as the administration of the oppressor and/or foreign occupier. This was precisely what my friends and I did in our struggle against the British Empire which led to the birth of the State of Israel in 1948.

What about an organization such as the PLO? Does the PLO also qualify as a national liberation movement?

The charter of the organization, known as the "Palestine National Covenant," stipulates in Article 1:

> Palestine is the homeland of the Palestinian Arab people and an integral part of the great Arab homeland. The people of Palestine are part of the Arab nation.

The aim of the PLO, then, is not to establish a national home for a portion of the "Arab nation" known as the Palestinian Arab people in a country known today as Israel, but to expand the existing "great Arab homeland," which already consists of 22 sovereign states, in order to accommodate those Palestinian Arabs who for some odd reason do not seem to be able to find a place to settle in the vast expanses of the existing "great Arab homeland."

The PLO claims my homeland, Israel, as its land. What does it wish to do with Israel's Jewish population of over 3.5 million? Article 6 of the above document stipulates that any Jew whose family did not live in Palestine prior to the "Zionist invasion" which began in 1917 must leave. Since over 90 percent of the Jews arrived after 1917, that means in effect that the PLO is pursuing Hitler's Nuremberg Laws. In other words, after committing a politicide against the State of Israel, the PLO would proceed to commit a genocide against the Jews of Israel, many of whom are survivors of a previous genocide.

A genuine national liberation movement does not commit genocides. It seeks to free people, not to destroy them.

The PLO is not a national liberation movement not only because of its aims but also because of its methods, which all self-respecting freedom fighters would reject as cowardly and dishonorable.

I recall the words of British commanding officers in my homeland who, after many battles between them and the Jewish fighting underground, would comment, "It was a fair battle." During nearly ten years of combat against a mighty power, which we had to engage in battle in order to save our people from the danger of utter destruction, no British child was ever hurt, no British woman ever injured, no citizen of Great Britain ever attacked. We only fought as armed men against armed men.

Our rule was never to hurt a civilian, be he or she Jewish, Arab or British.

Not so the PLO. The main target of their attacks has been the civilian population. During all these years they have never once attacked a military installation, only civilians. They have a long record of brutally killing children. They smashed the head of a four-year-old girl in Nahariya with a rifle butt. They blew up a baby girl in Petah Tikva. They machine-gunned 8 children in Kiriat Shmona. They killed 18 children in a school in Maalot. Only to mention a few examples. The national Hebrew poet, Bialik, wrote: "Satan himself has not invented a way to avenge the blood of a little child." We Israelis do not wish, do not know how to avenge the blood of our children. Or, for that matter, the blood of our athletes slain at the Munich Olympics. Or innocent civilians, Jews and Gentiles, mowed down at Lod Airport. Or those killed on a Jerusalem street or elsewhere, at the hands of PLO "freedom fighters."

I do not seek revenge. I only seek security, and peace. But there will never be peace or security until we set the record straight. Until we learn to distinguish between genuine underground fighters whose aims are historically justified and whose struggle is confined to legitimate enemy objectives, and those who distort historical fact for their own ends and destroy innocent lives in the name of "freedom" and "liberation" which, clearly, are empty slogans on their lips.

The PLO today, instead of seeking to solve the problems of Palestinian Arab refugees in Lebanon, Jordan and elsewhere, has become the leader of an international terrorist movement funded, trained and equipped by the Soviet Union in order to destabilize Western democracies and facilitate takeovers by Moscow-controlled regimes. It is both instructive and ironic, that while my friends and I fought against a world power in order to gain national independence, the PLO has sold out to a world power which subjugates rather than liberates nations. Thus, instead of fighting for the "Arab nation," the PLO now serves the interests of Soviet Marxism.

Finally, the question is still being asked: wouldn't the British have left my country in 1948 without the armed struggle of the Jewish underground? The answer has been given by a senior official of the British Mandate: "The underground did more than anyone else to force us to leave the Land of Israel."

My fondest hope is that my book will be used as a textbook by national liberation undergrounds everywhere in their struggle for freedom.

Y.E.

ONE

The Road to the Underground

In the summer of 1929, as I was about to turn twelve, I remember standing at the door of my parents' house in Tel Aviv early one morning when suddenly a truck stopped across the street and unloaded a group of women and children. The women were crying and wailing for their loved ones who had been brutally massacred in Hebron, the biblical town south of Jerusalem.

One of the refugees who had arrived in our neighborhood, Mrs. Lazarowsky, was a friend of my parents. They invited her to stay in our small apartment. She was broken in body and spirit. For days she did not stop talking about the murder of her brothers by the Arabs during the massacre of the Jews of Hebron. I sat in my corner and her words cut through me like a knife. I was consumed with the fire of revenge.

I recall the following parts of Mrs. Lazarowsky's story:

"The massacre began on the Sabbath, August 24, 1929. As the Arab rioters gathered in the street, brandishing their weapons, the Jewish community rushed a delegation to the British chief of police in Hebron, to alert him of what was about to occur. The chief of police did not seem too concerned. He dismissed the group with some perfunctory remark, and ordered his men to put away their guns and only carry clubs. This was the signal for the Arabs to go into action. Their leader, Sheikh Talib Marqa, shouted at the crowd: 'Muslims! Kill the Jews! Drink their blood! Today is the day of Islam, as commanded by the Prophet! Follow me! Kill the Jews! Beautiful Jewish maidens are waiting for you!' Sheikh Talib inflamed the crowd with his exhortations. Before long the frenzied mob was heard boasting of the slaughter of entire families and, waving swords, axes and iron bars, the murderous mass proceeded to storm the gates of the Slonim house, where we had all taken refuge.

"We thought the house was safe, but the murderers broke in through a door in the roof. Two yeshiva students were killed on the stairs. The front door was shattered. Slonim fired his pistol. A heavy iron bar landed on his head. The pistol dropped out of his hand, and he collapsed in a pool of blood. Deathly silence fell on the house. The only sound we heard was the swishing of swords and the hacking of axes, landing on men, women and children. My brother Israel was stabbed and fell dead. Now Israel Kaplansky was pierced through after he had been shot. The old venerable Rabbi Abraham Jacob Orlinsky was writhing on the floor, wrapped in his prayer shawl, while his wife lay next to him, dying.

"Through the window," continued Mrs. Lazarowsky, "I could see British policemen and an officer riding by. At that moment the door opened and the two Heikal boys ran outside to ask the British for help. Suddenly the two found themselves cut off from the house and surrounded by the wild mob. Israel Heikal was encircled by five policemen on horseback when the murderers rushed at him from all sides and hurled their daggers at him. He fought them off bravely with his fists as long as he could, until he collapsed on the ground bathing in blood, at the feet of his police 'protectors.' His brother clung desperately to the officer's horse, as the mob began to sever his limbs one by one with their knives, mocking, 'Does it hurt, Jew?'

"All this time the beasts were continuing their work inside the house. They split open the stomach of Rabbi Zwi Drabkin and disemboweled him until he died. They stabbed Rabbi Zalman Ben-Gerson with daggers. They killed seven more yeshiva students and an old man named Gutlavsky, and then they killed my second brother, Bezalel, along with his five-year-old daughter. In this house alone, the Slonim house, they killed 24 people and wounded 13. Many Hebron Arabs took part in the carnage, including merchants and respectable citizens who were friends of Slonim. After they had their fill of blood, they plundered everything in sight and departed. Behind them they left death and desolation."

Mrs. Lazarowsky escaped death by hiding under a pile of dead bodies. After the assassins were gone she crawled out of her hiding place and scenes of horror unfolded before her eyes. The skull of one of the dead was shattered and the brain had spilled out. An old Jew died after he was castrated. The Jewish baker's head had been burned on a lighted primus-stove and his stomach slashed open with a dagger. Rabbi Grudzinski, tortured and ridiculed, had his left eye gouged out and his brain smashed. A young woman who had finished teachers' college in Jerusalem and came home for vacation was raped in front of her parents by thirteen thugs who then killed her father and left her mother and sister badly wounded. Another young woman was stripped naked and only death saved her from disgrace. She had pleaded with her murderers to take her life and in their mercy they slit her belly and ripped out her intestines.

In this way an old-established Jewish community in Eretz-Israel was eradicated. Their Arab neighbors had put them to the sword simply because they were defenseless. Sixty-three Jews lost their lives in Hebron and over 50 were wounded.

The Hebron riots were part of the renewed attempt by the Arabs to snuff out any hope for a Jewish national home in Palestine. On August 23, 1929, a crowd stormed out of the Aqsa mosque, their passions fanned by the notorious mufti, Haj Amin Al-Husseini. Carrying sticks, knives and daggers, they set out to attack Jewish neighborhoods in Jerusalem. The British, following the ancient principle of "divide and rule," condoned and even lent their support to such acts of violence. The first to suffer were the Jews of the Old City, but most of the new town was soon engulfed: from Sanhedria in the north to Makor-Hayim, Talpiot and Ramat Rahel in the south; from Mea Shearim in the east to Giv'at Shaul, Montefiore and Beit Hakerem in the west.

Most prominent in the looting and killing were the fellahin of Lifta, northwest of the city, who were soon joined by the Arabs of Deir Yassin, a village overlooking the western suburbs of the capital. The death toll after seven days of rioting reached 30 Jews dead in Jerusalem and Motza. At the same time, some 20 Jews were killed in Safed. The Jewish quarter in that town was plundered and largely destroyed.

Tel Aviv and Haifa also came under attack, as well as a number of agricultural settlements in various parts of the country. Some of these settlements, such as Hulda, held out and even inflicted casualties on the enemy. Others, such as Ein-Zetim near Safed, offered no resistance. The settlers abandoned their homes and ran away. By the end of that week, 133 Jews had been killed and 339 wounded. In most cases, the security forces did not intervene even when the attacks were carried out right in front of police or government officials. Arab police often actively assisted the attackers. The Mandate judiciary toed a line similar to official British policy. Out of twenty death sentences given to murderers caught in the act, only three were carried out. The rest were pardoned or sent to prison.

During that dreadful period, Mrs. Lazarowsky's tale left me no respite. I could not sleep at night and was awake the night my baby brother, Herzl, came into the world and uttered his first cry. Herzl was to follow me in the resistance movement.

During the 1929 riots, our neighborhood organized itself against a possible Arab attack. Adults kept guard in shifts day and night, but all they had for arms were sticks, which they took to a nearby workshop to be fitted with sharp metal points, like spears. I also found myself a stick and embedded nails in its head, my very first weapon. I was very proud of it and quite prepared to use it.

One Sabbath, while the Arabs were firing on Tel Aviv from the surrounding orange groves, a rumor spread on our street that a nearby neighborhood had been infiltrated. A group of people immediately rushed to the defense of the area, grabbing everything they could find—knives, hatchets, spear-sticks, anything to ward off the attackers. I remember a small, slightly hunchbacked Jew, beard down to his waist, running toward that neighborhood with his ritual-slaughterer's knife in his hands. To me he symbolized the new Jew who was prepared to defend his homeland. The rumor proved false, but I was filled with pride and I knew we would prevail.

As I recall those days I realize that here lie the seeds of future events narrated in this book. The parent generation rose to defend itself, and I followed them. The difference was, that while they only sought to defend themselves against a possible attack, I, their son, prayed for a chance to turn the tables. I came under the spell of such biblical activists as the judge Ehud ben Gera, with whom I completely identified. It is written in the Book of Judges:

And the people of Israel served Eglon the king of Moab eighteen years. But when the people of Israel cried out to the Lord, the Lord raised up for them a deliverer. Ehud, the son of Gera, the Benjaminite, a left-handed man. The people of Israel sent a tribute by him to Eglon . . . and Ehud

made for himself a sword with two edges, a cubit in length; and he girded
it on his right thigh under his clothes. And he presented the tribute to
Eglon king of Moab. Now Eglon was a very fat man. And when Ehud had
finished presenting his tribute, he sent away the people that carried the
tribute, but he himself returned from Pesilim, near Gilgal, and said, "I
have a secret message for you, O king." And he commanded, "Silence." And all his attendants left his presence. And Ehud came to him as
he was sitting alone in his cool roof chamber. And Ehud said, "I have a
message from God for you." And he arose from his seat. And Ehud
reached with his left hand, took the sword from his right thigh, and thrust
it into his belly, and the hilt also went in after the blade, and the fat closed
over the blade . . . Then Ehud went out into the vestibule, and closed the
doors of the roof chamber upon him, and locked them . . . When he
arrived he sounded the trumpet in the hill country of Ephraim and the
people of Israel went down with him at their head . . . And they killed at
that time about ten thousand of the Moabites, all strong, able-bodied
men . . . So Moab was subdued that day under the hand of Israel. And the
land had rest for eighty years.

Ehud, like Moses who did not hesitate to slay the Egyptian, did not
wait for official sanction for his plan. I, the child of the redeemed
generation, never had any doubts or qualms about my future actions. My
duty to hasten the redemption was always self-understood.

At age 15 I joined the National Youth Circles. I was attending the
Herzliya High School in Tel Aviv, probably the best high school in the
country at that time. One of my favorite teachers was Dr. Hayim
Bograshov. Ten years later, in 1942, when I was brought before a British
military court in Jerusalem after I was wounded and captured at 30
Dizengoff Street in Tel Aviv by British detectives headed by Officers
Morton and Wilkin, Bograshov testified about my character. It was at
the end of the trial, before the sentence was read. He said that I had a
good character, I helped others and did well in school. My three judges
smiled at him after he finished, and the presiding judge told him: "His
character must have changed somewhat since then." Bograshov remained in the court until I was given my life sentence. When the British
led me out of the court to the armored car with my hands and legs in
chains, our eyes met. I could feel his admiration for what I had done, and
I felt great pride.

The National Youth Circles had been active in several Tel Aviv high schools since 1928. They defined their purpose as "organizing, educating and activating the youth in order to establish a Hebrew state on both sides of the Jordan," and in time they gave rise to the National Cells which produced the commanders of the IZL underground.

In October 1930 I went out with members of the national movement to demonstrate against the British authorities. On October 9, 1930 the deputy of Lord Passfield, the British colonial secretary, arrived in Tel Aviv in order to discuss local affairs with the authorities. His name had been associated with the White Paper which was issued after the 1929 riots, restricting Jewish immigration and land purchase. As he arrived in Tel Aviv we arranged a demonstration in the center of town, in front of his hotel. The demonstration was preceded by fliers in which we denounced the visitor, and we carried banners stating "Long Live Immigration" and "Down with the British Government." When the deputy and his entourage came out of the hotel they were greeted with boos and whistles. At first the visitor thought he was being welcomed by a friendly crowd and, as an English gentleman, he tipped his hat to thank us for our friendly gesture. But when the shouts were accompanied by stones he realized what the crowd's true feelings were. I remember how calm I felt when I threw my first stone at the representative of the foreign rulers of my country. My wish to become like one of Israel's ancient heroes who fought for the freedom of their people and their country was fulfilled.

A police officer quickly escorted the astounded deputy to his car, and the police began to disperse the crowd and arrested some of the demonstrators, including Dr. Abba Ahimeir and Moshe Segal (the latter would cast his lot with the IZL and LHI undergrounds and take part in many of their operations. He willingly allowed me to hide in his apartment after I escaped from jail in 1943, albeit he had a large family and ran the risk of a long jail term). They were beaten with a truncheon by Officer Schiff and transferred to the Tel Aviv police. After a short investigation they were released, in order to minimize the importance of the demonstration. In reality, it was a turning point: for the first time Jews carried banners against the British rule and clashed with the police.

In 1933 the British High Commissioner published new decrees against Jewish immigration, and the police initiated an all-out search for immigrants who had entered as tourists. British police patrols would stop suspects on the street, take them into custody and deport them. The pleading of the Jewish Agency proved futile. A group of us, 15-year-old boys, decided to compose a strongly worded statement to denounce the decrees. We printed a wall poster at the print shop of one of our friends—without his father's knowledge—and went out at night to paste copies of the poster in the streets. The pasting method we used became later on a standard practice of the underground: one person would smear the paste on the wall with a brush and run away to hide in a nearby alley, while another person would come by and attach the poster as others were on the lookout. The poster made an impression and rumor had it it was put out by a large underground. We were inspired by the results to publish additional posters.

The historical significance of those posters lies in the fact that they were the first ever issued against the British rule by a would-be underground. They taught me that the important thing in fighting the ruling power was not the number of people one could count on but the timing and the impact of one's action.

In early 1935 our group was invited by Moshe Rosenberg, second-in-command of the underground organization which was known in those days as Haganah Leumit (or Haganah-bet, as distinguished from the main Haganah organization, or simply the Irgun, the Hebrew word for organization), to a meeting. As a result of that meeting our group was admitted to the Irgun. We were only 17 at that time.

From its inception and throughout the years, the Irgun was guided by three principles—respect for and dedication to arms, military activities, and confidence in armed force. The Irgun sought to create a new national spirit and teach Hebrew youth new values, strongly advocating the idea of militarism which the Haganah rejected. I joined the Irgun in order to fulfill those goals, and I considered my joining a turning point in my life. I believed the Irgun to be the force that would bring security and ultimate redemption to our people. I felt reborn, and I was prepared to work for the Irgun with selfless dedication.

After a short trial period, I was summoned to be sworn in as a member of the organization. My commander gave me a broken pencil, and told me to hand it to a person who waited for me on a Tel Aviv street corner, and had a description of me. I met this person at the appointed time, and after he matched the two pencil fragments he took me in a roundabout way to the swearing-in place, making sure no one was following us. The door opened after the secret knock. The guard showed me inside. He took me through dark corridors to a large, completely dark room. In the middle of the room there was a lectern, like the lectern used by the prayer leader in the synagogue. On the lectern there were two burning candles and between them there were a Bible and a pistol. At each corner of the room an Irgun member stood at attention, casting a shadow across the room. One of them ordered me to approach the lectern and place my right hand on the Bible and the pistol and repeat the oath which was spoken in a mystical voice, as if coming from the netherworld.

With holy dread I put my right hand on the Bible and the pistol, and the flames lit up my face. From a parchment scroll written by a scribe I read the following oath:

> Of my own free will and consent, and without any coercion, I swear to be a loyal soldier of the Irgun Tzva'i Leumi in the Land of Israel who will defend national property, life and honor, and will help to bring about the full restoration of our people in the land of their forefathers. I accept obedience without any reservations, and promise to keep total secrecy in regard to all I know about the Irgun. I will obey my commanders and carry out all their orders at any place and at any time. So help me the Guardian of Israel.

After I was sworn in I became a full-fledged member. I was assigned to a cell of ten Irgun members.

At this stage we learned general principles of conspiracy, how to behave in special situations, such as arrest, police search and investigation, precaution measures during unit meetings, signalling and first aid. We also held ideological discussions in which it was emphasized that unlike the Haganah, which took a purely defensive posture in its training and use of arms, the sole purpose of the Irgun's military training was preparation for war leading to victory. Commanders had to bear in mind during training that the prime function of the training was the cultivation of morale, which encompassed fighting-spirit and discipline. The Irgun regarded fighting-spirit as the cornerstone of the military unit, while drill was considered essential for building morale as well as total, unswerving obedience.

It soon became clear that the "fighting-spirit" of the Irgun was limited to self-defense, passively awaiting enemy attack which "hopefully will not take place," without taking any political or military initiative. I realized that the difference between the Irgun and the Haganah was only in form, not in essence. The Irgun stressed military ceremonies, drilling exercises, discipline and field training, but had no intention of going on the offensive.

   The principal weapon of the Irgun was the handgun. It was available in sufficient quantities to allow training and exercising by all members, and was considered the "ideal weapon" for self-defense as well as for potential reaction. The Irgun arsenal had a large variety and types of handguns, and each member had to know how to use all of them. It was not enough to know how to load, unload and fire. One also had to know how to assemble the weapon and take it apart, how the mechanism worked, the names of the parts, and many other theoretical details.

   In those days our main activity was getting prepared to act each time it seemed that a Jewish settlement might come under the threat of an imminent Arab attack. This activity was coordinated with the Haganah. Two-thirds of the defense positions were taken by the Haganah, and one-third by the Irgun. The positions were located in strategic points around the threatened community, and in each post there were a few boys with personal weapons and one or two concealed hand-grenades. This was done in shifts around the clock. Food was supplied by neighbors or by the Irgun headquarters, either daily or in a quantity sufficient to last for several days in case of a siege. We also had a first-aid station supervised by one of the girls.

Avraham Tehomi (Gideon).

In the spring of 1937 I was sent for training with 25 other members under the command of David Raziel. The training took place in the evenings and on Saturdays, when the members were out of work, at the Bialik Elementary School on Levinsky Street in Tel Aviv. For training with live ammunition we would go out to Ramat Tiomkin in Natanya, where the residents were members of the Irgun.

I found Raziel to be an outstanding commander. He instilled in us a martial spirit, faith and vision, and was very popular. He kept his distance from us, yet he took personal interest in each one of us and was aware of our individual needs. Raziel was both knowledgeable and dedicated. In our course he introduced three innovations, which in time became an inseparable part of basic training. First, the use of the Finnish submachine-gun which was an exact replica of the American Thompson, to which we referred as Wash, in order to pretend it came from Washington. Second, a basic course in sabotage, the use of explosives and the making of bombs. Third, the use of the grenade not only for defense but also as an offensive weapon. Raziel taught us all this and also taught us how to teach it to our men. The positive military spirit he imparted to us was passed on to those who followed us.

The course lasted for six months, and was superior to anything we had done in the past. But it was also the last course under the Irgun as it was constituted at that time. A short time thereafter the split took place, and the new Irgun Tzvai Leumi emerged.

TWO

The Irgun Emerges from the Split

During 1929–1936 the Land of Israel went through an interim period of growth and development. However, murderous attacks on Jews did not cease altogether. In April 1931, three members of kibbutz Yagur near Haifa were killed. The way the attack was organized indicated it was a political act. In June of that year, two young men were murdered as they left Tel Aviv for a trip north. Their mutilated bodies were found almost five months later, at the Sidni Ali beach in Herzliya. A member of kibbutz Balfouriya in the Jezreel Valley was shot dead in his house in January 1932. Two months later a resident of Kfar Hasidim was shot and killed. In December, Arabs threw a bomb into a home in Nahalal, killing the head of the family and his young son. These murders were often accompanied by acts of sabotage, such as the uprooting of trees, the destruction of crops or the burning of granaries.

The unrest increased as waves of immigrants began to arrive from Nazi Germany. The disturbances culminated in a series of riots known as the 1933 uprisings. In March, the Arab Executive Committee adopted a sharp anti-government slogan which, combined with the incitement in the Arab press, soon bore fruit: on October 13 a stormy demonstration took place outside government offices in Jerusalem; on the 27th an angry crowd rioted in the streets of Jaffa and the police fired shots which claimed dozens of victims. That same day, public buildings in Nablus were attacked and policemen were stoned. Police stations in Haifa were also attacked.

When Italy invaded Ethiopia in 1935 England did not react. Italian gains in Africa reduced Arab fears of the British lion. Those fears were further abated as Nazi Germany continued to consolidate its power. "The English understand when there is shooting," remarked Britain's political representative in Iraq, Sir Arnold Wilson. To the Arabs, it seemed that the time was ripe for the *coup de grace* which would crown their ambitions with victory.

On Sunday, April 19, 1936, rumors began circulating in Jaffa that Arabs in nearby Tel Aviv had been murdered. An excited crowd surged toward the town, armed with knives, daggers, clubs and stones, and hurled itself on the Jews. Nine Jews were killed and over 50 wounded. Police who arrived on the scene dispersed the throng and imposed an even-handed curfew on both Jaffa and Tel Aviv. A "state of emergency" was subsequently declared through the country. The curfew did not induce calm, nor did the state of emergency stop the disturbances. The outskirts of Tel Aviv came under attack again. Jews were killed, homes and shops were looted, factories and workshops were set on fire. Thousands of inhabitants began to leave the area under attack for the more secure center of town.

An organized Arab political movement was emerging. On April 25th, what later became known as the Arab Higher Committee, was founded in Nablus, headed by the notorious Jerusalem mufti and Nazi collaborator, Haj Amin Al-Husseini. This new body announced a general strike and asserted that violence would not cease until three basic conditions were met: a halt to Jewish immigration, a ban on the sale of land to Jews, and the establishment of a national government which would be responsible to a "representative council."

These announcements were accompanied by more violence. Telephone lines and railroad tracks were ripped out, bridges were blown up, roads were blocked. Jews were ambushed and killed, fruit trees and forests were cut down, crops were destroyed in the fields. In the hills, the Arabs organized themselves into gangs augmented by volunteers from Syria and Iraq. The more indecisive the government appeared, the more the Arabs intensified their attacks. Highway attacks increased, bombs went off in Jewish settlements, forests were burned down, crops destroyed and orchards and vineyards cut down.

The wave of destruction and bloodshed reached its peak in August.

Fauzi el-Kaukagi.

Araf Abdul Razek.

On the 13th, a father and his three children were murdered by a band which infiltrated the Jewish quarter in Safed. The next day, a car was attacked near Haifa and all four Jewish passengers were shot dead. On the 16th, shots were fired from a train crossing Tel Aviv on its way from Jaffa to Jerusalem, as the train slowed down at the barrier on Herzl Street. A child was killed and 13 Jews wounded. On the 17th, two Jewish girls were killed on their way to work at the government hospital in Jaffa. On the 20th, a lecturer in Oriental studies at the Hebrew University was murdered at home. On the 21st, four Jewish workers were killed in Kfar Saba by Arabs from neighboring villages.

By the end of the month, foreign forces had joined the local gangs. Fauzi el-Kaukagi, the experienced commander who had served in the Turkish and Iraqi armies, infiltrated the country and appointed himself head of the "army of liberation." He made his base at Tul-karm from whence he supervised the raids on Jewish settlements.

Jewish Agency figures for losses at Arab hands show 80 Jews killed and 369 wounded by the end of October 1936; over 2000 attacks on Jews and 900 on Jewish property were recorded; 1369 bombs and mines were exploded; 380 buses and trains attacked; 17,000 dunams of crops were ruined; 200,000 trees were uprooted or set on fire; hundreds of houses were destroyed, including factories and workshops; three cemeteries were desecrated; nine nursery schools and orphanages were attacked; three old people's homes and 19 schools also suffered damage.

When in August 1936 the Arabs mounted direct attacks on Jewish settlements with the express aim of annihilating them, the Jews were forced to organize their tactical defense and try to foil or minimize the damage as much as possible. There were only two alternatives: either to carry the attack into the Arab heartland and spread panic among the inhabitants until they sued for peace, or to pursue the armed gangs and engage them in battle. In the end neither option was adopted. The first was discarded by the Jewish leadership on moral and political grounds (the policy throughout the period was one of restraint). The second was rejected because the leadership trusted the Mandate government implicitly in all security matters.

Small wonder that when the Arabs began to kill and plunder the defenders were at a loss. They had no choice but to remain in their defensive positions. The Haganah's top priority in those days was to defend the settlements until the arrival of the police. Fields, forests, crops and travel routes were not included in the Haganah's perimeter of responsibility, and, needless to say, the Haganah did not dream of crossing the line and attacking the Arab gangs.

The same was true of the political leadership of the Irgun, who, like the Haganah, refused to consider an all-out attack on the gangs. When the hostilities started, the Irgun was no less at a loss than the Haganah. In most respects there was no real difference between the two defense forces.

After a child was killed when shots were fired on Hacarmel School in Tel Aviv, the Irgun commander approval reprisal-raids on the outskirts of the southwestern suburb of Kerem Hatemanim. Binyamin Zeroni and Avraham Buchman were assigned the task. They threw a hand-grenade and fired their guns into a nearby Arab neighborhood. One Arab was killed and one wounded. But the climax of the series of reprisals organized by the Irgun in 1936 was the grenade attack on the Jaffa-Jerusalem train that became known as the Train Operation (17 August 1936).

Those reprisals notwithstanding, the Irgun continued to conform to the *havlagah* (restraint) policy of the Establishment, while some of its military commanders clamored for action. As a result, some members of the Irgun led by Avraham Tehomi returned to the Haganah, while others, under the ideological influence of Avraham Stern (Yair), formed the

Irgun Tzvai Leumi as a fighting underground force. Thus in the summer of 1937 the so-called "Gideon Split" (Avraham Tehomi's *nom de guerre*) took place.

Stern, who headed those of us who opposed the union with the Haganah, knew how to instill in us a great faith in the new way of the organization. He formulated the ideology of the independent Irgun, as expressed in the following internal circular which he wrote and distributed to the members on 23 April 1937:

To Those Who Honor the Oath!
The Irgun Tzvai Leumi in the Land of Israel was created because we believe that the Hebrew state will not become a reality without relying on an independent national military body.
The Jewish Agency now hopes to obtain approval for free action for those under its command in return for subjugation to the foreign rule and surrender to the cantonization plans for this land. The IZL in the Land of Israel is charged with the duty of acting as the only real force that will be called upon and will be able to fight for the reestablishment of the Hebrew nation in the Land of Israel in the face of the plotting of the external enemy and the surrender to those who are willing to betray us from within.
The IZL in the Land of Israel has been forced by political reality to decide whether to surrender to the power of the government and the Jewish Agency, or to redouble its sacrifice and its risk-taking. Some of our friends were not up to this difficult task. They surrendered to the Agency and left the battlefield. The large loyal majority continues to uphold the original policy of the IZL. All the attempts by the former command of the Irgun to reach a merger with the leftist organization have failed, since the left has not negotiated on the basis of joining forces but of imposing one group's will on the other. Putting the IZL under the authority of the Agency whis is ruled by the left is the end of our organization.
There are two organizations today in this land: one is leftist, run by the left, and to our regret some of our men have joined it. The other is the IZL, which continues to fight for the dignity and the life of the nation being reborn. We believe in the mission of our movement and in its power to reestablish the full independence within the historical borders of the Hebrew state. We believe in Israel's youth's willing to fight and to sacrifice, having set as its life's goal the might and the independence of the nucleus of Hebrew power.
Anonymous soldiers!
The nucleus of Hebrew power is prepared for any order or sacrifice. "Only death releases us from duty!"

David Raziel.

On 24 April 1937 each member was asked which side he wished to join. The results were important to both sides, since they determined how our arsenal was going to be divided. By mutual agreement, the arms were divided according to the number of members who joined each side. It turned out that nearly the entire high command opted for the union, while all the activist groups, including commanders and subordinates, chose the separate organization. This human element determined the character and spirit of the organization in the new era following the split.

I myself said no to the union in no uncertain terms when I appeared before the local command in Ramat Gan. I was convinced that Arab murderous acts called for vigorous reaction, and that such reaction was a moral and political imperative which outweighed any arguments about the importance of communal unity and discipline.

Avraham Stern (Yair).

The split brought a good feeling to the organization's rank and file. People were now looking forward to long-overdue action. The main issue that had caused the split was: restraint or retaliation? While the split took place during a low point in the Arab hostilities, the general feeling among the members was that the lull was only temporary. We all felt that the Irgun did not see the end of the bloody conflicts. The new policy of the Irgun was set forth in the principles enunciated by Stern: a) The fate of the Hebrew nation will be determined by the force of Hebrew arms on the soil of the homeland. b) The Irgun considers any Jew who supports this goal an ally. c) The Irgun consider any member of any other nation who recognizes the right of the Hebrew nation to independence in its homeland an ally. After these principles were formulated, a new command was chosen for the Irgun. David Raziel was unanimously proclaimed our new commander.

THREE

The Jerusalem Garrison

In early 1937 my family moved from Tel Aviv to Jerusalem. We were three children. I was the oldest. My sister Sarah was three years younger than I, and Herzl, the youngest, was thirteen years my junior. My sister accompanied me during all my years in the underground. She was a member of the Irgun and later LEHI and worked fearlessly for both.

In Jerusalem I decided to study chemistry at the Hebrew University, in order to help the underground, especially in the area of explosives. I was put under the command of Yosef Hakim, whom we called Kushi (Negro), since he came from the Sudan and was dark skinned. I became the commander of Group 81, which carried out most of the attacks in Jerusalem during 1938–39.

As commander of Group 81 I chose the underground name Etan (Hebrew for strong). I wanted my men to be strong and eager for action and sacrifice. I developed those qualities through training, exercise and action.

Training focused on the following subjects: light weapons (handgun, rifle, grenade), explosives (detonators, means of ignition), and explosive devices (regular and electric).

The guiding principle of the training was practicality. The study of weapons had one practical purpose: hit the enemy and destroy him. I

28

concentrated on the revolver, the sawed-off rifle, the Wash submachine-gun, and the grenade, all of which could be concealed on one's person and be drawn out quickly in order to hit the enemy with accuracy. The experience gained in those courses was not theoretical, as it used to be in the old Irgun, but intended to be applied effectively in real life situations. Similarly, the study of explosives, detonators, fuses and firing devices led to the making of bombs and mines, to be used for destruction. Thus the training program was kept strictly practical.

During exercises I trained the members to use the limited weapons we had at our disposal at that time. I would pick an objective such as an Arab gang leader, a gang headquarters, an arsenal, a munitions factory, etc. We would then work in stages: first we would gather information, then make a plan, study the area, check our information before the operation, carry out the operation, retreat, disappear. All this was done under difficult conditions, with few means, keeping total secrecy.

Those who went through the training successfully and passed all the tests and all the stages of execution would in time be sent out on actual missions.

The door to our place of training would open after the secret knock. A guard would let the member inside, after he looked out to check the area. After a second indentification, the entering person would go through corridors and rooms, each under surveillance, until he reached the training room. The guarding and the precaution measures prevented any unwanted persons from breaking in on us.

Field training included target shooting with handguns, rifles and submachine guns, tossing grenades, and detonating explosive devices. This took place around Jerusalem, mainly at Nahalat Yitzhaq.

In those days the Arab gangs concentrated on harassing Jewish traffic on the single road connecting Jerusalem with Tel Aviv. The narrow road, turning in the mountains in a predominantly Arab area, was an easy target. The most vulnerable spot was the sharp turn near Mount Kastel, 9 kilometers outside Jerusalem, but the danger did not cease until one went past the village of Abu Gosh. In order to protect Jewish traffic, a guard post was built in the fall of 1937 11 kilometers outside of Jerusalem, manned by Betar recruits. This post, known as the "road unit," was also called Nahalat Yitzhaq.

The place soon became a training base for the Irgun in Jerusalem. The units and their commanders would come to Nahalat Yitzhaq on Friday nights and on holidays and train in the mountains with rifles, which could not be used in the city. The basement of the guard post was used for practicing with small weapons, and the dynamiting of rocks in the nearby quarry was used as a cover-up for tossing home-made bombs and Mills grenades.

I would take my group to Nahalat Yitzhaq on Friday afternoon and train until Saturday night. The training was practical, either with live fire or without. The men would practice quick drawing of pistols against enemy dummies, proper holding, cocking, firing, completing the drawing, and the proper aiming of the weapon for instinctive firing. We also played duel games: men with unloaded pistols would search through the house, the corridors and the basements for their comrades-in-arms, and when they found them the first to draw would win.

We also practiced throwing grenades. A grenade used as an anti-personnel weapon must have a short fuse, so that the grenade explodes immediately and does not linger on the ground. The military grenades we used at the time, such as Mills, burned for 4 seconds. This was enough time to pick up the grenade and toss it back, so that you ran the risk not only of missing the target but also of having the grenade thrown back at you.

In order for the grenade to explode at the right time and hit as many persons as possible without allowing time for someone to throw it back, it had to explode at least three feet above the target. For this purpose I would shorten the fuse to 2.5 cm, allowing it to explode after 2.5 seconds. Furthermore, in order to time the explosion accurately, the thrower would have to hold it in his hand and slowly count 21, 22, 23. Then the grenade was tossed, exploding three feet above the target. To perfect this operation, the trainees had to keep practicing and exert a great deal of self-restraint. They would often count too fast, and the grenade would explode on the ground after a short pause. In order to slow down their counting, I would hold their hand as they held the grenade and together we would count until it was time to throw it.

FOUR

My First Operation—
A Burst of Hand Grenades

Jerusalem in 1937 was a mixed town, with Jews and Arabs living and working side by side. The mayor, Rageb Bey Nashashibi, and most of the city councilmen were Arabs. The majority of the population was Jewish but was represented by only a few councilmen, led by Daniel Auster. Palestinian Arabs made Jerusalem their political capital. The Supreme Arab Committee met here. Its leader, the mufti Haj Amin al-Husseini, lived there. Haj Amin had been an artillery officer in the Turkish army and as soon as the British conquered the country he gained attention as a vociferous opponent of Zionism. He placed himself at the head of the extremists, preached violent opposition to the Zionist endeavor, and distinguished himself throughout the Mandate years by his bloody anti-Jewish campaigns. In 1938, fearing arrest, the mufti fled Jerusalem and joined the Nazis in Germany where he collaborated with Hitler on the "final solution to the Jewish problem," as a prelude to liquidating the Yishuv in the Land of Israel. When the war was over, I set an ambush for the mufti in France but it was not successful.

Jerusalem is the third holiest city in the world to the Muslims, following Mecca and Medina. Thus it was the most important Arab city on either side of the Jordan, a city ruled by Arabs, while serving as the seat of the British administration. The Arabs were aware of the preeminence of Jerusalem in world opinion, and of its unique significance for the rebirth of the Jewish state.

Because of all this, the Arabs made Jerusalem the focus of their terrorist activities. They sought to show all parties at home and abroad that since they controlled the capital, they also controlled the rest of the country. The British authorities were receptive to this idea, since they were wary of the drive of the Jews to reestablish their national home in the Land of Israel.

Indeed, on October 14, 1937 armed Arab attacks against Jewish communities and travellers resumed throughout the country. The unarmed and defenseless Jewish population of Jerusalem suffered many casualties. Passanger cars and buses were attacked, and individual Jews were shot at, resulting in many wounded and several dead. On October

The five victims of Arab terrorist attack near Jerusalem (the "Maale Hahamisha victims") are eulogized by Yishuv leaders Menahem Ussishkin, Chief Rabbi Herzog, and Moshe Shertok (Sharett). The attack elicited reprisals against the Arabs in which Eliav took a leading part.

29, Jewish worshippers were attacked on their way back from praying at the Western Wall. One Jew was killed and two seriously wounded.

The British police opened an investigation, but naturally "nothing was found." Fifteen Arabs who were detained and questioned after this last attack were released. The Arab rioters understood that the British authorities were on their side, and they geared up for new assaults.

On the morning of November 9, two groups of farmers from Ma'ale Gordonia, a pilot settlement temporarily lodged at Kiryat Anavim, left for work at a Jewish National Fund forestation and road paving project some 5 kilometers away. As soon as the first group of five men arrived, they were shot and killed and their guns were taken away. (In 1938, kibbutz Maale Ha'hamisha was named in memory of the five.) The mood among the Jews of Jerusalem was grim. The graveside eulogies reflected the general anger and pain. All the victims were members of the Haganah, but the feelings of outrage were not translated into action. The official Jewish leadership continued to hope that self-restraint would result in political gains. Our leaders failed to realize that Arab aggression made the British respect the Arab cause, and increased the chances of the Arabs to become the dominant political force in the country.

On November 9, the authorities issued an official communique announcing the establishment of military tribunals in the Land of Israel. Three kinds of offenses would come under the jurisdiction of those courts:

1. Shooting with live ammunition at any person will be punishable by death.
2. Carrying arms, bombs, etc. will be subject to the death penalty.
3. The same applies to acts of sabotage or terror.

The Irgun ignored the new rules and the military courts. Furthermore, David Raziel, as the commander of the Jerusalem garrison, decided to wipe out Arab terror in the capital, using new tactics which had already proved effective. Similar tactics were subsequently employed in Irgun operations throughout the country.

The method, derisively called by its opponents "the Black Sunday method," was based on carefully timed attacks occurring simultaneously at different parts of the city. The idea was to spread panic by giving the impression of a huge and well-organized Jewish force. The simultaneous actions were also designed to confuse the police, who would find it hard to cope with the attackers. The targeted areas were chosen after long and painstaking reconnaissance. The participating units were made up of three individuals: one who brought in the weapons before the operation, one who fired them or threw the grenades, and one who hid them afterwards. The reason for this division of labor was that if the attacker was caught, he would not have the weapons in his possession, and since he did not know where the weapons were taken to, he could not tell the police. Operations were usually done at street-corners to facilitate the escape. Arms were brought to nearby hiding-places after the operation and thoroughly cleaned to remove all traces of use. The men would even collect the empty cartridges and scrape the rifle barrels with sandpaper or a thin file in order to foil any ballistic examination if the weapon fell into the hands of the police.

One of Raziel's innovations was a statement issued after each operation and distributed to all the commanders. These internal memos, which ran counter to every instinct of secrecy followed by the old Irgun, were read in all the branches of the Irgun and raised everyone's morale. In time these memos becamse a prominent feature of the expanding propaganda war.

The Black Sunday reprisal actions were scheduled to being on Sunday, November 14. But the first and decisive action was set by Raziel for Thursday, November 11. I was put in charge. Here is how the Jerusalem correspondent of *Ha'aretz* (November 12, 1937) described it:

It happened behind the offices of the National Arab Bus Company, in the empty square facing the International Cafe, frequented by British soldiers and policemen. The bomb was tossed at a group of 4 Arabs who sat on the porch of the bus company office, facing the depot. It is hard to determine where the bomb was thrown from because of the sudden and loud explosion. No suspicious person had been seen in the area before the attack.

A British soldier who had stood at the door of the cafe told our reporter that at exactly 4 o'clock, two minutes after the cannon signalling the end of the Ramadan fast was fired, a loud explosion was heard and smoke rose from a place where Arabs were sitting on stools. He did not see where the bomb was thrown from, but it seemed to have been dropped from above. Seven Arabs were hit by fragments, and two died later. Telephone lines were cut and a telephone pole was damaged. The glass door of the cafe was shattered. A nearby bus was pierced by fragments, but no one was wounded on the bus.

One fragment entered a Jewish flower shop nearby and landed next to a customer, but no one was injured and no damage was reported. A terrible panic ensued on Jaffa Road. High police officers headed by the Inspector General of the police arrived shortly after.

How did I do it? When I was first put in charge of Group 81 I told my superior, Yosef Hakim, that I could not accept the command until I took part in the reprisals. "I will have no moral right to send anyone on a mission until I go on one myself," I argued.

At first, Hakim was surprised to hear that the newly arrived young student from Tel Aviv was itching for action. But as I kept insisting he finally agreed, and a few days later told me I was chosen by Raziel for a very important mission not attempted thus far, which would be the first in a series of similar operations.

The Arab bus company grenade attack was planned for the Jaffa Road Company headquarters, which was a meeting place of Arab gangs. Two of us were to climb on the roof of the three-story building above the restaurant and drop the grenades on the bus station down below. As my partner I chose the son of a Sephardi rabbi, Avraham Duek.

I visited the place ten days earlier disguised as a plumber. In addition to my "working clothes" and tools, I dirtied my face and hands and put on a mustache. Duek dressed as a yeshiva student in a black suit and hat, beard and sidecurls. We picked an approach route, a plan of action and a getaway. We went over everything the day before the attack to make sure there would be no surprises. I also checked the grenades to make sure they were in perfect working order. I adjusted the safety-fuses to make sure the grenades exploded exactly three feet from the ground, causing maximum damage and casualties.

On November 11, 1937, a few minutes before 3 p.m., I met Hakim at the home of his assistant, Miriam Robovitz, on Melisande Street. Miriam's family was long established in Jerusalem, and she had been active in the Irgun since her childhood. She and Hakim handed me the grenade device. It consisted of a large shoe box with four fittings (*mufas*) embedded in the corners. A plumber's fitting was a connecting-pipe 6 inches long, which could screw at either end. Closed at one end, the fitting served as a stopper for fuel pipes in buildings. We used to remove those stoppers for our purposes. In the box I found four *mufa* grenades, made from pipes 2½ inches thick. They were tightly screwed down front and back. There were grooves in the fittings to increase the amount of shrapnel during the explosion, and the stopper had a hole in it for the fuse to go through.

This is how we prepared a *mufa* grenade: we took a fitting securely closed at the bottom with a stopper, filled it with dynamite and stuck a primer into the dynamite to increase its force. Into the primer we put the detonator and into the detonator we put the safety-fuse which passed through the aperture in the other stopper and came out. This other stopper would be tightly closed with a special screw thread which had to be thoroughly cleaned so that no traces of dynamite remained which could spark an explosion by friction when you screwed down the stopper.

The length of the safety-fuse varied according to need and the tip of the fuse was unravelled in the form of a cross for maximum exposure of the gunpowder concealed inside it. Ignitable material, such as potassium chlorate which could be purchased at any pharmacy, would be mixed with sugar and placed on the tip of the fuse, covered with waterproof paper and tied with a thread so that the explosive material would not scatter or get wet. The fuse had to be lit gently, with a burning cigarette, for instance, to allow the flame to spread gradually through the fuse. The fire would progress one centimeter per second until it reached the dynamite which would set off the grenade.

The four grenades in the box, tightly packed, were tied together by special knots. The spaces between them were filled with steel nails, intended to produce additional shrapnel. All the fuses were pointed toward the center of the box and the cords were tied together. They were prepared in such a way that they would all burn at the same time and go off together.

I wrapped the box in paper, as if I had just bought myself a pair of shoes in the store. Placing the box under my arm, I went outside and walked down the street. Duek was strolling behind me as if we were strangers. He was prepared to disappear if I were stopped by the police. We were near the Russian Compound, which housed the police head-quarters, and the area swarmed with policemen and detectives. I walked briskly past the Generali Building, past the Central Post Office and the Anglo-Palestine Bank, until I reached a crowd of Arabs at the site of the action. They were middle class Arabs—government officials, mer-chants and proprietors. I crossed the road by the municipal park and entered an office building and climbed up the stairs. I was acting like a messenger boy bringing a parcel to one of the offices. I climbed up to the roof. The door was open, as my earlier check had indicated it would be. Nobody was on the roof and nobody saw me reach the railing which overlooked the bus company. Duek was right behind me.

The railing was three feet high. I placed the box on the floor of the roof and looked down. The bus company directors were sitting on little stools, sipping Turkish coffee. One was smoking a nargileh. Now came the moment to raise the box with both hands as Duek put a match to the concealed fuses, and drop the box on those people. I had just given Duek the order, when a woman and a child came up on the roof, carrying a basket of laundry. They turned to the clothes lines at the other end of the roof, without even seeing us, but Duek was alarmed. Instead of igniting the fuses, he retreated to the staircase and disappeared.

So I had to do it alone. I propped the box on the railing and lit the fuses myself. A sheet of flame leaped up immediately, singeing my hair. But I held on to the box with both hands and aimed it at the middle of the group below. As soon as I dropped the box I turned to leave. The woman at the clothes lines still did not see me. Calmly, I descended the stairs. As I passed the third floor, I heard a loud explosion. The building shook. I was filled with pride. The operation was a success.

Meanwhile, people were tearing out of various offices, so I mingled with them and made my exit. Outside, the street was like a madhouse. The police were already on the scene, an ambulance siren was wailing around the corner. I crossed the road and retraced my steps towards the Post Office, intending to return to Melisande Street and report the success of the operation. Opposite the entrance to the Post Office I saw Yosef Hakim coming toward me. I was about to express my jubilation to him when I noticed he was white as a sheet and was firmly shaking his head, letting me know I should not greet him. I accepted the secrecy, but failed to understand why he was so pale. Only afterwards I realized he had been deeply worried about us. Soon I would share his anxiety, whenever I sent people on dangerous missions. But on this occasion Yosef had an extra reason to worry: he had seen Duek leave the building and thought the operation had failed, and when he heard the explosion he thought I had been caught. His face had betrayed his fears.

The operation had succeeded beyond Hakim's wildest hopes. The Jerusalem gang leaders were severely punished. One hour later, the city was under curfew. I watched the curfew gleefully from our balcony in the center of town.

David Raziel later singled me out as he praised the operation at a secret commanders' meeting. I believe it was the only time he ever praised anyone in public in Jerusalem, and the memory has been with me all my life. Raziel invited Hakim and me to a private meeting at which we analyzed the operation and he offered a toast. I learned to appreciate and emulate Raziel's courteous manner.

The curfew continued over the weekend. As soon as it ended on

Sunday, Raziel's command executed a series of operations that same day, which subsequently became known as Black Sunday, November 14.

Lo and behold, rather than increase Arab hatred, the reprisals seemed to achieve quite the opposite. The Arabs began to realize they had to face systematic, well planned reprisals, carried out by a fighting body that had to be reckoned with. The Arab press suddenly understood that self-restraint is not only good for the Jews. Thus, for example, the Arab paper *Al-Jama' a al-Islamiya* in its November 15 issue condemned all terror: "We have known that crime is a two-edged sword which harms the perpetrator as well as the victim. Ambush and murder do not bring glory to the perpetrators, and Arabs should despise such odious acts." This attitude became more evident among the Arabs as Irgun activities intensified.

November 14 became known among the members of the Irgun as the day on which official restraint was challenged, marking the beginning of the shift from passivity to action. Other branches of the Irgun also adopted the Jerusalem Method. The British police reacted with a wave of arrests. Only publicly known members of the Revisionist Party were put behind bars, while the ranks of the underground Irgun remained intact. The clandestine nature of the Irgun was paying off, although the degree of secrecy was quite lower than what it would soon become.

FIVE

Facing the British Police

The British CID (Criminal Investigations Department) head-quarters were located in the heart of Jerusalem, inside the Russian Compound. It consisted of eight sections: the Jewish Section, the Arab Section, the European Affairs Section, the Censorship Section, the Legal Section, the Detention Section, the Telephone Listening-in Section, and the Political Archives.

The Jewish Section was by far the largest of the eight. It had the most manpower, equipment, and the biggest budget. The British were more worried about the Jews than the Arabs, and did everything they could to suppress the Jewish ''national home.'' This section was staffed by a large number of Jewish officers and policemen and a considerable number of Jewish informers. In time, the Jewish personnel of the CID's Jewish Section was reduced, as it was found out that Jewish police officers showed allegiance to the institutions of the Jewish community, including the Irgun and the Haganah. The police would rely instead on private informers, some of whom were on its payroll, while others were paid a fee for any verified bit of information.

The key positions in the Jewish Section were held by British officers. Most of them had served for several years on the Palestine Police force and were carefully screened for the new job. The main criterion for their selection was their hatred of Jews. The CID at that time was headed by Colonel Arthur Giles, addressed by both British and Arabs as Bey, an honorary title he had received from the Egyptian Government for his services with the Port Said police. After the British Police was disbanded in Egypt following the Anglo-Egyptian treaty of 1936, Giles was transferred to Jerusalem as an expert on Arab affairs. Soon he became the head of the CID and dedicated himself to shape its character. He brought experts from Scotland Yard in London to train his men, sent British officers for special training in England, and saw to it that his subordinates stayed on and made a career out of their police work.

In order to upgrade the department, Giles would raise the salaries and promote those policemen who met certain specifications. Those specifications, according to Giles, included hatred of Jews to the point of wishing to liquidate them. Among those promoted by Giles to high rank were Morton, Wilkin and Cairns. The first two would later kill some LEHI members and liquidate their commander, Avraham Stern (Yair), while the third, Ralph Cairns, became the head of the Jewish Section in 1939, and excelled in torturing members of the Irgun. For this, and in retaliation of the publication of the White Paper, I was ordered to execute Cairns in August 1939, shortly before the outbreak of World War Two. Wilkin was liquidated later on by the LEHI while Morton fled the country after three attempts on his life. Giles came on January 21, 1942 to 30 Dizengoff Street in Tel Aviv to witness the slaughter of LEHI members by Inspector Morton, who took his orders from Giles, and enjoyed seeing me near death, on a stretcher, as will be told later on.

As was mentioned before, Giles used private informers for the Jewish Section of the CID. They came from various walks of the Jewish community. Some were ex-convicts and other persons of questionable character. Some were merchants and salesmen who did business with the government. Some were well-educated people who offered their services for a good fee.

We protected ourselves against the CID with the aid of our Intelligence Section (MESHI in Hebrew), which was established after the April 1937 split as one of the Irgun sections at headquarters. MESHI monitored CID activities and found out what the police knew about the Irgun and what it was planning to do against it, in order to avoid searches and arrests. MESHI used various sources of information, including Jewish policemen who considered it their duty to help the two armed bodies of the Yishuv. Each member of the Irgun had to pass on information to his superiors, as part of his ongoing duties. From its inception, MESHI did not spare any efforts infiltrating the CID and making use of its employees, who provided us with first-hand information on political affairs, lists of men about to be arrested, copies of various documents, etc. MESHI also kept an eye on other important departments in the Mandate government and did all it could to obtain classified information.

In the first half of 1938, as the Irgun was preparing for drastic retaliation against Arab gangs, MESHI services in Jerusalem became urgent. Our main targets were the British administration, the CID and the Jerusalem Police.

On a cool Jerusalem evening I was summoned by Raziel, the commander of the Jerusalem garrison of the Irgun, and was ordered to head the MESHI operations in Jerusalem. I agreed on the condition that I continue to head Group 81 and carry out missions against Arab marauders. Raziel agreed, and allowed me to include some of my men in the new assignment.

An important method of obtaining information in those days was through interception of mail. I developed a method of monitoring VIP mail, and was later sent to teach my method at the Tel Aviv branch. Another important source of information was the listening system we established in Jerusalem. One of our main targets was the Schneller Orphanage, a German institution with Arab students and teachers. It was known to offer its technical installations to the Arab gangs, and as a German institution it enjoyed political immunity and provided good cover for their activities. Needless to say, we were quite interested in what was going on inside its walls.

We arrived in the neighborhood one day driving a small telephone company van. We were dressed in the company uniform and had the tools and accessories of the company. One of us was a legitimate employee of the company, who came along as our guide. Our experts connected a wire to the Schneller House telephone line outside, attached it to a nearby roof and from there extended it to another roof, where we had rented a room for that purpose. During the operation a man and a woman kept a lookout in the street to alert us of any suspicious movement, or of a real telephone company van that might come by to do some work.

When we finished the job we posted men in the room who listened in around the clock, writing down all the conversations, which were mainly in Arabic, German and Turkish. Outside we kept constant guard.

The important conversations were recorded. Those included calls to the Jerusalem mufti's house, to Dr. Yusuf Qna'an and certain gang leaders, as well as Arab police officers who collaborated with the gangs. A second listening station was later installed on Haturim Street, in the same neighborhood. As a result of our listening we obtained valuable information about the Arabs and their British contacts.

Our main interest, of course, was gathering information for the practical execution of our missions. To this end we divided Jerusalem into two areas. I was put in charge of the area north of Jaffa Road. Here we became acquainted with all the streets, alleys, lanes and courtyard passages, as well as the access across roofs from one street to the next, for fast withdrawal. We carefully studied the possibilities in order to thwart enemy action and achieve our own objectives. We figured out where the Arabs might try to strike at the Jews, how they could reach the place, how the police could get there, etc. For our own purposes, we recorded places we could attack, access and egress routes, and storage spots. For our reconnaissance assignments we would dress as local workers, beggars or yeshiva students, or even as idlers who sit on a park bench and read the newspaper while peeking through a hole in the paper in order not to arouse suspicion. Another effective cover was a young couple in love trying to be inconspicuous.

Despite the fact that the places we were interested in were always under strict surveillance by the police, our men never aroused any suspicion. The intelligence gathered would be brought to me, and I would analyze it and draw the necessary conclusions and make contingency plans. Those plans were kept in my memory like files in a professional archive. Nothing was written down. Everything proved valuable as we intensified our operations.

SIX

Fighting Arab Terrorism

In the spring of 1938 acts of Arab terrorism increased throughout the country. Jews were killed, their bodies mutilated, Jewish women were savagely raped, and babies' heads were smashed. On June 29, 1938, Shlomo Ben-Yosef was hanged by the British at the Acre jail for attacking an Arab bus in the Galilee to avenge Arab terrorist acts. He was the first Jew to go to the gallows in the Land of Israel.

The Irgun stepped up its campaign around the country, especially in Jerusalem. Throughout the month of July we conducted a series of operations against the Arabs in the capital, with various degrees of success. Here are two examples:

On July 15, 1938 we scheduled a major attack which had taken a long time to prepare. We were anxious to avenge the murder of Jews in the Old City and to strike near the Temple Mount, where Jews were not allowed to worship in peace. We chose Friday, the day when Muslims left the mosque after being incited by their religious leaders to kill Jews.

The question was how to gain access to the place without risking one's life in the hands of Arabs as well as British patrols. After numerous checks I found out it was not necessary to walk through the throngs or past the police guards. Instead, one could go up on the roofs of the Jewish quarter and reach the Arab quarter without being noticed. I also noticed that the main alleys of the Arab quarter were covered with stone roofs which had openings for daylight through which one could easily place a bomb.

I began to transfer materials to the Jewish quarter for making the bomb. Since the police conducted searches in the area, I smuggled the materials into the quarter with the help of old Jewish men and women who were supportive of the Irgun, and could carry those things in without arousing suspicion. The materials were hidden under the ark in the Hurba synagogue, a place never searched by the British. In one of the Jewish homes near the synagogue I put together the largest bombs I had ever made. It consisted of a tin can $12 \times 12 \times 16$ inches which I filled with blasting gelatin weighing 33 pounds. The explosive charge was put into an inner tin tube to increase the blast. Between the tube and the can I put steel nails soaked in sulphatic acid as an anti-personnel measure. I attached electric detonators to the explosives and connected them to primers and electric batteries connected in a row. I attached press-button switches on the outside of the can, so that when the bomb dropped from the skylight onto the pavement below at least one of the switches would be pressed, close the electric circuit and set off the bomb. I checked the electric system before the final installation in the bomb and found it to be in working order.

I made a wooden tripod with an iron pulley on top to hang a rope which would hold the bomb over the open skylight. To the rope I attached a stick of dynamite, and an alectric detonator connected to an electric battery and a clock which would close the electric circuit and smash the rope at a given moment, allowing the bomb to drop.

On Thursday night, July 14, we transferred the bomb to one of the roofs in the Arab quarter. As my men kept guard, I installed the bomb over the skylight at the intersection of David, Hashalshelet and Ha-basamim Streets, almost directly above an Arab cafe teeming with Arab youth.

At noon on Friday, July 15, the place would be jammed with men returning from prayer at the mosques on the Temple Mount, most of them gang members whose hands were defiled with Jewish blood. Meanwhile, it was an enchanted moonlit night. We worked quietly over the empty streets. We installed the tripod and put the rope through the pulley, attached a hook to a slab of stone on the roof and tied the rope to the hook. We timed the explosion to 12 noon the next day, and wrapped the device with insulating material to protect it from humidity which might cause a short circuit.

We returned to the Jewish quarter and slept there. I was assisted in this operation by Hayim Corfu, later Israel's transport minister, Rahamim Cohen and Ephraim Ben-Eliyahu. At dawn we returned through the Armenian quarter to the new city, some by bus and some on foot. We planned to meet later on to discuss the results. I arrived early at the Jaffa Gate, before 12. I milled about, my watch and my heart ticking, not hearing a sound. Twelve o'clock passed, and nothing happened. No explosion. No police cars speeding by with their sirens going, no ambulances picking up the casualties.

We soon found out that our bomb had been discovered at dawn by the police. To this day I have no idea what had happened. According to one hypothesis, the can had shaded some of the light people were used to get out of that skylight, and so they found it. Another theory has it that the can had made the passage too narrow for a cat to slip by. The cat had caused a pebble to fall and caught the attention of the peddlers down below. Be it as it may, the police came and dismantled the bomb. The British bomb expert would later pay with his life for one of his successful bomb jobs.

Despite the fact that the bomb failed to explode, it was not a total loss. The presence of a powerful explosive device near the Temple Mount, which could have killed hundreds of Arabs, sobered up the gangs and slowed down their attacks. But I was not ready to let go of my prey.

Haaretz, July 24, 1938
10 ARABS KILLED, 31 WOUNDED
In Shocking Explosion at Arab Vegetable Market in the Old City in Jerusalem.
One of the most terrible, if not the most terrible explosion since the riots started, took place last Friday afternoon in Jerusalem. Ten were killed and over thirty wounded. At 1:20 a frightful explosion was heard in the Old City and its vicinity. A bomb had exploded at the entrance of the vegetable market on David Street. The chaos at the place of the explosion was total, and only much later the extent of the tragedy became known. Eight Arabs were killed on the spot and thirty were wounded, nineteen serious. Police, soldiers and ambulances of the government hospital rushed to the place. The transfer of the dead and the wounded lasted until 2 in the afternoon. Seven ambulances stood at the entrance to David Street and the casualties were brought over and placed side by side on the street before the wounded were taken away.
It is hard to describe the panic that seized the Old City, as well as other

parts of the city, after the explosion. People fled in all directions, stores were closed, ambulances and cars transporting the casualties sped through the streets and went up Jaffa Road. A large Arab crowd gathered near the hospital, greatly agitated. It was scattered by the police. Army and police patrols were reinforced throughout the city.

As a result of the bomb, an Arab strike broke out in the Old City.

I was quite dismayed by our fiasco, and decided to plan an alternate operation for the following Friday, July 22. The plan was based on reports I had received from Yaakov Shabtai, the head of our Arab intelligence. He had found out that the Arab merchants in the Old City bought goods in the new trade center in the Jewish area. Arab porters would load the merchandise on their backs and bring it to the stores in the Old City. It seemed to be a ready-made opportunity to strike at the Arab gangs and avenge the murder of the Jews in the Old City.

I recalled that next to one of our members' homes in the trade center there was a warehouse of kitchen utensils, which had been shut because the owner had gone abroad. We made keys for the warehouse lock and on the day of the operation, at 7:30 a.m. I went over there and opened the warehouse as if I were the new owner of the place, about to start my business day. A crate arrived with the bomb, which resembled last week's hanging bomb, but was not operated by a pushbutton, but rather by an electric detonating circuit consisting of a detonator which connected at one end to an electric battery and at the other to a clock, connected to the battery. The clock would close the circuit at the right time. The clock was my innovation, and was subsequently used in all the elctric explosive devices used by the underground. I replaced the glass cover of the clock with a plastic one and drilled a hole in it through which I put a small well-fastened screw, to be touched only by the hour hand. I removed the minute hand, and attached the other end of the screw to the battery, connecting the time-setting button to the detonator. Under the screw I smeared insulating material to prevent any contact prior to the moment when the hour hand touched the screw. Shortly before the operation, I set the clock for 12 o'clock. I did not trust this job to anyone else because of the special expertise and caution it required.

At 11:15 one of our men, dressed up as an Arab merchant, arrived with a porter. No one could tell from the looks and speech of that man that he was not an Arab merchant. He had agreed on a fee with the porter beforehand. Now he began to haggle with me over the price of the merchandise. The bargaining lasted for ten minutes. He went out without buying anything, checked the price in the next warehouse, and came back, to convince the porter he was a genuine merchant. We finally agreed on the price. He paid cash. I took out the crate and checked the merchandise. I arranged the sets of knives, forks and kitchen utensils on top of the crate, and at the same time set the clock. I then nailed the crate and helped put it on the porter's back, which was protected with the thick mat the porters in those days used to carry.

It was 11:30. We synchronized our watches with the bomb clock, to the second. We calculated the time necessary for the merchant to walk the porter to the corner of David and Hashalshelet Streets—the place where the bomb had failed to explode the week before—find a place to put down the bomb, and come back. The merchant would tell the porter he had to go somewhere to get directions and would come right back to let the porter know where to go.

After the two left I closed the warehouse, and at 12 o'clock I was at my observation post at the Jaffa Gate. This time the thunder did not fail to come. At exactly 12 noon a deafening explosion shook the area. The stunned crowd scattered and disappeared. Ambulances and police cars rushed towards the Old City. On Jaffa Road, on my way to the Russian Compound, I saw the ambulances coming back loaded with casualties. There was continuous traffic going to the government hospital, which resembled a beehive when I got there.

I went to see the hero of the operation, the "avenging merchant." It was not an easy thing for him to do, either emotionally or operationally. But when I saw him his face was glowing. We shook hands, congratulated each other, and toasted L'chayim.

Operations of this kind, in retaliation for the murder of Jews by the Arab gangs, made the Arabs aware of the severity of their actions. As a result, from the end of 1938 until the outbreak of World War Two in 1939, the Arabs stopped killing Jews and even sued for a cease-fire.

The "Messiah" and I Are Saved by a Miracle

Another operation we planned at that time was inspired by a report that a large number of Arab gang members from villages near Jerusalem were about to converge on the courthouse in the capital, where some of their leaders, who had been caught by the police, were standing trial. We were going to attack those on trial, their guests and their lawyer, Henry Katan, a well-known gang supporter and a personal friend of the mufti,

Haj Amin al-Husseini. We decided to hide a bomb in the courtroom at the Russian Compound in Jerusalem.

Again I prepared a time bomb. This time I used a large glass jar, 6 inches in diameter and 14 inches high, the kind Arabs used for keeping pickles. The bomb itself was made of a tin cylinder, which I put inside the brine and pickle filled jar, so it could not be seen from the outside. We welded the tin to make it waterproof. Inside the tin we had put four sticks of high explosives and steel nails. Inside the explosive charges I installed the electric detonating mechanism, which, as usual, included an electric detonator, a primer, electric battery timer and a switch, which, if necessary, could be used to break the circuit. I set the timer so that the bomb would go off fifteen minutes after it was placed in the courtroom.

I chose a young man named Mashiah (Hebrew for messiah) to carry out the mission. He was swarthy like an Arab, and spoke fluent Arabic. We dressed him like an Arab worker, and crowned him with an Arab headdress. The jar of pickles under his arm was quite natural looking. What Arab villager ever comes to the city and fails to buy a jar of pickles for his family? I briefed Mashiah and showed him how the bomb worked, and how he could turn it off if necessary. We arranged to meet on Haneviim Street. I would walk ahead of him and he would follow me at a discreet distance. I would enter the court, find out where the trial took place, and give him a signal by passing my hand over my hair, letting him know where to go.

When I went into the courthouse I was stunned—the place was empty. I did not give the agreed signal, which meant that Mashiah had to switch off the bomb. I proceeded down the long corridor and went up to the second floor, to find out if the trial took place in another room. Mashiah kept following me, both of us finding it difficult to come to terms with the fact that our mission had failed. I finally realized the trial had been postponed and we went outside. We kept walking, Mashiah a few steps behind me, to our original meeting point. As we reached the Jewish Quarter I noticed how Mashiah had taken off his Arab headgear. I slowed down and he caught up with me.

"Everything okay?" I inquired.

"Everything's okay, too bad we couldn't pull it off."

We kept walking with the bomb between us, held by Mashiah, and headed for an Arab ruin on Habashim Street. There Mashiah would take off his Arab outfit and remain in his regular clothes, which he had worn underneath. Mashiah entered the ruin as I waited outside. Suddenly I heard a terrific explosion and part of the ruin collapsed. Stones flew in all directions. I was engulfed by a cloud of dust. I stood there, paralyzed. I was sure Mashiah had died. A moment later Mashiah came walking out of the debris. He looked like someone coming out of the netherworld. He was pale as a sheet and his eyes were burning. I found out that what had saved his life was the fact that he had put the bomb in the front room of the ruin and went into a back room to change his clothes.

We quickly left the place before anyone would stop us with any questions. After we walked for a while we calmed down, and I was finally able to ask the question which had been bothering me: "Didn't you switch it off?" To my amazement, Mashiah told me he had pressed the switch not once, but twice.

I need not add that the second time he pressed it, it was on again. He could have caused a disaster in which not only the two of us would have been killed, but many innocent passersby as well.

This narrow escape taught me an important lesson: those who engage in this type of work must go over every detail over and over again, or else their lives are in danger and their death is certain. Many of our members lost their lives because of carelessness.

The Bomb in the Drawer and the Three Dignitaries

We were about to give up the idea of going after the gang leaders who had been put on trial, when we decided that, at a minimum, we had to eliminate their lawyer, who was one of our main enemies. Attorney Katan had an office in the same building from which I tossed the grenades on the bus company office. I went one night to visit the office after work hours, and let myself in with a special key. It was a sumptuous office, lavishly done with Damascus furniture, a scene out of the Arabian Nights. I took a special liking to the huge desk, surrounded by leather-lined chairs. In the middle of the desk there was a large drawer, clearly meant to hide a bomb. It was locked with a special key, and after many efforts we found a way to open it. We made a bomb, tied inside the drawer with a string, which was made to go off when the drawer was opened, stretching the string. We took out the drawer, installed the bomb in the drawer space inside the desk, and then put the drawer back in the desk and locked it.

We worked with gloves, so as not to leave any fingerprints. After we finished we cleaned the room, locked the office door behind us and slipped out of the building. The next day we waited for the news about the explosion, but we were disappointed. After three or four days we became genuinely concerned about the welfare of our lawyer. We asked around, and found out he was away for a month on vacation. We became concerned lest someone else might open the drawer, and since we did not wish to harm any innocent person, we returned to the office one night and dismantled the device.

Our intelligence reports, however, were not always faulty. To balance the picture, let me mention two instances in which good intelligence did help us achieve our objective.

The first instance was our attack on Engineer Martin Huri, director of the above mentioned Schneller institution. Huri, like Attorney Katan, was also a leader of the murderous gangs and a supporter of the mufti. He was personally responsible for making the institution he headed a center for terrorists who were responsible for many fatal attacks on the Jewish population of Jerusalem.

He had been on our hit list for a long time. He seemed to be an easy target, since he lived in a mansion opposite the Schneller House, and each day he would cross the street on his way to work. But since he did not hide his subversive activities, Huri feared an attack on himself, and used roundabout ways to go to and from his office. At first I suggested to lower a bomb through his chimney into his living room. But we decided against it, since the bomb would have killed his entire family, and we only wanted to settle accounts with him. We finally decided to attack him with personal arms. Using our previously mentioned listening station, which was connected to the Schneller House, we found out that Mr. Huri phoned his office each time he left the house. We waited for his call, and lay in wait for him in the basement of a nearby house. When he left his home we charged out of the basement, fanning out across the street, and attacked him with all our weapons. He was seriously wounded and became an invalid. He could no longer do any harm.

We did the same thing with Dr. Canaan, a third member of the club of professionals involved in gang activities. We connected a wire to his phone line and listened in, finding out about his comings and goings. When we found out he was about to take a ride in his car, we drove our car in front of him and shot him behind the wheel. We put him out of circulation for a long period of time.

The execution of gang leaders, or putting them out of commission, has a disastrous effect on their organizations in several ways. It takes years of experience and political maturity to become a leader, and it is not easy to replace one.

Moreover, an attack on a leader results in confusion, a feeling of inferiority, fear of subversion and provocation. The attacked organization suffers deep trauma which can paralyze its activities for a long time. Our successful attacks on some of the gang leaders contributed to the cessation of their activities and saved many Jewish lives.

SEVEN

The Hero Who Took His Secrets
to the Grave

Yaakov Raz was a member of Group 81 which I commanded. He was born in 1919 in Afghanistan, and when he was ten the family emigrated to Jerusalem. His family was so poor he could not finish grade school, and had to start working for a living. But he had a thirst for learning, and continued to study at night. He was small and shy. I remember him riding his old bicycle delivering milk and other products. After he finished work early in the morning he would report to me with his bike for duty, or would show up in the evening for training. He did not stand out in the group, hardly said a word, and I did not get the impression he was listening to what I was saying to the group. But this was an outer cover hiding the soul of a saint, and a man who was prepared to fight for the redemption of Israel and avenge the blood of the innocent.

Raz was able to move freely among the Arabs because he looked exactly like one of them. He spoke all the local Arab dialects, and was often sent on missions in Arab areas.

Late in July 1938 two Jews, Moshe Tzaban and his son, Haim, were murdered in the Old City. They had gone there to buy merchandise and were stabbed to death. This caused great fury among us and required immediate action. I summoned Raz, and found him ready to act. He knew what was involved, and was glad to do it. He remained quiet when I told him about the operation, but his face was eager, and he was anxious to find out what the mission was. I spread a map before him and showed him the place where the murder had been committed. I had previously scouted the area disguised in a British uniform, and found out that the alley was crowded with shops and connected to another alley by a courtyard. The second alley was higher, continuing behind a stone wall to the Tower of David. After careful study I worked out the plan of action. The bomb-thrower would go through the Tower of David to the high side of the wall, toss the bomb into the alley below where the murder had been committed, and quickly retrace his steps.

Raz was disappointed. When I asked why, he said, "This operation is nothing. I thought you were going to give me something more complicated." I slapped his shoulder and promised him I would give him something more complicated next time. I kept my promise, and he paid with his life.

In the meantime we proceeded with this mission. Raz was well acquainted with the alleys of the old city, including the targeted area. But to be on the safe side I went there with him to doublecheck. I walked ahead of him, as if we had nothing to do with each other. At the designated place I stopped and marked the spot I thought would be the best position to throw the bomb from, and we continued to walk. We later met and went over all the details. The mission was set for noon the next day, Wednesday, July 27, 1938. I made the bomb from a *mufa* cast-iron tube, 10 inches long and 4 inches in diameter. I crisscrossed it with deep grooves to increase the fragmentation. The safety-fuse was only one inch long, to prevent anyone from throwing it back. To ignite it, Raz was going to use a burning cigarette.

Raz dressed up as an Arab, took the bomb and left. I walked behind him at some distance and saw him arrive at the place without any difficulty. When he entered the courtyard I turned back and left. I immediately heard a terrific explosion. Great confusion ensued, with Jews, Arabs and British police all running into one another. We were able to leave the place without difficulty. Fifteen minutes later we met and shook hands. Raz's face was ecstatic. I told him he did a good job and deserved praise. He did not say anything, but before he left he said, "The Irgun is everything to me, and you are like a father to me." There were tears in his eyes, and he quickly left.

The operation was successful. Several Arabs were killed and many wounded. Everyone knew it was in retaliation for the murdered father and son.

Less than a week later I was able to keep my promise to Raz. This time it was joint action between Group 81 and another unit of the Irgun in Jerusalem, under the command of Gamliel (Gami) Halpern, whose operational zone was south of Jaffa Road. Since there were no suitable objectives at that time in his area, Gamliel was given the task of planting another bomb in the Old City. We had to assist him, because he did not have the right personnel for the job. He had to plan and execute the bombing, while I provided the bomb and the personnel. Gami decided that a time bomb would be placed in the Old City near the Nablus Gate, and would be brought over in a large vegetable basket, carried on the back of a man disguised as a porter.

On Monday, July 26, 1938, Raz waited for us early in the morning near the Italian Hospital, at the entrance to Meah Shearim. He sat on the sidewalk, dressed as an Arab porter, and played with marbles, like an Arab porter his age would. I arrived there with Tzvi Meltzer, a member of our technical section. A few moments later Yaakov Kemara arrived, driving his car, bringing over the vegetable basket with the bomb. Kemara parked his car on a side street. Meltzer and I went inside, prepared the bomb and set the time. Yaakov Shabtai waited for us nearby. Shabtai played the part of an Arab landowner, who had hired the porter to bring over the basket. When everything was ready we called over Raz, the porter, to take the produce. We helped him take the basket out of the car, load it on his back, and tie it to his forehead. From there he was going to go down Prophets Street to the Nablus Gate. Shabtai was going to walk ahead of him. They had about half an hour to bring over the bomb and put it in place. I said goodbye to them with a heavy heart, since this time I was not in charge and I was not able to accompany them. I had no choice but to go back. Still, I waited for them at the place of reassembly. When they did not show up on time I had a bad feeling. Finally Shabtai came and told us what had happened.

As bad luck would have it, the porters at the Nablus Gate had decided to call a strike that day. They were for the most part Horani immigrants from Syria, who were either protesting their extreme poverty or being incited against the Jews. We were at fault for not finding out about it beforehand. Nor were we aware of the fact that those porters considered that place their turf and resented any intruders. When Raz showed up as a new competitor while they were on strike, they surrounded him with curses and threats. He knew he was having problems, and should have turned around and left. But it seems that he decided Yaakov Raz does not retreat. Like Samson, he was prepared to die in the line of duty. He carried on. He put down the basket and stood in the crowd, waiting for the explosion. Something about the look in his eyes must have betrayed him. Someone noticed it and yelled, "Jew! Bomb!" No one had to say another word. The Arabs attacked Raz with their daggers and forced him to the ground, stepping on him. The bomb was not going to go off for another 20 minutes. After they thought they had

Yaakov Raz.

killed him, his attackers left the scene. In the meantime Shabtai went to the police station nearby and called for help. The police found Raz in a pool of blood with the basket next to him, as the Arabs kept pointing at it and saying "Bomb, bomb!" The Arab police alerted the CID who sealed off the surrounding streets and brought over a bomb expert, who dismantled the bomb and took it to the CID headquarters. When the package was opened it turned out to be a large tin can, filled with explosives, nails, bits of metal, detonators and primers, a timer and an electric detonating mechanism. The bomb weighed 77 pounds, and the experts reported it was the largest bomb ever found by the police, which could have killed dozens of people.

Raz had suffered thirteen knife wounds, and was brought under heavy guard to the Hadassah Hospital on Prophets Street. As soon as he arrived at the hospital the police came over to investigate him, and the next day the order came to transfer him to the government hospital, under heavy guard. Some of the doctors and nurses at that hospital were members of the Irgun, and we had plans to free him by force. I started working on a plan to free him, but was told he was in critical condition and had to start recovering before we could free him.

We had to wait, and in the meantime Raz underwent a difficult operation. He needed repeated blood transfusions, and was barely conscious. Not only was he heavily guarded by the British, but as soon as he was taken out of the operating room the CID started questioning him, and kept questioning him day and night, in shifts. Some of them stood next to his bed with pad and pencil ready to record any word he might say in his semi-conscious state. I can imagine how much he must have suffered, knowing he might say something inadvertently which would jeopardize the Irgun, albeit we on the outside kept changing things in case Raz might be tricked into saying something. Raz felt a sense of responsibility to the very end. When the questioning intensified and he felt he could not hold out much longer, he decided to put an end to his life. He tore off his bandages which covered most of his body, and after much suffering he died, taking his secrets with him to the grave.

The death of Raz put the Irgun into deep mourning. But at the same time we all felt proud of the example of the little anonymous soldier, whose "soul departed in pristine silence." The Order of the Day of August 18, 1938 issued by Irgun headquarters, extolled "The first casualty of our offensive operations, the exemplary selfless person, model of discipline and total loyalty to the highest degree," and his act of sacrifice was described as a symbol of ''step by step victory won with the blood of anonymous soldiers who go out to conquer or die ... with a mighty willpower which cannot be broken or stopped, not even by death.'' Among the ranks, the exemplary death of Yaakov Raz became an educational asset and an object of admiration.

Immediately after the death of Raz, Yaakov Shabtai came to me and demanded revenge. He proposed we put a bomb in the place where Raz was assaulted and asked that he be the one to do it, without delays. At first I was going to refuse, because I felt we needed to plan this mission more carefully since Shabtai was vital for more specialized tasks and I did not want to risk his life when someone else could do this mission. But Shabtai insisted, and I finally agreed, particularly since he argued that it would give him an opportunity to train his own men.

Again I prepared an electric bomb, this time in a large jar of jelly. Shabtai checked out the place and proposed that he go and sit at a cafe and leave the bomb there. I went there myself and studied his proposal. It seemed acceptable.

On the appointed day, one week after the death of Raz, Shabtai took the bomb and went to that cafe. He picked the same time of day when Raz was attacked, to let the public know there was a connection between the time and place of Raz's death and this attack. He took along with him six of his men, who came along to see how he operated and also to provide cover in case of an emergency. They went, of course, in a scattered formation, each taking a separate table at the cafe. I walked part of the way with them, as far as the Nablus Gate, and we decided to meet again 45 minutes later at Meah Shearim. When we met we heard a powerful explosion from the direction of the Old City. Shabtai had no difficulty placing the bomb next to his table while he was having coffee, and was able to leave the cafe without arousing any suspicion. The operation was successful. Everyone knew Raz's blood was avenged.

EIGHT

An Army of 40,000 for the Liberation of the Land of Israel and the Rescue of European Jewry

As I reflect on the events narrated in the last two chapters I am amazed at the scope and impact of our activities during that period. Not only in Jerusalem were we so active at that time. The electric bomb method which I invented was copied in Haifa, Jaffa and Tiberias, and resulted in hundreds of casualties, dead and wounded, among the Arabs. It appeared that once the Jews decided to take the initiative, the war against terror became an offensive against the Arabs, the originators of terrorism. As the offensive started in the Land of Israel, Avraham Stern (Yair) began a political offensive in Poland, where he sought to develop political ties and work out practical plans for the liberation of the Land of Israel by combining the uprising of the Irgun at home with an invasion of 40,000 Jewish fighters from Europe who would arrive by sea at the shores of the homeland.

Avraham, the oldest son of Mordecai and Leah Stern, was born in 1907 in Suvalki, Poland. When the town was occupied by the Germans in World War One his mother took him to Russia and left him with relatives. Avraham wanted to return to his home, and, risking his life at a

58

time of Communist military rule, the 14-year-old boy wandered through the Russian countryside without money or documents until he reached his home town. He entered the Hebrew high school in Suvalki, and soon became one of its best students. He excelled in languages, literature and history, and became the leader of the local scout movement.

In 1925 he asked his parents to let him go to Jerusalem to further his studies. They agreed, and as soon as he arrived in Jerusalem he became a Jerusalemite to his core. He was admitted to the Hebrew University, where he excelled in classical languages and literature. Despite its meagre funds, the university awarded him a grant to study in Florence, Italy. Before he left he took part in the defense of Jerusalem during the 1929 riots, and was deeply affected by the experience. In late 1932 he decided to stop his studies and devote his life to the war for the liberation of Israel. Quite naturally he joined the Irgun, but after the split he became one of the founders of the new Irgun Tzvai Leumi, under the new name of Yair, after the zealot leader of Masada, Elazar ben Yair. When David Raziel assumed the command of the new Irgun, Yair became the theoretician, the brain, the man who inspired the members and fired them up.

After the trial and hanging of Shlomo Ben-Yosef, Yair decided it was time to fight the British, rather than the Arabs. He called it the "fight against the foreign occupier." He went on a mission to Poland and made direct contacts with the Polish authorities. At his suggestion military courses were arranged under the supervision of Polish officers. He also bought Polish weapons and sent them over to us. Yair's name began to circulate by word of mouth among Polish Jewry. Secret cells were formed, and free immigration was organized. Two papers began to appear in Poland—*De Tat*, in Yiddish, the official weekly of the Irgun, and *Free Jerusalem*, in Polish, a monthly for assimilated Jews who were being brought closer to Zionism by Yair. Everything seemed ready for the revolutionary act, but at the last moment the entire command of the Irgun was arrested and the Germans invaded Poland.

When Yair arrived in the Polish capital in November 1937 as the foreign representative of the Irgun, he had a daring political plan for liberating the Land of Israel by force. His plan was based on the assertion that if the Land of Israel was indeed our exclusive homeland, and if only there our people could be free, it followed that any non-Hebrew rule in the Land of Israel deprived the people of the freedom they deserved. In our case the foreign rule happened to be British. Hence we had to fight it until we expelled it and replaced it by Hebrew rule. This could not be achieved through petitions and protest meetings, as official Zionism tried to do, but only through the force of arms, which was the task of the Irgun, the national liberation movement of the Hebrew people. The Irgun was forging its force in the Land of Israel, but that force was not enough. The masses of Jews in Europe had to be organized as the reserves for the war of liberation. Time was of the essence. The state of the Jews in Europe was getting desperate. We had to act quicky and follow a clear plan which would lead us to our goal through the shortest way.

Yair's plan, then, was to establish branches of the Irgun in every Jewish community in Europe: in Poland, Rumania, Czechoslovakia and Austria, in the Baltic and in the Balkan countries. In every city and town secret cells of the Irgun would be organized, which would attract the elite of the Jewish youth. Those cells would teach underground skills which they would use after their arrival in the homeland. They would train with different types of weapons. In time the cells would become platoons and regiments and eventually, after all the conditions were ripe, some 40,000 young men, trained and armed, would head for the harbors of Europe, board ships and sail for the Land of Israel. At that time the Irgun would declare war on the foreign occupier and fighting would start. The British would have to mobilize all their forces, including the police and the coast guard. While the fighting went on, tens of thousands of young men would land on the shores from Rosh Hanikra to Gaza, and would overcome the British forces stationed in the country.

Yair operated on the assumption that when it came to *real politik*, one had to disregard the anti-Semitic sentiment of the other party. On the contrary, not only did we not regard anti-Semitism as an altogether negative force, we actually had a common interest with the anti-Semites, since we wanted to bring the Jews to their land from their dispersion. Moreover, denouncing anti-Semitism only strengthened it, since it showed that Jews continued to have the unhealthy need to cling to their lands of exile, whereas the national political plan of redemption pulled the rug from under the anti-Semites. As for the desired political relations, this plan could turn the enemies of Israel into friends.

Yair's premise was fully vindicated in his contacts with the Poles. This is not the place to go into the hatred and contempt of the Polish nobility towards the Jews. Yair, however, with his proud and unrelenting nationalism, was politically acceptable to them. Better yet, they respected and admired him. Later on the Polish government recognized, albeit not officially, that it was in its interest to support the Jews in breaking the British policy of preventing Jewish immigration, and if it took an armed uprising to liberate the Land of Israel, it was in Poland's interest to assist in such an uprising.

Against this backdrop Yair reached an agreement with the Polish government based on the following principles: The Irgun would take care of the evacuation of the Jews of Poland and would bring them to the Land of Israel; it would help Poland gain influence in the Middle East; and it would enlist the support of world Jewry for Poland's struggle against Nazi Germany and Communist Russia. The Poles for their part promised to provide large quantities of weapons, offer professional military training in camps inside Poland, and help Jews to emigrate. According to this agreement the Irgun was to receive 20,000 rifles and 20 million rounds of ammunition, hundreds of Hutchkies heavy machine guns, thousands of pistols and bayonets, many tons of explosives and large guantities of grenades. The arms and ammunition were given directly to the representatives of the Irgun in Poland out of the Polish army's arsenal and were transfered to warehouses. They remained under the control of the army until they were shipped to this country. The rifles and the pistols were smuggled in double bottom crates. Machine guns were packed inside road construction equipment, such as steam rollers, along with the ammunition for the long barrel French rifles, later re- placed by Polish-made rifles. Many of the weapons were sent on ships which also brought over illegal immigrants. The news about the flow of weapons infused the members of the Irgun back home with new faith in the high command, and it was understood that the shipments were only a fraction of the huge quantities of modern arms temporarily stored by the Irgun in Warsaw and waiting to be shipped home. At the same time, in order to implement the invasion plan, Irgun members went to Europe to train soldiers and officers who in time would leave Europe and raise the banner of the war for national liberation.

As part of the agreement with the Polish government, a course for Irgun commanders from the Land of Israel was given in Andrikhov, in the Carpathian Mountains, by experienced officers of the Polish army. Twenty-six Irgun officers were given regular military training as well as instruction in guerrilla tactics. This nucleus of officers was to become the high command of the invasion army of 40,000.

The course participants met with David Raziel in Tel Aviv. I was invited as a candidate from the Jerusalem branch. Raziel spoke briefly.

He went over the accomplishments of the Irgun during the past year. He praised his men for their action against the Arab rioters, told us about the fame of the Irgun around the world, and stressed the fact that we were only in the first stage of our operations, the main objective of which was the war for the independence of Israel. He made it clear that the Irgun leadership was determined to establish a military force to achieve that goal. He then alluded to the political gains of the Irgun and its new allies. Only at the end of his remarks he informed us about the course about to take place in Europe, and told us we, the assembled commanders, were the candidates. He stressed that the Irgun command trusted us, and the trust should make us aware of the gravity of our responsibility.

The next day I was feverishly preparing for the trip. I was a legal traveler, a 21-year-old man going to Poland to visit relatives, and had no difficulty obtaining a visa. All our passports were handled by the secretary of the national staff, Moshe Hasson, who arranged transit and tourist visas for the various countries. None of us at that point knew where we were going or where the course would take place. Only after we boarded the ship were we given our documents and found out they were stamped with visas for Egypt, Greece, Turkey, Rumania and Poland. The men had been divided into small groups, each departing on a different date. The person in charge of each group was given the address of a contact at the point of arrival.

We sailed on the ship *Transylvania* and arrived in Constanta, Rumania, on the shore of the Black Sea. After a 24-hour journey by train we arrived in Cracow, Poland. A few days later we took the train to southwestern Poland and got off in a small town. A wagon driver waited for us. He gave us warm blankets and a shot of vodka. We traveled slowly through snow and forests and arrived at night at a three-story house atop a mountain, surrounded by a large yard. This was our training base. The house had been divided into a lecture hall and a dining room, bedrooms, instructors' quarters, arms depot, and down in the basement a kitchen, pantry and living quarters for the kitchen and cleaning staff, the gardener and the chauffeur, all of them Poles who had been brought over from remote places to attend to the needs of the Irgun officers.

The instructors were introduced to us on the first day. They were Polish army officers, some of them veterans of Pilsudski's legions, some former members of the pre-World War One Polish underground, and the rest Polish army career officers. The instruction was divided into two: underground fighting and regular army fighting. but the distinction between the two was not altogether clear, since the Polish war of independence did not distinguish between them but rather had used underground activities as a preparation for its open armed uprising. But even as an auxiliary method we found the underground course quite useful, not only in terms of clandestine behavior and the principles of conspiracy per se, but mainly becaue of the technical aspects of bombing, sabotage and personal attacks. The regular military training complemented the above by preparing us, through rigorous exercises, to serve as commanders in a war between large military units, in field conditions, while putting special emphasis on the problems of a force in an uprising against an occupation army. The military subjects included individual training, platoon and company training, lectures on the operations of larger formations, military tactics, fortifications, communications and topography. The underground subjects included terrorist bombing, conspiracy, secret communications, partisan warfare, and underground planning of terrorist activities against various objectives. Sabotage was taught on a scientific basis. Many hours were devoted to calculating the quantities of explosives needed for destroying targets made of different materials. We learned mathematical formulas for demolishing objectives made of cement, iron, wood, bricks, soil, etc.

Each day we would go out to the woods for training. The vicinity roared with thunderous explosions, automatic fire and gun shots. The program was ambitious and our time was limited, so we had to do a great deal in a short time. We would go out at dawn on a long hike and come back at night, tired, frozen and dirty, but joyous and hopeful. Our spirits were high, and the Polish instructors were impressed by our endurance and eagerness to learn.

The lectures were given in Polish with a simultaneous translation into Hebrew by one of our men. Some of the lecturers were senior officers or high government officials, who were old enough to have taken part in the underground fight for national liberation. We could tell by their tone of voice and by the spark in their eyes that they were reliving their past and were anxious to impart to us that fighting spirit. They wished us success from the bottom of their heart, although they knew from personal experience that not too many of us would live to see the day of deliverance.

Dov Rubinstein and I kept records of the instruction material, and later published it in our internal instruction pamphlets. This material was used for training our men back home and abroad.

The course lasted for four months. Our Polish instructors gradually became more and more supportive of the idea of the liberation of the Land of Israel by the Jews. Their anti-Semitic feelings were dissipating, and they were filled with admiration for the rebirth of the Hebrew nation.

Midway through the course Yair came to see us and check on our progress. He spoke to us about his plan of national liberation and explained that if we did not act expeditiously the British would implement their plan of putting our country under Arab rule and reducing the Yishuv to a ghetto they could easily control. Yair also expressed his fear for the fate of the Jews of Europe and his explicit conviction that Hitler indeed was going to carry out his plan against the Jews in all its details without delays. Yair concluded that on both counts time was running out and we must waste no time in starting our war of liberation before our enemies got ahead of us. He added a word of thanks to Poland for its support and pointed out its importance as an ally. He urged us to make the most of the course in which we were fortunate enough to take part. He left us with the feeling great things were in store for us.

In this spirit we continued our training, but we never finished the course. Before it ended we were finding out that the world situation was rapidly deteriorating. Back home the Yishuv was bracing itself for the publication of the White Paper, and there was great urgency to bring us back to active duty, either as instructors in training camps in Poland or as trainers and commanders on the home front.

The course was shortened and was scheduled to end before Purim. Before the day of the final test we were told we would be tested by high ranking officials and our scores would determine our tasks in the underground. The testing was done by senior officers headed by a general and representatives of the Polish government, who brought Yair along with them. There was a festive parade, the general walked past us with Yair, chatted with each one of us and shook our hands with great feeling, as if he were about to send us on a dangerous mission and was deeply concerned about our success.

We did extremely well on the tests. The examiners did not hide their admiration for our high level of achievement. The head instructor said frankly that although he had trained many officers among his own people, he had never gotten so much satisfaction as he did training the boys from the Land of Israel.

Yair spoke last. He compared Poland's struggle for national liberation to our own, and we could tell his words made a deep impression on the Polish officers. They sat hypnotized, as if they were still going through their own struggle. Yair went on to talk about acquiring allies, and about conquering the land with the combined force of Hebrew youth at home and diaspora youth. He repeated his plan for landing a force of 40,000 men and liberating the homeland from the foreign occupier. He added that we now had large quantities of weapons which awaited shipment. Thousands of our men were training for the military invasion. And last but not least, our group was going to be put in charge of implementing the 40,000-soldier plan in Europe and at home.

We were living in a dream. The plan, its success, its practical gains, all made us hopeful and confident. We felt the presence of historical decisions, entrusted to our hands, the liberation of the homeland, the rescue of the Jews of Europe.

The officers' course in Poland was a turning point in the instruction and training of the Irgun, and the impact was felt even at a later date. During the revolt against the British, after the publication of the White Paper of May 1939, I made extensive use of the electric mines and the various types of contact mines, the assembly method and the placing method. We also made use of the instruction in building secret transmitters, organizing tracking operations, etc. At a later stage we made use of the platoon attack, street fighting, fortifications and trench digging, and even capture and occupation of objectives. The practical and theoretical aspects of the training in Poland helped with all the above.

The day after the emotionally charged parade we each went back to our duties at home, except for a few who remained abroad to prepare the 40,000-man plan. I had to return immediately to Jerusalem to my assignment as operations officer in that city. On the way I stopped in Warsaw and witnessed the feverish preparations in that major Jewish center for the war of Israel's independence, which included the organizing of large numbers of fighters, increasing the flow of immigration, and launching a large-scale propaganda campaign. I was under the impression of what I saw in Warsaw as I boarded the ship in Constanta to go home. On the ship we received the news about Hitler's occupation of Czechoslovakia, which had ceased to exist as a state.

NINE

The Blowing Up of the Rex Cinema

When I returned home from the officers' course in Poland I was filled with an optimistic faith I had never felt before. The decrees of the British White Paper, however, quickly sobered me up. This document clearly stated that the "objective of His Majesty's Government is the establishment within ten years of an independent Palestine State," which would maintain relations with the United Kingdom that would meet the trade and strategic needs of the two countries in the future. The White Paper decreed drastic reduction of immigration for several years, at which time it would cease altogether. It forbade Jews from buying land in nine-tenths of the mutilated territory left to them, and in effect was designed to reduce the Yishuv forever to the status of a national minority and put an end to its aspiration to live as a free nation in its own land.

It was now obvious that the only way to a free state was by fighting Great Britain and overthrowing its rule. Until that time, this belief was not shared by many. The leaders of the Yishuv had believed in the idea of a "national home" which would come into fruition under the patronage of Great Britain's Mandatory government. I thought that Albion's perfidy, which now shattered the illusions of those people, would help us recruit fighters for the Irgun and gain public approval. Only by ridding ourselves of foreign rule could we hope to be able to open our gates to the doomed Jews of Europe. The White Paper was indeed a severe blow to the Jewish Agency, the Vaad Leumi and the

Zionist leadership, all of whom based their policies on cooperation with Great Britain.

I was about to assume the job of planning attacks on the British in Jerusalem when we heard that David Raziel had been arrested. Hanoch Kalay took over Raziel's command. He had headed the Jerusalem branch of the Irgun since July 1938. I knew him well from my days as operations officer. He had always given me a free hand and sanctioned even my most daring schemes. When I came back from Poland, I went straight to Hanoch in Tel Aviv. He made me company commander (Gundar), the youngest in the history of the Irgun. In Jerusalem I had under my command an elite corps, intelligence squads, arms depots, caches, and underground headquarters in the Zikhron Moshe neighborhood. I started working day and night on planning and carrying out attacks.

The Irgun now decided to embark on ''acts of war'' against the British. I was ordered to strike at the heart of the British government in Jerusalem. The Rex Cinema explosion was planned as our opening salvo in this new campaign.

An underground operation is generally planned as follows:
1. Intelligence.
2. Plan of action.
3. Practice and maneuver.
4. Preparation of accessories.
5. Intelligence updating prior to the operation.
6. Withdrawal and disappearance.

The Rex Cinema was in the center of town in the middle of the government office complex known as the Triangle. Government offices, national police headquarters, the CID, the courts, all were there. The high British officials as well as the Arab leadership frequented the new movie theater. An attack on that center of entertainment meant a psychological blow to the government and a way to undermine its prestige.

My preparations had to be very thorough. I began by gathering intelligence on the location, a crucial phase of any terrorist operation. I chose three men and a woman from our Arabist group. Two men were assigned to the orchestra, and the ''couple'' to the balconies. They looked exactly like Arabs and spoke perfect Arabic. I always sent people in pairs on such missions, to check their reports against each other afterwards. We dressed the men in suits with colorful handkerchiefs in their breast-pockets, and had them use hair lotion and perfume. They carried Arab ID cards and the documents of government officials, all forged, of course, by our documentation center.

The theater had two entrances, from two different streets. One led to the orchestra and the other to the balconies. The orchestra was guarded by ushers who carefully checked and even frisked everyone who came in, and examined every bag or package. But the balconies were not checked, since they were used by the British and Arab dignitaries, their wives and mistresses, who would be offended by the searching.

Our people had no difficulty in gaining admittance through either entrance. They brought me two important pieces of information: a British detective sometimes accompanied the Arab doormen during the downstairs checks, whenever a film was particularly popular with the British, and the seats inside were unnumbered. It was first come first seated, so it would be easy to take a good position from which to launch a bomb. There was an interval during the performance and one could go outside for a quick snack in the street (no refreshments were served on the premises) and return to the theater. Jews rarely attended that theater.

I studied the disposition of the balconies. This area had no security check, and the audience preferred to sit in the boxes, so it was easy to find seats in the first row. There was a railing, with the orchestra immediately below. I then checked out the Mamilla cemetery near the theater. It was surrounded by a wall of hewn stones about the height of a man. Anyone standing behind that wall would be hidden from the people entering or leaving the theater, and would have a direct firing line. The cemetery was unguarded. One could go in and out at will.

I decided we would need sophisticated time-bombs. After much thought I came up with the idea of an "explosive coat." I invented a device which several years later I used in the LEHI operations in London.

Despite the free access to the balconies, I decided that our team should look and sound as authentically Arab in dress, speech, behavior and documents as possible. They would toss their grenades, carried inside the girls' handbags, so that they would explode over the audience down below at the same time as the coat. The follow-up attack from behind the cemetery wall presented no particular problems apart from getting the weapons in and out. Having picked my people, I sent them on ostensible intelligence missions, which in reality were rehearsals of the operation. The reason for that was to keep the operation a secret from the participants until the last moment. Once they were about to start the actual operation, no one was allowed to leave, except in the direction of the objective. Man's natural instinct is self-preservation, albeit in the underground there is a strong spirit of self-sacrifice. This often causes a conflict which is usually overcome, and the fighter's idealism takes over when the moment arrives. But it is obviously better to shorten this process as much as possible. Moreover, leaving the point of assembly before an operation is always dangerous, hence strictly forbidden.

I found a tailor who agreed to sew my special coat. He worked in a small shop in Mahane Yehuda. I explained to him the importance of the operation in view of the recently published White Paper. He was delighted to cooperate, although he had no idea where or how that coat was going to be used. He had to start from scratch, since we were afraid the police might later on trace back the remains of the coat if we bought a ready-made one. He made a new coat, and, together with my electrician friend, I attached the accessories of the time-bomb. We stuffed the shoulders with blasting gelatin instead of the usual shoulder pads. This was the most powerful explosive substance available at that time, and you could shape it as you wished, like plasticene. We lined the coat with layers of blasting gelatin and added about ten fingers of dynamite. The tailor had made a small pocket inside one of the shoulder pads for inserting a timer at the last moment. Two wires connected that pocket to the electric firing device. The other shoulder pad contained four small batteries joined together. The batteries were connected by wire to the device, supplying the necessary power. We inserted electric detonators into the explosives, also joined together, and wrapped them with a primer to augment the explosion.

The electric firing system, then, included the following: dynamite stuck with detonators wrapped in primers; detonators connected to wires, one leading to an electric battery, the other to the timer; and another wire connecting the battery to the timer and thus completing the electric circuit. When the clock reached the set time, the current would reach the explosives, setting off the resistance which would cause the fulminate of mercury to explode. This explosion in turn would cause the explosives to go off. The most delicate of all the components was the timer.

Before inserting anything into the coat, I carefully checked each item and calculated the combined power of the batteries. I made sure the electrical system was working. I tried out the timer with a test lamp.

Before concealing the bomb mechanism, we connected it to a switch which was hidden in a matchbox. This enabled us to turn the whole thing off if something went wrong. The tailer sewed in everything beautifully and made a double lining. The only opening was in the timer-pocket, so that it could be withdrawn and set at the last minute. The coat was tried on and it fitted perfectly. I passed my hand over it—no telltale bulges or lumps. We hid the coat till it was time to use it.

The next step was the preparation of the chocolate-box bombs. A member of the Irgun who owned a candy store agreed to donate three different sizes of chocolate-boxes into which bombs could be fitted. We chose imported English *bonbonnieres* in their original wrapping. I removed the confections, replaced them with a tightly-fitting tin and welded a roll of wire to the tin. We put nails and bits of iron between the wire roll and the sides of the box, in order to aggravate the impact, and we added dynamite inside the roll. Here, too, electricity was provided by small batteries, electric detonators and primers, plus an electric switch. If you pressed the wire connecting the switch to the current, the bomb would go off.

I put all the bits and pieces into the tin box and fitted the box inside the chocolate-box. The wires were concealed in the ribbon around the wrapping and I did not forget a proper bow. The ribbon was measured according to the distance from the theater floor to the railing, minus 4½ feet. This meant that when the box was thrown down, with the ribbon tied to the railing, the electrical mechanism would close off the circuit and cause the chocolate-boxes to explode above the heads of the public. We prepared three boxes and hid them until needed.

Now we had to select the participants. The most important person was the one who would carry the coat into the theater. I chose the tailor himself for this task. He was a Sephardi, looked like an Arab, spoke fluent Arabic, and was familiar with Arab customs. No one could tell him apart from an Arab, and the coat fitted him perfectly. It was also important to guard the secret of the sewing of the coat, since I considered the coat idea an important invention and did not wish to divulge it. For all the above reasons I chose the tailor, whose name was Mazliah Nimrodi.

I picked six of our Arabists to go up on the gallery as three couples. Rahel Ohevet-Ami, who had participated in all the operations in which we needed a dark skinned, Arabic speaking woman, was one of them. She was later caught in another exploit and was sentenced to life imprisonment.

The day before the Rex was to be bombed I personally visited the place—my standard practice—to make sure my intelligence was accurate and nothing had changed in the meantime. I was disguised as a British detective. My English was fairly fluent and I did not expect the Arab doorman to suspect my accent. I was only 21 years old, but most of the British detectives at that time were also very young, or at least looked young. I had my hair cut short, I dressed the part, and I carried the appropriate papers and entered the theater after passing all the checks. I examined the hall, made a mental note what to tell Mazliah, and waited for the next show to begin, at which time I went up to the gallery from Shlomzion Street and decided where the three couples should sit. I went to the Moslem cemetery to see where our people should position themselves in order to attack those fleeing the theater. I went over the plan once more. Everything seemed to click. I felt confident we would succeed.

The date was set for May 29, 1939. The show was scheduled for 19:15. We set our time-bombs for 20:30, at which moment the MGM lion would be roaring for Tarzan at the Rex. Working backwards, I set the meeting with Mazliah for 18:00, with the couples for 18.30, and with the machine gun squad for 19:45. First I went to the tailor shop. The coat, removed from its hiding place, was hanging on a dummy. Mazliah had no idea why I had come. I said: "Let's see how the coat looks on you," and he put it on. As expected, it looked great. I then said: "You have been chosen to take the coat into the movie theater, the same movie theater you have visited. You know how to get there and how to reach the spot picked for the action." I added that the Irgun had chosen him for a most important protest action in the wake of the White Paper, aimed at both the Arabs and the British.

Mazliah listened intently and remained perfectly calm. I could tell he was going through an inner struggle to remain calm in the face of this new situation I had just presented him with. I assured him the operation had been carefully planned down to the last detail and I knew he would have no problems and would perform one of the most complex and sophisticated operations the Irgun had ever undertaken. I reminded him he had to adhere to a timetable calculated to a fraction of a second. A time-bomb, after all, goes off on time, regardless of external circumstances. We synchronized Mazliah's watch with the timer in the coat, so that he would know exactly when the bomb was due to go off, and act accordingly.

Mazliah was groomed like an Arab, perfumed, his hair sleeked, a colorful handkerchief in his chest-pocket, his shoes glistening. He had expensive English cigarettes in his pockets, an Arab favorite. I shook his hand warmly and told him as I always did on such occasions: "Mazliah, your name is a good omen, and the Almighty guards his warriors." I shook his hand again and wished him success. I reminded him we would meet after the operation to congratulate each other on our success.

I asked Haim, my electrician, who was with me, to accompany Mazliah to the door of the movie theater. It was our custom to accompany those sent on a mission to make sure all went well and to protect them before, during and after the mission. Haim had the added task of pressing the switch and starting the mechanism just before Mazliah entered the theater.

After Mazliah departed I drove quickly to my meeting place with the couples carrying the cholocate-boxes. They were all there when I arrived. We brought the boxes out of the hiding place. I told the couples about the operation, its importance and its plan. They were receptive, and did not seem to have too many doubts. They listened eagerly and were anxious to get started. The women hid the boxes in their bags. I took one last look at them. They all looked like Arabs in every way. I shook their hands and wished them good luck. Each walked away, taking a different route to the theater, as one of my assistants accompanied them at a short distance.

Now I had to meet the third detail, assigned to open fire on the people fleeing the theater. This group was headed by Refael Saban, a fearless fighter whom I fully trusted. Here too everything was ready. We used our Finnish "Wash" submachine guns, each with hundreds of rounds of ammunition. Our men also carried pistols for self-defense, as well as grenades, to increase their firepower.

This is Mazliah's report of the operation:

"The walk to the theater seemed endless. I kept looking around to make sure I did not arouse suspicion. I did not carry anything, but my coat was very heavy. I arrived at the theater. Haim pressed the switch and left. He told me not to become absorbed in the movie and keep track of time. I went to the box office and bought a ticket. The cashier gave me my ticket and my change without looking at me. I waited till the entrance became crowded and joined the crowd. The ushers frisked me and felt my pockets, and the British detective sized me up. I was waved inside. My heart beat violently. They showed a Tarzan film. The theater was not too full. I looked for a suitable place to sit. Arabs were sitting all around, chatting and smoking. I preferred to sit near a group of Britons. I was so nervous I began to chain-smoke, and one of the Arabs remarked, 'Perhaps he's in love, that one, who knows?' I hardly looked at the screen, I was so tense. It was almost 20:30, and and I was still wearing the coat. I didn't know how to take it off, it seemed to be stuck to my body. The timer was ticking away. I couldn't think of anything else. Seven minutes to go. I finally took the coat off and hung it on the back of the seat in front of me. I got up. I couldn't move. Somehow I managed to apologize to the people next to me and got through and went outside. I was afraid someone might get up and yell I had forgotten something, but apparently the film was holding everyone's attention. I left the hall. I asked the usher for a ticket so I could get back in, and told him I had to see someone outside. He was very friendly. I spoke Arabic, of course, and no one suspected anything.

"I don't know how I arrived at the meeting place. I was so tense and excited my feet did not seem to touch the ground. I did not pay attention to the traffic and to the crowds. I finally reached the meeting place. Etan had been waiting for me. I gave him my hand for a strong handshake. He kept holding my hand as if examining the results of the operation. At that moment we heard a loud explosion and then more explosions and gunfire. We embraced and Etan said, 'Go home and rest.' "

The three young couples had arrived at the theater separately and took their seats in the gallery, next to the railing, away from one another, as couples in love would. The gallery was not crowded. In the dark the women were able to unravel the ribbons of the chocolate boxes and tie them around the railing. They kept the bombs in their bags, ready to toss them into the hall below as soon as the coat exploded.

At exactly 20:30, as the famous lion opened its mouth, the coat exploded with a deafening noise. The couples immediately threw the boxes down, where they hung over the heads of the panicked crowd. The ribbons tied to the railing pulled the switches and the candy boxes exploded.

The place became a pandemonium. Screaming people ran outside trampling one another in their haste to get away. Those who managed to get outside were greeted with gunfire and grenades from the direction of the cemetery. The operation resulted in 18 wounded and 5 dead, and the damage to the theater was estimated at 20,000 pounds.

The news of the attack spread quickly in the city and around the country, and became the main topic of conversation and news commentary. The military commander of Jerusalem, Major General O'Connor, ordered all Jewish movie theaters, restaurants and places of entertainment closed "until further notice."

The Campaign Against the British Continues

The Rex Cinema success boosted my men's spirits and instilled in them self-confidence and derring-do. It also taught them how to carry out a complex, professionally executed operation. They were flying high. Success begets success, while failure leads to inaction. In light of my successes, the high command gave me complete freedom of action. I was determined to do everything I could to fight the British. I began to select objectives in Jerusalem, choosing the most convenient ones. Blowing up the telephone system appeared to be the most convenient.

One June 2, at 7 a.m., we blew up three telephone junction boxes: near the Italian School Terra Santa on King George Street, near Eden Hotel off Ben-Yehuda Street, and in Meah Shearim. As a result, some 1750 phones were disconnected, including those serving the army and the police in the capital.

The operation was followed by a wave of attacks in Tel Aviv, where our men destroyed most of the telephone lines in the city. Over 1100 phones were paralyzed.

Before we blew up the telephone boxes, we carefully studied their locations. They were buried in the ground at main intersections in the city, covered with a metal lid. My intelligence unit surveyed the location, access routes, and the subscribers of each exchange. We chose the ones with Arab and British subscribers.

At the appointed time my men, dressed as telephone company crew, went to the three locations, spread a tent over the underground box, and began their "repair work." Other men stood guard around the place. The workers lifted the lids and put a load of 11 pounds of explosives in each box. It was more than enough to blow up the entire works.

My success prompted me to expand my operation, and four days later, on June 6, I took on eight more boxes, ten public phones, and five transformers. The transformers were property of a British company. That day we attacked 23 targets, each relatively small, yet all adding up to a major complex operation. In each place we needed five men, to put in the bombs and to stand guard, totalling 115 men. Add the lab team, who made the bombs, and the one who assisted with the logistics; we had engaged no less than 150 men that day.

Handling such a large quantity of explosives was problematic. We needed at least 242 pounds—11 pounds for each underground box, 4.4 pounds for each public phone, and 22 pounds for each transformer. We had to divide the stuff and put small portions of it in special containers in order to conceal it and to protect the men from the poisonous fumes. We had to train the demolition teams on location, which required great effort, since they had to go there one at a time, pretending to be casual passersby, in order not to draw any attention to themselves.

Each of the three groups of objectives was assigned a commander, while I commanded the entire operation. The three commanders briefed their men, using a scale model of the objective. I attended all three briefings, and saw the men leave on their mission. I went along with the group that went out to blow up the largest transformer, in the Arab section.

At 9:30 in the evening Jerusalem was rocking with powerful explosions, heard at different ends of the city. A dark cloud rose over the city. In several places fires were started because of the explosions, and the night sky was bright with flames. During our withdrawal we ran into police forces rushed to the scene. They did not notice us, but I could hear the shouts of alarm: "The Irish are coming! The Irish are coming!" It was their way of letting their own men know it was a major attack.

Our forces returned safely.

In 1939 I used to read a weekly magazine called *9 Baerev* (9 PM). One time as I leafed through it I saw a cartoon showing a little boy trying to put into the mail box an illegal pornographic publication. It gave me an idea for an attack on the British. Mail boxes in those days were cast-iron cylinders, placed on street corners. One stood on the corner of Mamila and Julienne. It was an Arab neighborhood with many British residents and few Jews. It seemed to me to be an excellent target, provided one could put in sufficient explosives and a good firing device. Next to the mail box there was a public phone. I decided to install a small time bomb in the phone booth and let it explode so it would attract a crowd of curious people. Ten minutes later the bomb in the mail box would go off. I made the two bombs—the small one for the phone booth and the larger one for the mail box. I gave the small one to Nachshon, who hid it inside the phone booth, and the larger one to Yitzhak Miller, to put in the mail box. Miller ran into some unexpected difficulties.

Miller rode his bike and waited in the vicinity until Nachshon was done. When he saw Nachshon come out of the phone booth he went to mail his letter. The envelope, it turned out, was too thick to go through the opening. As he was trying to push it in, the owner of a nearby vegetable store came running out and yelled at the top of his lungs, "Bomb! Bomb!" A crowd materialized and grabbed Miller, about to tear him apart. Fortunately, A British army patrol walking down Princess Mary Street heard the tumult and came over to find out what was going on. Miller was a South African who spoke perfect English and was dressed like an Englishman. He explained to the British Sergeant he was a government employee who was trying to mail an official letter. He showed the envelope to the soldiers. It was an official envelope, British royal seal and all, which one of our men who worked in a government office had stolen. Miller said he could not understand all that nonsense about a bomb. To prove his point, he said he was willing to throw the envelope against the rocks across the street. There was a moment of silence, and without further ado Miller threw the envelope. The edge tore, showing some of the paper wrapping the explosives. The soldiers were convinced. They derided the Arabs for being so suspicious, and told Miller to take the envelope to the central post office, where the openings are larger and the public is less suspicious. Miller willingly agreed, picked up the envelope, mounted his bike and came back to our hiding place fast as an arrow. When he arrived he staggered, nearly fainting.

I was watching the whole thing from a nearby rooftop. I was dying to go down and help Miller, break through the crowd and rescue him, but could not come up with any useful ideas. I stood there and saw how he was saved by a miracle. I went down and quickly returned to our place, then helped revive him, and dismantled the letter bomb, five minutes before it was due to explode. I took the bike and sped to the phone booth, where I disconnected the time bomb moments before the explosion, preferring not to let it go off and reveal our plans. When I returned to our room Miller was still greatly agitated. "I saw the hanging rope and my mother's face when I spoke to the soldiers," he said. "Both gave me the strength to control myself and carry this thing through."

Following Miller's lead, I decided to put the advice the British soldiers had given him to good use. The idea of putting the letter bomb in the central post office was appealing for several reasons. First, it would mean a direct attack on a government institution. Second, the building was next to the CID headquarters, hence an attack on that place would shake the secret police. Third, an explosion next door would attract the top CID investigators, including their bomb expert. This man had dismantled many of our bombs, and discovered our methods. It was extremely important to put him out of action.

The central post office had four large mail boxes with large openings. They were located in pairs at either side of the main entrance, with a slot both in the front, on the streetside, and in the back, inside the post office. It was clear that a bomb detonated inside the boxes would go through the wall of the post office. I used this fact to determine the size of the bombs, and decided to mail the letters late in the evening, when the place was nearly empty, after the mail had been collected, so that the Jewish mail collectors would not be harmed. I prepared four letter bombs—three for the mail boxes, and a special fourth one for our friend, Clark, the bomb expert. In this envelope I put a trap. It was not the usual electric circuit, which our expert already knew how to dismantle by cutting the wire before the time of the explosion. This time I installed a double wire, so that by curring one wire, the cutting instrument would touch the second wire and close the circuit, causing the explosion. This bomb was my special gift for the expert, who, I assumed, would be anxious to dismantle it, not realizing it was intended for him personally.

Miller, who in the meantime had recovered from his harrowing experience, was anxious to carry those envelopes, to make up for his fiasco. I readily agreed.

The post office operation was set for June 10, the day after one of our female members, Rahel Ohevet-Ami, was arrested. We wanted to show the British we were not lying low. The effectiveness of subversive activities lies not only in the impact of each one, but in the continuity, which paralyzes the occupation forces. And so at 9 o'clock on the evening of the 10th, Miller and his escort left a house in Zichron Moshe and rode their bikes towards the central post office. They carried the envelopes which contained 5 sticks of blasting gelatin and a firing device, consisting of an electric detonator, a battery and a wrist watch. When they arrived they deposited the letters in the mail boxes in the front of the building. Three letters exploded on time, destroyed the front wall, and caused serious damage to the main hall. Furniture was blown up and the electric system was destroyed. A police inspector, a British soldier and several Arab guards nearby were wounded.

The fourth bomb, with the booby trap, did not explode. The next day, at 8:30 a.m., as the debris was being cleared, one of the employees found the envelope. Fred Clark was immediately alerted at the CID. The day before he had dismantled Rahel Ohevet-Ami's bomb at the Russian Compound. He began to work on the envelope, when the bomb exploded in his face. He was killed on the spot. His head was thrust in the air and stuck to the ceiling, with his eyes staring down. The explosion and the ghastly sight scared the CID personnel away, except for the eight who were wounded and needed help. It took the police a while to recover and come back inside to offer first aid to their wounded friends. The post office chief was told to come over, but when he saw the severed head he went into shock and had to be taken to the hospital. One Jewish police officer named Silver, who happened to be there, was also wounded. Since we did not have anything against him, we sent him a large bouquet of flowers with a get-well card. The daily press reported it, and after he left the hospital we found out that he was terminated by the police.

Officer Silver was not the only unintended casualty of the operation. I myself nearly got caught. At that time I lived in a small underground room in Zichron Moshe. We used to live in the religious neighborhoods of Jerusalem, because we assumed that Jews who said every day in their prayers, "Let there be no hope for informers," would not turn us in. We were right. Those neighborhoods did make us safe.

It was a good room and my landlady was a good pious woman. Under the cover of a university student, I was able to work on my bombs, including those letter bombs. The day after the post office explosions, however, the British, for the first time since their arrival, blocked the Jewish neighborhoods which they suspected might be harboring the terrorists. They went up on the roofs with machine guns, imposed a curfew, and started to search every Jewish house. Fortunately, they did not come into my neighborhood but rather encircled it, so I had time to leave my room and go into hiding. Before I left I hid my notes from the course I took in Poland. When the British came in and searched the room, they found some explosives which the person who used the room before me must have left without my knowledge. They continued to search and found the notes. After questioning the landlady, they found out that the room had been rented by a yong man named Dov Tamari, who lived in Motzah (now a math professor at the Technion in Haifa). He was caught, put on trial, and sentenced to seven years in jail for possession of explosives. The military court also studied my notes and decided they were most dangerous. The presiding judge remarked that the author of the notes deserved 15 years in jail. I need not mention I did not return to that room, especially since our men found out that the British kept watch over it, waiting for the tenant to return.

The curfew and the search at Zichron Moshe marked the shift in CID efforts from the Arab to the Jewish community. An Irgun member always had to use caution, but now he had to redouble his watchfulness, go into a deeper underground. This was particularly true in Jerusalem, since the capital of the British rule was full of British soldiers of the best units as well as British, Arab and Jewish police. The latter were probably the most dangerous, since they could obtain information about the underground more easily. There were also Jewish informers, who for money were willing to sell their own brothers and sisters.

But the intensified activities of the CID did not deter us. On the contrary, each day the authorities found out that they had to spend more and more resources in their fight against us, since Irgun attacks were becoming a daily occurrence. This pattern continued unabated since, whenever we did not have a spectacular operation like the ones I have just described, we filled the gap with a small one in order to keep up the frequency and the continuity.

TEN

Stepping Up Our Attacks

In June and July 1939 we stepped up our attacks against the British and the Arabs. Our exploits included blowing up telephone and electric installations in Jerusalem and Tel Aviv and the bombing of the central post office in Jerusalem. On July 12 the British colonial secretary announced in the British Parliament that as of october 1939 all Jewish immigration would be stopped, in light of an imminent world war and in order to appease the Arabs. The decree came in spite of the desperate efforts of the Zionist leaders in London to prevent the British government from implementing the White Paper. The Vaad Leumi announced a general strike of the entire Yishuv on July 17.

The Irgun reacted in its own way. I started a campaign in Jerusalem aimed directly at the government in order to send a loud message of the Hebrew reaction to the strangulation policy. I targeted the government radio station Kol Yerushalayim on Melisande Street. My objective was to cause as much damage as possible to the studios and stop the broadcasts for a period of time. This interruption would be concrete evidence of the power of the Hebrew underground.

In order to carry out this attack I needed an inside person. It was very hard to enter the station because of the British guard at the door who checked everyone and only admitted employees and those who had a pass. One of the employees, a man named Meir, was an Irgun member. I arranged to meet him and I found out it would be easy for him to place letter bombs anywhere in the building. I decided to use official government envelopes for the letter bombs. In addition, I ordered another explosive coat from Mazliah. In each of the envelopes I put six sticks of high explosives, an alectric detonator, a battery and a timer. In the coat I put twelve sticks with the same mechanism. The timers were set for 17:20.

On the morning of August 2, 1939 Meir was driven to the station wearing the explosive coat and carrying the envelopes in his attache case. He entered the building without difficulty after a short search by the guard. He hung up the coat in the control room and put the envelopes in the studios. He proceeded to another wing of the station to do his work. At 17:00 I was sitting on a park bench near the Russian Compound, next to the band stand, where each Wednesday the band played for the public, in keeping with good British tradition. At exactly 17:20 the radio station reverberated with mightly explosions. The building was badly damaged, and the broadcasts were stopped and later transfered to Radio Ramallah. Maya Weisenberg, a young Jewish woman from South Africa in charge of the Youth Hour in English, who used to help the Irgun and was not supposed to be there at that time, was seriously wounded and later died at the hospital of her wounds. Adib Mansur, an Arab engineer working at the control room was fatally wounded, and one of the technicians was

Arab gang leaders, fully armed.

lightly wounded. The building was evacuated, and I was still able to see our friend, Meir walking home. A few days later three of the station workers, including our man, were detained for questioning. Two were soon released, but Meir was sentenced to one year administrative arrest for lack of evidence. His sentence was later extended, and in time he was exiled to Eritrea.

After the bombing of the government radio station in Jerusalem the Irgun command announced a short lull in its operations on the occasion of the forthcoming Twentieth Zionist Congress, which was to take place on August 16 in Basel. The heads of the Jewish Agency and the Vaad Leumi looked forward to this congress as the opportunity to consolidate the campaign against the political decrees which threatened to put an end to the Jewish national home. In honor of the festive occasion we decided to slow down our activities, but in our hearts we knew that the British were unimpressed by the congress. We were convinced that only by force we could put an end to the occupation, and only an all-out war against the British could bring the redemption.

I used the lull to prepare material for the future. I decided to confiscate explosives from a store belonging to a Jew named Nadav, also on Melisande Street, near the police and CID headquarters. The store sold all sorts of weapons, but mainly dealt in explosives, used in quarries. The trade in explosives was, of course, under strict government control. For this reason, and not only because of the cost, we had to find unofficial ways of obtaining those things.

The store was bolted and locked day and night, and a policeman always stood outside. At night special security measures were used, and it was extremely hard to break in. The back door, in the inner court, was even more secured. But I found out one could enter that court from a side street without being seen by the policemen who were always in the neighborhood. From the court it was not hard to break at night into the paint shop which had a common wall with Nadav's store. The son of the paint shop owner, Zvi Aharonovitch, was a member of the Irgun. We decided not to implicate him, which was the right move, since he was later arrested and tortured. I set the time of the break-in for Friday night, August 4, 1939, since Jews were home welcoming the Sabbath, and we could do our work without interruptions. Breaking into the paint shop was not hard, but breaching the common wall was extremely difficult and required great expertise. Rahamim Cohen, an expert stone-cutter, was put in charge. He was assisted by Ephraim Ben-Eliyahu, Gershon

(Top) an explosive device ("infernal machine"), (right) a submachine gun, and (bottom) weapons used by the underground.

Abramovitch, Hayim Corfu and myself. Only before dawn were we able to make a large enough hole to take out the merchandise. At that point we were exhausted, our hands were bleeding, and we nearly passed out from lack of air in the closed paint storage room. But when we went through the hole we discovered such large quantities of explosives that we nearly jumped for joy.

Now we had to transfer the loot to our warehouse. At first we were going to use a car which was coming from Tel Aviv, but at the last moment it broke down and got stuck on the way. We had no choice but to use Binyamin Zeroni's car, our newly appointed commander, and it almost cost him his life. We took out about one ton of explosives. When we finished loading the car it was almost 4 o'clock in the morning. Because we were running out of time, we decided to hide the explosives temporarily in the basement of an unfinished building in Rehavia, a respectable neighborhood where Jewish Agency officials lived. Those officials were not on the CID's list of suspicious persons, since they did not oppose the British and at times even collaborated with them. We usually stayed away from that neighborhood, but this time it turned out that we did the right thing hiding the explosives there. When the authorities found out the explosives were missing they naturally suspected us. They looked everywhere, except in Rehavia. In the meantime we kept constant guard at the place, and on the third night, when the searches subsided, we put the forbidden stuff in tightly sealed milk containers and transferred it to our cache in one of the caves in Emek Hamatzleva. We used those explosives for several years in operations throughout the country.

ELEVEN

The British Method of Torture

Seeking to uncover the secrets of the Irgun, the British did not shy from using physical torture in their investigations. They were confident the Irgun would not dare retaliate. For some reason it took the Irgun a whole year to start reacting to repeated incidents of torture.

The first one to be tortured by the British was my first commander, Yosef Hakim, one of the senior commanders of the Jerusalem district. Hakim was sought by the police immediately after my attack on the National Arab Bus Company. He had to leave Jerusalem and take residence in Zikhron Yaakov, where he commanded the operation in Samaria. He was caught by the CID, brought to Jerusalem, and was severely tortured. Hakim did not tell his tormentors anything and was released after he agreed to leave the country. I vigorously condemned his action.

When the Irgun renewed its attacks after the publication of the White Paper, torture became more frequent. The head investigator and torturer was Ralph Cairns, assisted by British and Arab policemen at CID headquarters. In one of the statements issued at the time, the Irgun command revealed to the Yishuv what it knew about the infernal torture used by the CID:

> They beat them with rubber sticks all over their body; they squeezed their testicles; they pulled out their hair and their beards; they burned them

with cigarettes; they hanged them by their thumbs and by their feet; they poured kettles of water into their stomach and lungs, nearly choking them; they beat them with bamboo sticks on the bottom of their feet.

The torture was supervised by Cairns, who would question the prisoner and personally torture him. He also took active part in torturing women, and did not stop at anything. The torture of women was one of the most serious crimes committed by him, which were counted against him when I executed him in August 1939.

At one point Cairns tortured four of our members who were caught by the police. The first was Menahem Levin, a chemistry student, who was arrested on June 11 with his friend Oscar Buchwald and accused of illegal possession of explosives. The detectives found a key in Levin's pocket to a room where the Irgun had a small laboratory for explosives. Cairns was sure he could get out of him important information about the local command, its mode of operation and its plans. He subjected Levin to intense beating and warned him he "would not come out alive" if he did not cooperate. Levin kept quiet throughout the investigation, and when his investigators despaired of getting him to talk they sent him to the central prison, where his wounds were allowed to heal so that the military court would not see them. He was sentenced to four years in jail.

The British had a fiendish method of picking their victims. They would go after those who seemed an easy mark. They did not usually torture operational commanders for fear of retaliation. This fear seemed to be the only thing that stopped them. Thus, for example, when I was wounded and captured by the British in 1942 they knew I was the commander of a combat unit of the LEHI and was responsible for many operations in which British police and soldiers were killed, yet they did not dare touch me. I made it clear to them they would pay for it if they did, since my men would go after them and kill them.

On July 16, 1939 at 7:20, our member Mordecai Fecho was arrested in Jerusalem. A few days before his arrest I went out with him to the Jaffa Gate to look into placing a bomb. We walked slowly when suddenly he asked me, "Tell me, Etan, how will I be able to endure the torture if they catch me?" His question surprised me, since I was absorbed at that moment in the operation and it never occurred to me I might get caught. I quickly responded, "Trust in the Lord. The Lord guards his warriors." He was a religious boy and when I saw him after he had been tortured at jail he told me that my words had helped him bear his pain. He was frail and had sidecurls and a beard. He bravely endured the torture and did not say a word about the Irgun.

He had been stopped on King George near the Jewish Agency building by a detail of secret police headed by Cairns and was taken into the CID headquarters. Cairns gave him a list of names and told him to identify them. When he said he did not know any of them they began to torture him. They did not let up for a week. Cairns took part in it himself. In his letter to the Mandates Committee in Geneva Fecho wrote: "Three times he put a burning cigarette next to my ears." The tormentors made use of bamboo sticks, a legacy from the Turks. When they failed to learn anything from him they sent him to the central prison of Jerusalem where he spent 11 days in solitary confinement. Cairns had warned him that if he revealed anything about the seven days of torture he would be severely punished.

Fecho was the first victim of the "third degree" method which Cairns introduced against our members. But in torturing Binyamin Zeroni, the commander of the Jerusalem district, whom he caught, Cairns pulled all the stops. Zeroni recorded the experience after his escape:

I was arrested on August 5, 1939 at 10:30 as I drove my car on King George in Jerusalem. As I crossed the King George-Jaffa Road intersection, an Arab policeman ordered me to stop. I thought I was being stopped for an ordinary traffic violation and I saw no reason to escape. But I told Refael Saban who sat next to me to leave just in case. He left and the traffic policeman took his place. He took me directly to the CID headquarters in the Russian Compound. Here I was surrounded by British detectives with drawn guns who took me to Officer Gordon to make a statement. When I refused to talk and asked for a lawyer, they handcuffed me and chained my legs and took me to the cellar to be investigated. Officer Cairns sat behind the table. When he saw me he growled, "You better talk, or you will be sorry." As I stood there I was seized by three Englishmen who stood behind me, held back my hands and stepped on my feet so I couldn't move. Cairns got up and began to strike me on my head, my nape and my neck. He hit me with the flat of his hand under my ears, left and right, then on both sides at once. The pain entered my brain cells. After fifteen minutes of constant beating I was in shock. My hand and leg muscles contracted, I became deaf and I fell on the ground. The Englishmen picked me up. The same thing was repeated and I kept hearing the question: Who is M. R. who was mentioned in a report found in my room? As I was about to pass out they locked me up in the cellar. On the morning of August 6, 1939 they took me back to the torture chamber. Cairns came over to me, pulled me by the hair and tore out some of it. He finally made me look at him. "Listen, are you crazy, you want to die? Here you don't die so fast. You will die, but slowly, very slowly. We will torture you three times a day, morning, noon and night." He beat me till I went limp. I told him, "Aren't you afraid to torture me? You know I have many friends on the outside and they will surely kill you." He slapped his pistol and said, "Though I walk through the valley of the shadow of death I will fear no evil for Thou art with me." He then slapped his chest as if to say, I am protected.

Meanwhile Cairns called the government physician, who checked me and pronounced me healthy. After he left, the torture resumed. Cairns is the master tormentor. He is the overseer and also the inventor. He is assisted by Officer Gilpin, who seems to derive sadistic pleasure from the whole thing. From time to time Giles, the head of the CID and his deputy, Shaw, came to witness the inquisition.

The tortures continued. I was stripped naked, my shoes and socks were taken off and I was made to lie flat on the table with my face up. Once again Cairns tried to make me talk, pinching and hitting me. My hands and legs were tied, my underpants stuffed into my mouth, as Cairns put a rubber glove on his right hand, and began to squeeze my testicles, one at a time. A sharp pain shot through my body, went into my head, dimmed my eyes, went back to my legs, repeating itself. He keeps squeezing, lifts me by my genitals, drops me and continues to squeeze. I lost the sense of time. A moment seemed an eternity. He sees my eyes glaze and he drags me across the table until my feet reach the edge. He begins to swat the table with a crop and reaches the bottoms of my feet.

I managed to push my underpants out of my mouth with my tongue. I released my right hand, and started to scream at the top of my lungs, protecting my genitals with my right hand. They were startled by my screams, stopped the torture for a moment, closed the windows and the shutters, and started again. Cairns was standing next to my head all this time and when he saw my face contorting with pain he pulled my hair and said, "You bloody Jew, you filthy dog, are you crazy, you want to suffer? Start talking!"

I don't know how long it lasted. I had lost my notion of time. I was taken back to my cell naked, wrapped in a blanket held by three Arabs. I was not able to walk.

On the morning of August 7, 1939 they had to carry me to the torture chamber, since I couldn't walk. Cairns always spoke first: "Binyamin, you see this picture? Look at me, you bastard, you want more torture? Are you crazy?" He accentuates his words with blows, slaps, kicks and pinching. He shows me the picture they had found in my room, my girlfriend's picture. "You see this picture? What a beautiful lassy, what a beautiful body." He smacks his lips. "Must be heaven to go to bed with such a girl. We will find her and bring her here. You know what we will do to her, you stinking bastard? We will rape her in front of you. I will rape her right here in this room. It will be my pleasure. We will then strip her naked and do to her what we did to you." Suddenly the blows come down and I begin to bleed from my mouth and lips. "You think we are finished with you, you're crazy? We have only started." He waved at two Arabs to come over. They take me into a long room. Again they undress me and put me down on a table. Cairns, expertly, attacks my testicles and the bottoms of my feet, but this apparently is not what he had in mind. Cairns and Gilpin press my head between two desk drawers, like a vise, and I can't move my head. The Arabs hold and squeeze my hands and legs. Cairns wraps a bandage around my nose and fastens it with a clothespin. I cannot breathe through my nose, and I have to open my mouth. He goes out and comes back with a large kettle full of water and starts pouring the water into my mouth. I try to close my mouth but I can't breathe. I open my mouth and it fills with water. I try to breathe and the water goes into my lungs. I have no choice but to swallow the water. I drank one and a half kettles of water and my stomach began to swell. My head was pounding. My lungs filled with water. My heart was about to burst. Through all this the voice of that English gentleman, Cairns, reached me, droning as usual, "Ben, you think we are short on water? We have a full supply. We have enough water for the rest of your life. You bastard. You stinking louse. You want to talk? You crazy? You want more torture? Life is good. How old are you, eh? Twenty-five? You are still young. The world is yours. You can still do a lot for yourself and for your Jews. You are stupid, Ben. Your friends are now sitting on the beach in Tel Aviv, eating ice cream and hugging girls, and you are going to die of torture. But we won't let you die, Ben. We will keep torturing you for days and weeks until you tell us who your bastard friends are." He slowly empties into my mouth the seventh, the eighth, the ninth kettle. After an hour and a quarter I felt I couldn't bear it any longer. A stream of foul water burst out of my mouth and my stuffed nose, mixed with stomach and lung juice. With great effort I released my right arm and started waving it. I grabbed the kettle and swung it in the air. I freed my legs and started to kick. Finally I fell back and lay motionless, swooning, water gushing out of my mouth. Cairns was telling to his aides he was afraid my lungs might burst. They checked my pulse and took me back to my cell on an old blanket.

Cairns came to see me at noon. Again he squeezed my testicles, again he spat on me, cursed me as usual, then turned me over to his aides.

They drag me to the torture chamber and tell me that since I kept insisting I wanted a lawyer they decided to bring Attorney Goitein. They dress me, wipe the blood stains, and comb my hair. They pour cold water on me to help me recover my consciousness and to hide the blows, and take me into the office. A man comes in who introduces himself as Arieli, a Jew, and says he works for Attorney Goitein. They leave me in the office for half an hour to consult ''my lawyer.'' I ask him where Goitein is and he says he is in the office and in the meantime he has sent him to get my personal data. He asks me for my name, address, activities etc. I ask him: ''Do you have a document that shows that you work for Goitein? I don't want to talk to you because I don't know you, and if Goitein wants to see me tell him to come over and bring an ID. Otherwise, I won't talk to anyone.'' The young man leaves in embarrassment. The provocation did not succeed.

Cairns starts again. As usual, he kicks, he pinches, he curses me, my mother, my race, all my people. He promises to torture all the Jew pigs and send them back to Hitler, ''who knows how to take care of them.'' They take me back into the torture chamber. Since I can't stand or sit they lay me down on the table. Cairns, as usual, goes for his favorite place. After he kneads my testicles and pulls me up by gripping them, he huddles with his aides and conducts a consultation. They whisper so I won't hear, and as they finish they look pleased with themselves. Cairns, the expert, approaches me, this time without cursing, and occupies himself with my thumbs. He wraps cotton around my thumbs and ties a cord around the cotton. The cord is tied at the other end across the room to the tin roof. He says ''ready'' and the others pull the bench from under me and now I hang in midair by my thumbs.

My face slowly turns blue and my head drops on my chest. Cairns comes over, checks the cord and grips my pulse, to make sure it still works. The blood leaves my arms and gathers in my head. A pain radiates from my thumbs into the rest of my body, total pain. Vague pictures swim before my eyes. My head pounds and seethes as if the whole universe is squeezed into it. Black and red circles dance before my eyes, and I begin to sink into a bottomless pit. Cairns, the grand inquisitor and the medical authority, checks my pulse which has nearly stopped. His concerned aides take me down. They put me on my side and revive me by pouring vinegar into my nose and mouth. My thumbs are dead. The blood inside them has coagulated and they no longer are part of my body.

Cairns puts his hand next to my nostrils and finds out whether I am still breathing. They hang me up again, this time upside down. They tie my feet together with a rope and hoist me by the rope, leaving me hanging with my head leaning on the bench. After they secure the rope Cairns takes DDT, wets my naked feet and begins to whip them. The blows keep coming sharp and strong, endless. The blows intensify, the pain gets worse, the blows subside and intensify again. Cairns keeps pouring DDT on my feet as his aides applaud his wisdom. The whipping changes rhythm, and my feet are drying up. The blood flows into my head. My head keeps swelling. It seems to fill up the entire room. The flesh on my feet turns to a pulp. Through a fog I hear Cairn's voice, telling Gilpin to lower me down a bit, to start the whipping again. Between whipping he pulls my testicles, as if it were some kind of private privilege. I lose control of my body. Only my mind is clear and I am aware of everything. They untie my legs and take me down from the hanging. I fall from the bench to the floor. Cairns and Gilpin begin to kick me, step on me, spit on me, and when they get tired they call the Arab prisoners to take me to my cell, wrapped in a blanket.

I haven't eaten in three days. I cannot eat. My lips burn and bleed constantly. My throat is swollen from the blows on my neck and nape, imparted to me by Cairns, the medical expert, each time he decides to revive me after each torture. I can barely drink the water brought to me by the Arab inmates. I relieve myself in a pot brought to me by an Arab inmate, and when he is late I relieve myself on the floor. I lie on a rickety bed with a torn, foul-smelling mattress. I am not able to smoke. My lungs are full of water. I cough from time to time, a piercing cough which causes me great pain and shakes my aching body. I cannot move my arms and legs. My leg muscles have become too tender. Any slight movement makes me aware of their existence. My feet burn, swollen and wounded. I cannot talk, and only manage to whisper a few words when I must say something.

The torture continues. Each day they take me to the torture chamber. I cannot walk. They hold me under my arms, with my feet dragging across the floor. I cannot sit on a chair, and if they do not prop me from behind I fall down on the floor like a sack of potatoes. Cairns does not believe I am so weak, and checks me according to his method—four men turn my hands backward, break them at the joints till they seem to be pulled from my arms. They twist my hands until they crack. Cairns is startled. They tear open my shirt and suddenly pour ice water on my neck and back. They put ice cubes inside my shirt, pour ice water on my ears, burn my hands with cigarettes. It doesn't work. My head rests on my chest, my eyes bulge out of their sockets, my mouth is foaming, but I don't say a word.

Cairns is desperate. My genitals resist his pressure and blows and I don't budge. All his questions are dashed against my wall of silence. His anger is burning: "Listen here, look at me, I tell you. Are you crazy? Look at me!" More hair is torn out of my head, but when he lets go my head drops again on my chest. "Are you crazy? Listen! You want us to bring your family and torture them in front of your eyes? You want us to rape your sisters right here? You want us to bring Abu Ali, the negro, to rape them right here, in front of your eyes? Are you crazy? You don't want to talk? All right. We will bring your old uncle and aunt, we have no pity. You Jew bastard!" And he spits on me, kicks me, puts a burning cigarette against my skin, but it's all useless. I won't talk.

The torture continues. He presses his handkerchief against my nostrils and I begin to suffocate. My lungs strain against my ribs. My pinned down hands twist. My eyes sink in their orbits. Cairns looks at me with sadistic joy and removes the handkerchief from my blue face.

And now he invents a new torture: he won't let me sleep. He orders the Arabs not to let me sleep. They are happy to comply and arrange day and night shifts. Nothing is worse than lying on your back with your eyes open. The Arabs change every two hours. The guard is not sleeping on the job. He sits on the edge of my bed and does not take his eyes off of me. When they start to close he punches me in the stomach with his fist and yells, "Wake up, don't go to sleep." The hours drag on, my open eyes are smarting. I am drowsy, my entire body pleads for sleep. The Arab inmates are snoring, mosquitoes buzz in my ears, and a voice full of hatred and vengence pounds in my ears, "Don't sleep!" I nearly lost my sanity. Fortunately, the Arab inmates were getting tired and began to doze off, and I was able to take a catnap now and then.

On the fifth day, August 10, 1939, they left me alone. They might have gotten tired of it, or they might have taken time out to decide what to do with this strange person they couldn't break down. I noticed a change in their approach. They started to bring me food and helped me eat. I used the opportunity to ask them to take me to another cell away from the john, since the smell made me faint. Miracle of miracles, they took me to the other end of the hall, next to the guard room. I was transferred to that cell on the morning of August 11, and here is where I decided to escape.

At 21:00 I decided to go to sleep in order to wake up at midnight and try to escape. I slept well. The food I had eaten made me feel better. At 00:10 I woke up, got out of bed, paced the room to get used to walking again, and climbed the wall. Around me the Arab inmates are snoring. Outside I hear the guards' steps. My task is to loosen the wire net above the wall separating my cell from the guard room, go through the opening, get to the door, open it with the guard's key, go outside, climb the high wall with the bits of glass embedded on top of it. I quietly start bending one square of wire. I keep bending it. The wire gets hot, my fingers ache and I have to stop. Half an hour, an hour, an hour and a half go by. The Arabs toss in their beds, and the symphony of snoring is joined by the guard, who snores like a trumpet. I am about to give up my idea. I am filled with despair. Suddenly I see a rusty razor on the edge of the wall.

I start working again. With the razor I make a groove in the wire and start bending it again, left and right. Suddenly the wire bursts with a loud noise. I hold my breath. An Arab stirs in one of the cells.

Now I have to take apart the net. The work is hard and noisy. I open the squares one by one, straining not to make noise, sweating all over. My arms are weak, and I make a superhuman effort to go on with my work. Dawn is breaking and the cell brightens. In a few minutes the guard will wake up, they will catch me attempting to escape and start torturing me again.

The hole is now as big as my head. I put my right arm and my head through it, and push my shoulder and left arm through. The net is making a loud noise, and I am sure all the inmates will wake up. It is too late to go back. My right hand finds a beam near the ceiling. I take hold of it and pull my entire body through. My shirt and pants are caught in the wire. The noise does not stop. I pray to God to help me. I slowly slip through, going down, holding on to bumps in the wall, and now I am standing on the guard room floor shaking and sweating. The Arab guard wakes up, sits up in bed, scratches the back of his head, lies down and puts his blanket over his face and goes back to sleep. I tiptoe to the door. Luckily, the key is in the door. I have to unbolt the door and then turn the key in the lock. I don't have much time. The bolt squeaks loudly. I quickly open the lock. I carefully open the iron door so it won't screech. Fresh air fills my lungs and revives me. I am in the police courtyard. I close the door behind me.

Now I have to climb the high stone wall. It is studded with broken glass and barbed wire. An iron pipe leaning against the wall comes to my aid. I climb it and scale the wall, cutting my arms and legs in several places. I am now on a tin fence which groans and crackles. I am waiting for a bullet to whistle in my ear and hit the escaped prisoner.

Now I am standing in another police courtyard, surrounded by tall buildings with lights in the windows, although it is daylight. I can see police personnel at work. One goes to the window and looks outside. I squeeze against the wall and wait. I quickly cross the yard and come against a second fence. I barely manage to climb this fence, I stop for a second to rest on top, and go down. I am on a Jerusalem street. I am free.

At this point we can pick up the thread of the story.

Zeroni went directly to Yosef Dukler's apartment. Dukler was then the second-in-command of the Jerusalem district. Dukler did not want to leave Zeroni in his apartment and took him to the roof apartment of Shoshana Shimonovitch (Abulafiya), a supporter of the Irgun. Zeroni hid on the roof and even saw the police dogs in the streets looking for him. In the evening he was dressed up as a woman by Shoshana, and went with Refael Saban to Binyamin Cohen's home in Bet Hakerem.

Cohen was the secretary of the French Consulate in Jerusalem, and an active member of the Irgun. His apartment was perfectly safe. Zeroni stayed there for two weeks, recovered from his wounds and became stronger. He was then transferred to Tel Aviv by Ephraim Ilin and by Avraham Stern (Yair), who was now the commander of the Jerusalem district. He hid for a while at the home of Ilin's sister, where two weeks later the entire command of the Irgun was arrested.

TWELVE

The Outbreak of the Revolt Against the British

Our military operations, aimed at thwarting the White Paper and its threat to the Jewish national home, were now expanded to include the task of liquidating the heads of the British secret police, who had set out to capture the leaders of the fighting underground and inflict upon them a slow death by torture.

I met Zeroni shortly after his escape and he told me about the torture he had endured. The man was physically broken, but his spirit was strong. He had obviously overcome his pain and was determined to seek revenge. After I saw him I went to our headquarters and I insisted that we execute the head of the Jewish section of the CID, Officer Ralph Cairns. This would be the opening salvo in our revolt against the British rule. We would also avenge the torture of our people and put a stop to it.

Nothing had been done until then about this matter. The command of the Irgun had learned about the torture from Jewish policemen, but all it did was appeal to public opinion at home and abroad. Bulletins were issued, calling on the Yishuv to protest "the inquisition against the Jews on their own soil" and demand a stop to torture as well as disciplinary action against the perpetrators. In a special flier to "Jewish youth," the Irgun held "Cairns, a British secret police officer," responsible for the sadistic acts. The flier mentioned Cairn's role in torturing "two Jewish girls by pushing fingers into their eyes and pinching their nipples." But the protests and the denunciations, as could be expected, were of no avail, and the torture continued. I did not believe in that "paper war"; I demanded action, and I threatened to resign if my demand was turned down. I was given the go-ahead and was put in charge of the operation.

As a prelude for Cairns's liquidation, I decided to eliminate a Jewish police officer named Gordon. Gordon was in charge of gathering information about our people and had many connections with informers. He made arrests and also took part in torture. I was afraid that after we killed Cairns he might use his information against us and cause us a great deal of trouble.

Gordon was totally committed to the British cause. He was married to an English woman, and they lived at the end of Zephaniah Street in the Kerem Avraham neighborhood in Jerusalem. One evening I rang his bell. His wife answered the door, her two little children hanging on to her at either side. I changed my mind and drew up a new plan to attack him on his way to work.

I put together the usual team: a signaller, a gunman, and a girl who takes away the weapon. The operation was set for Friday, one week after Zeroni's escape, near Gordon's home. The signaller was dressed as a yeshiva student on his way home from the synagogue. The gunman was David Ilan, who had taken part in a previous attack. Tikva, the girl, and Ilan played the part of two lovers taking a stroll in the direction from where Gordon was expected to appear. A bicycle was waiting for the gunman around the next corner, held by a youth waiting for his friend.

Gordon did not suspect anything as he walked into the trap. The quiet of the Sabbath was all around. The Sabbath lights could be seen in the windows. Ilan let Gordon come within fifteen feet, as I had told him. Suddenly he moved away from Tikva, who quickly disappeared. He spread his legs and leaned forward, aiming his gun. Gordon froze. He raised his hands, as if pleading for his life. He shook violently and his eyes bulged in mortal fear. Ilan pulled the trigger once, he pulled it again, but nothing happened. Two bullets jammed together. He did not have a reserve revolver, and I did not have time to come to his aid. As soon as Gordon became aware of the problem he turned away and ran as fast as he could. We were forced to leave without results. Since that day I made a rule not to use an automatic pistol in such attacks, only a revolver, to eliminate the risk of jamming. The rule was accepted throughout the Irgun. Two weeks later Gordon took his family and left the country without a trace. Our objective of removing him from the scene was accomplished.

I now became absorbed in the task of doing away with Cairns. To me this act signified the battle cry in our war of liberation against the foreign occupier.

First, I organized a special intelligence team. The team was headed by a student named Uriah. The key person was Zefati, whom I had previously planted as a telephone operator at the CID main office. He gave us a precise report on Cairns's schedule, his comings and goings, his talks with outside people and his habits. This helped us follow him and plan accordingly. Cairns was clever and extremely cautious. He suspected everyone around him, and was always on the lookout. He had a fulltime bodyguard, and his right hand was always in his pocket, holding his gun. I organized a group of men and women of our Arabist group to follow him. They were disguised as street vendors and shoe-shines, rode bicycles and motorcycles, and even stood on roofs, taking turns along the way, like relay racers, until we had a full picture of his route. We found out Cairns's residence was in a building in Gan Rehavia, on the corner of Shmuel Hanagid and Narkiss, opposite the Bezalel art school. On the way to his apartment he would take a shortcut of about 100 yards through a construction site. Zeroni had told me Cairns had a gun in his pocket and wore a bullet-proof vest. I concluded that we had to get Cairns inside Gan Rehavia on that shortcut. and blow him up with a powerful mine as befitted a man of his stature.

After going over all the details, operational as well as technical, I drew up the following plan:

The mine: the Fugaz type I had learned how to make in Poland. Coneshaped, made of tin, 2 mm thick. The tip of the cone planted in the ground. Base diameter 1.5 feet, height of cone 1 foot.

Explosives: Blasting Gelatin, 33 pounds. Three pairs of electric detonators in a row, total 6 detonators. The detonators implanted in primers to increase the explosion. This mechanism was put inside a well welded tin box with electric wires coming out of holes to be connected to the activating wire.

Fragments: between the explosive charge and the outer container of the mine we put nails and bits of iron. We welded a cover over the mine, to increase its effect.

Activating wire: a well insulated electric wire connected to the detonators' wires and extending some 50 yards to the stonecutters' hut on the site of the construction. The wire was buried in the ground. A socket was attached to the end of the wire inside the hut.

Firing device: three batteries connected together, with a plug to be attached to the wire. Before the plug we installed a switch.

Concealment: the mine is buried in the ground with its point down, supported by pressed soil and gravel, with about 2 inches of soil on top, aiming the explosion upward. The mine is placed in the middle of the lane between two trees, so that the moment the victim is lined with the trees he is passing over the mine.

Activation: the person activating the mine goes into the stonecutters' hut when he receives the signal from two comrades, letting him know Cairns is approaching. He plugs the batteries and puts his finger on the switch. When Cairns is directly on top of the mine he activates the mine.

Ohmmeter: after the electric mechanism is installed, the entire system, including the detonators, are tested with an ohmmeter.

The team: Uriah and Zefati—lookout. More persons to be added as needed. Tikva Israeli and Mati Gross—signallers. Yitzhak Miller, Shlomo Cohen, Mati Gross—mine placers. Haim—mine operator.

After I completed the plan I began to work on the mine. I made the tin mine at the shop of Refael Saban's father in Mahaneh Yehuda, keeping it a secret from the latter. I took the tin container to the apartment of our member Yaakov Knall, who lived near the place of operation. Yaakov played the harmonica as we filled the container with nails and iron fragments. That night we transferred the mine to a desolate ruin near the construction site and hid it in the ground. We defecated on top of it so that no one would poke around on that spot. We hid the digging tools nearby so that we could have them without delay when we needed them.

On Friday night, August 25, 1939, the eve of the operation, all the participants gathered. Last moment instructions were given and each person turned to his assignment. Uriah and Yitzhak went to the ruin to bring the mine and the tools. Shlomo, Haim and Mati went to the construction site to dig the hole for the mine.

It was pitch dark at the site. The neighborhood was perfectly quiet, and the diggers had to work without making any noise. But the soil was hard and the digging was slow. The diggers had to use their hands instead of their tools to keep it quiet. After a superhuman effort they finally made a hole big enough to hide the mine. They placed the mine in the hole and put gravel around it to secure it in the ground. They covered it with soil and each person stepped on it to make it look like an ordinary section of the path. Haim connected the end of the wire to the detonators' wires protruding out of the ground, unrolled the wire as he retreated toward the stonecutters' hut, covering the wire as he moved back with dirt and gravel. He buried the end of the wire next to the hut and put a stone on top of it as a marker.

They were almost done when suddenly they heard steps in the dark. They saw a man walking down the path toward the building. He turned on a flashlight and was heard speaking loudly to someone. Everyone lay flat on the ground and waited. The thought in everyone's mind was the same: Lucky thing the mine had already been put in the ground, and the wire was concealed. But what about Mati? He was still near the mine, but the man kept walking as if nothing was gong on. Mati joined the group, breathing heavily, all excited: the man was none other than Cairns. Mati, who noticed him when he showed up at the construction site, quickly took off his pants and squatted as if about to relieve himself. Cairns saw him, switched on his flashlight, and aimed his gun at him. But when he saw his naked butt he was persuaded everything was normal, as the place had been used for this purpose before. He put his gun back in his pocket and walked away.

The next morning, a few hours before the execution, a couple was posted nearby to make sure the mine had not been detected. There was nothing unusual. Moreover, Yitzhak walked twice up and down the lane and did not notice the mine. Everything looked perfectly natural.

At 11:30 Haim arrived at the hut. He wore an auxiliary policeman uniform and carried a lunch box containing the batteries. On his way to the hut he saw Tikva and Mati, who would signal him when Cairns approached the path. Haim had walked past them without acknowledging them, and the couple remained at its observation post.

Haim walked slowly around the hut and sat on a stone behind it, burying his face in a newspaper. As he pretended to read he dusted the soil off the end of the wire and the socket attached to it. The wire attached to the batteries in his lunch box ended in a switch and a plug which he would connect to the socket as soon as the signal was given Cairns was coming. We had learned that Cairns arrived at the place between 12:30 and 15:30. Haim waited for two hours but there was no sign of Cairns. Haim began to fidget and was about to leave, when suddenly he saw Mati and Tikva passing by as agreed, nearly running. He connected the batteries to the wire, his finger on the switch. Seconds later he saw two men walking down the path, typical Englishmen. Cairns wore a narrow-brimmed English hat with a feather. The finger is on the switch. The two British officers are lined with the two trees. The finger moves. The entire neighborhood is shaken by the explosion.

Haim almost goes deaf. Instinctively he clings to the wall of the hut. After a moment which seems an eternity he hears the rain of stones on the roof of the hut. The noise brings him back to reality. He peers at the lane. It has disappeared behind clouds of dust. He hears the cry of a little girl down the lane and regains his composure. He takes a wet handkerchief out of his pocket and wipes the switch and batteries, leaving no fingerprints, and buries them in the ground. Now he turns to the little girl who is lying on the ground, frightened, picks her up and carries her across the field to the Menorah Club. He puts her down on the sidewalk and walks toward Mahaneh Yehuda, crossing Jaffa Road and turning to David Yellin Street. At the corner of Yellin and Tachkemoni he is met by Rahamim Agay who offers him a bicycle. Haim smiles at Agay and mutters excitedly, "Everything is fine. He is gone." As planned, he takes the bike and rides as far as the Schneller Building. Yitzhak Miller waits for him there. They shake hands. Haim continues on foot to Meah Shearim where I am waiting for him. We shake hands and embrace each other. We look into each other's eyes. We know we have made history.

After the two officers, Ralph Cairns and Ronald Barker, were blown up, the place was surrounded by British police and soldiers. The whole neighborhood of Gan Rehavia was searched and the residents were questioned at length. Thirty men were arrested in the neighborhood. The military commander of the capital ordered all Jewish restaurants and movie theaters closed "until further notice." The next day, in a special announcement, the Irgun command took responsibility for the attack.

THIRTEEN

In Jail with the Irgun's High Command

After I saw Haim I left immediately for Tel Aviv. I had to get there before the police had a chance to block the roads, in order to present my report of the operation to the Irgun's high command. Leaving my hideout on Hahabashim Street was extremely dangerous. The police had been looking for me since they discovered my previous hideout in Zichron Moshe. They had my real name and my picture, and I generally avoided going out in the daytime. But in order to get to Tel Aviv I had to use public transportation, which only ran in the daytime, as the Arab disturbances had not yet ended. I put on a toupee, a mustache and sideburns, and wore glasses. As I reached Jaffa Road on my way to the cab stop I was recognized by Officer Shmilgovsky, later Commander Naor of the Israel Police. He was a friend of my family and he was not fooled by the disguise. "Are you crazy?" he snapped at me. "The entire police are looking for you, you are going to get 15 years in jail, and here you are parading down the street." I smiled at him, realizing I was lucky to be leaving Jerusalem, when another acquaintance ran into me. This time it was Zack, the journalist. He winked at me and nodded. I was safe again, since Zack was a member of the Irgun.

I arrived in Tel Aviv without any further incidents. After a hot bath at a friend's home I took a walk on Rothschild Avenue. Here in the new Hebrew city I felt secure. I enjoyed seeing young mothers taking their little ones out for a stroll. In my mind's eyes I saw them growing up in the free Land of Israel.

At the appointed time I took a roundabout way to the headquarters of the Irgun. The address was top secret and had been handed to me personally. It was the apartment of Ephraim Ilin's sister (who was in the United States at the time), on 6 Aharonovitz Street. Ilin had made the apartment available to the Irgun command.

I tapped the door with a broken pencil. A young man opened it. He had the other half of the pencil. After he made sure the two parts fit together he let me in. I was warmly welcomed by Hanoch. He expressed his admiration for the planning and execution of the attack on Cairns, and invited me to stay in the apartment for three days until it was time for me to go to Haifa. He noted that the apartment was the most heavily guarded hideout in Tel Aviv. As we spoke the leaders of the Irgun began to gather for their meeting. They were all there: Hanoch Kalay, the commander; Avraham Stern (Yair), in charge of foreign relations and indoctrination; Aharon Haichman (Dov), the Tel Aviv district commander; and Haim Lubinsky,who was going to Ireland the next day to meet with Robert Briscoe, former member of the Irish parliament and the Irish underground, a Jew and an Irgun sympathizer. My report was the first item on the agenda. I told them about the attack on Cairns, and they praised me and shook my hand warmly. Hanoch told me the command had decided to promote me to First Gundar and appoint me second-in-command for the Haifa and North district. He mentioned that I would become the youngest district second-in-command the Irgun ever had. I thanked the members of the command for the appointment and retired to the next room to resume my work. The command continued to discuss the second item on its agenda, which was Jabotinsky's plan for an armed revolt leading to the conquest of the Land of Israel.

The plan was conceived by Jabotinsky as a result of the July 1939 White Paper, in which Great Britain sought to put an end to Jewish aspirations for independence, proposing instead a Palestinian state. Jabotinsky had mailed a three-part coded letter to the Irgun command with his war plan. According to the plan, in October 1939 an immigrant ship would reach the shore of Tel Aviv and among the passengers would be Jabotinsky himself. The Irgun would see to it that the passengers got to shore, using force if necessary. At the same time an armed revolt would break out, the Irgun would take control of the government building in Jerusalem, where the national flag would be raised. Those positions would be held, regardless of casualties, for a period of at least 24 hours. During that time Jabotinsky would not be allowed to fall into the hands of the enemy. A temporary government of the Jewish people would be proclaimed during the short occupation, issuing a simultaneous statement in European capitals and in the United States of its formation. It would subsequently continue to work abroad as a government-in-exile, representing Jewish sovereignty in the Land of Israel.

During that time, Yair's 40,000 Plan was actively pursued by the commanders of the Irgun. Irgun emissaries in Europe were busy organizing immigrants, training soldiers and buying arms abroad as they prepared the invasion army of 40,000 for the armed revolt leading to the capture of the strongholds of the Mandate government. The timing of Jabotinsky's plan was discussed in great detail. Some commanders spoke against it, arguing that it would lead to the total liquidation of the Irgun. The main objection came from Yair, who considered it a futile demonstrative act. The summary of the discussion and the negative response of the command were to be sent to Jabotinsky by Lubinsky, who was leaving for Europe the next day. But the summary was never written and the response was not sent.

Halfway through the meeting I suddenly heard footsteps in the stairwell outside the door, and when I peeked through the keyhole I saw several men, whom I immediately made out to be British detectives, running upstairs. Apparently they went up to the wrong floor, as they soon returned and rang our bell. I did not open the door. Instead, I went inside and alerted the commanders. They began to destroy their papers. Haim Lubinsky climbed out the window and managed to enter the apartment below us. Aharon Haichman tried to follow him but came back in when detectives down below on the street pointed their guns at him. As the knocking on the door became insistant, Hanoch told me to open the door. The detectives stormed the apartment, clutching their guns. I recognized Officer Wilkin, and later on I found out he had replaced Cairns as the head of the Jewish section at the CID. I also saw Officer Herrington, the commander of the Tel Aviv police, and Officer Hackett, the commander of the Jaffa police. I suppose all those distinguished people wanted to see the high command of the Irgun being arrested. They immediately identified the members of the command, and ordered Haim Lubinsky to be brought over from the apartment below.

The detectives did not pay any attention to me. They must have been overjoyed to see the big fish they had just caught in their net. This worked in my favor, since the main reason for the arrest was the killing of Cairns. Before I opened the door, I had told Lubinsky my alibi. I was a new immigrant from Czechoslovakia who arrived a few days earlier on the ship *Katina*, which was discovered by the British only after the passengers had disembarked and scattered on the shore. I had known Lubinsky back in Czechoslovakia, and I ran into him on the street in Tel Aviv, and he had brought me to the apartment. I even picked a new name for myself—Ben-Ariyeh, which became my name in many police communications. My story and Lubinsky's coincided when the police questioned each one of us separately. They were satisfied, and did not ask me any further questions. After the initial investigation we were transferred under heavy guard to the police station in north Tel Aviv and were all locked up together in the same cell.

The first thing we had to do was contact someone on the outside to let our men know we had been arrested. There were several Jewish policemen at the station. One of them, named Bergman, was an Irgun member. We did not have to say anything to him. When he saw us being brought in under heavy guard he signalled to us with his eyes to let us know he understood the gravity of the situation. He suggested to Dov that our men free the command, but when he did not receive any answer he went to contact the Tel Aviv district command to let them know the high command had been arrested.

They did not bother us during the night, but in the morning they transferred us in armored cars under heavy police and army guard to the Jaffa jail. The British must have felt that in Tel Aviv an attempt might be made to free us from jail. We did not stay long in Jaffa. The next evening we were taken out again by armored cars, this time with our hands and legs chained to the inside of the vehicles.

I remember it was a full moon night. The road to Jerusalem glistened in the moonbeams. In the silence around us we could hear the swishing of trees and the chirping of birds, as we passed through Shaar Hagai. The cuffs on my hands were large enough for me to slip them off, and for a moment I thought of escaping. I was chained to Dov (Haichman), the Tel Aviv district commander. Inside the vehicle there were Englishmen armed with submachine guns. Another Englishman was in the turret, equipped with machine gun and searchlight. I would have to overcome all of them in order to escape. I asked Dov for his opinion, but he did not say a word. I could tell he would not even consider it. As a junior officer, I was not about to act without his approval.

For some reason I was in high spirits. Still, I was apprehensive. I was concerned the British might find out who I was. They might link me to the killing of Cairns, or at least to the explosives which they had seized at Zichron Moshe in Jerusalem. This alone could get me 10 to 15 years in jail.

Around midnight we arrived at the CID headquarters at the Russian Compound in Jerusalem. The entire convoy drove into the high fenced yard. We were immediately surrounded by police and detectives and brought up to the second floor for a special investigation. Each one of us was questioned separately, and we each waited our turn. During the investigation I was chained to Hanoch Kalay.

Before long I was taken in to see Wilkin, who spoke fluent Hebrew and knew a great deal about the underground. His main objective was to find out who killed Cairns and bring the perpetrators to justice. I repeated my story: my name is Ben-Ariyeh, I am a new immigrant from Czechoslovakia. I came as a illegal immigrant (the British definition) on the *Katina*, I had no connection to the Irgun, and only happened to be with the Irgun command by chance. Wilkin listened and did not ask me any further questions. He made threatening gestures, passing his hand across his neck, as if to say that I would be hanged (he apparently did the same thing when he questioned the members of the command) for killing Cairns. But it seemed that he was too thrilled to have caught the whales of the Irgun, and did not have much interest in a small sardine like myself. It never occurred to him the sardine was the person he was looking for.

As we were being investigated on the morning of September 1, 1939, a British officer walked into the room in a huff and told us that German forces had invaded Poland and World War Two had broken out. Silence fell on all of us, suspects as well as investigators. Everyone wondered what the future would bring.

September 1, 1939 is a day that should have been stricken from the calendar. Before dawn German troops crossed the Polish border and German planes destroyed most of Poland's airfields and aircraft. World War Two had started, about to engulf most nations of the world. That night, Yair's 40,000 Plan for the liberation of the Land of Israel and the rescue of the Jews of Europe from the imminent Holocaust, was dead.

We were taken into the cellars of the CID for night detention. They chained us to our beds and left us heavily guarded. The next day they resumed the investigation. They took our pictures, front and side, fingerprinted us, and looked for special marks of identifiction. When I was arrested in 1947 on an underground mission in Belgium they tried to identify me on the basis of that information.

As I was taken around to the various departments, I was guarded by a Christian Arab detective who without a doubt knew who I was. During 1937-1939, when I headed the Irgun operations in Jerusalem and studied chemistry at the Hebrew University, I lived with my family at 16 Ben-Yehuda Street in Jerusalem. We had an extra room in our apartment which we rented out. We rented it once to a Christian Arab detective who stayed for a long time. He worked at the time at the CID headquarters. It appeared that his relations with the Arabs were not too close, since most of his friends were Jewish policemen and detectives. We had become quite friendly. If he had told the police who I was, he would have been praised and promoted. As for me, I would have been given a long jail sentence, and, needless to say, would have paid with my life if my part in the Cairns affair had been discovered.

When my guard and former friend first saw me, he was quite surprised. I looked at him without saying a word, and I could tell he understood what was going on. I could see in his face the inner struggle he was going through. But it only lasted a second or two. His face became sealed, and he did not reveal my identity to the British. As he guarded me between investigations we would exchange looks from time to time and communicate without words. This man had spared me a great deal of trouble and saved me from infernal torture. He might have saved my life.

The questioning went on during alternate days and nights. We would be awakened early in the morning, as if there were some special urgency. We were not allowed to dress properly and wash up, and were rushed out of the police cellar. In this disheveled state it was easier to make the investigated person feel self-conscious, isolated, foredoomed. The more self-esteem he lost, the easier it became to make him talk. The British made the most of this rule.

After they rushed me out of my cell they would take me into different rooms. In each room there was a British detective who would make gestures which meant that soon I would be hanged, or tortured, or given a long jail sentence. Several times the British hinted that I had been turned in by the Agency and the Haganah. They wanted me to become incensed at those bodies and reveal their secrets. On other occasions they implied that some of our own members informed on us, hoping that we would turn in our own men. We had to keep telling ourselves, "They won't make me say anything! They are leading me on and trying to confuse me. . . . No way! I won't let them do it to me! If I can keep my dignity and get through this ordeal, I will prove I am stronger than they are, and my future is secure."

They took me at all hours to be questioned by Wilkin. In essence, what I gathered from what he said was that he wanted to discover who killed Cairns and Barker. It was inconceivable that high ranking British officers could be murdered in a British colony and their murderers go free! His words were accompanied by threats, which did not impress me, because I could tell Wilkin was more scared of us than we were of him. I could also tell that he did not know who I was, and was not too interested in a 21-year-old boy when he had men like Avraham Stern (Yair), Hanoch Sterlitz (Kalay), and Aharon Haichman (Dov), the top commanders of the Irgun.

We went through a cycle of questioning, during which the CID gathered all the information they could get and put it in their files. We would go back to our cell, eat and rest briefly, then be questioned again. For a short time we were together, and we were able to exchange a few words on our way to the toilet or when we were served our meal. As we sang or prayed we would blurt our instructions or bits of information to one another to make sure we did not tell the police anything we shouldn't say, albeit we had expert advice from criminal lawyers. We knew we were not supposed to let the police investigators in on anything. We would say, "We don't know, we haven't heard it, we don't understand," and deny everything. If the investigator said to us, "If you don't talk we will put you on trial," we would reply, "Fine, if you are going to put me on trial, according to the law I have to consult my lawyer before I say anything." The Mandate law clearly stated a suspect did not have to tell the police anything. Moreover, the police had to warn the suspect that anything he said could be used against him later on in court, hence one was not obligated to say anything. We were well aware of the law. The British completely overlooked that law, but we kept reminding them of it. This kept us from getting into trouble. Without hard evidence, all the British could do was exercise administrative arrest (which did not require any legal procedure). They investigated us for five days, but seemed to reach a dead end. They decided to transfer us to the central prison of Jerusalem, next to the CID headquarters in the Russian Compound, a higher security facility.

At the prison we were separated. Each one of us was put in a different cell, so we could not communicate with one another. Apparently the police had not yet given up, and wanted to go over the evidence they had gathered and see if they could come up with anything. I had the distinct honor of being put in a special cell known by its Turkish name, *Zinzaneh*. It was in the center of the prison, surrounded by high walls and by the other sections of the building. There were ten such cells, about six feet by four and a half feet, with barely enough room for a mattress and a bucket for relieving oneself. The heavy iron door led into a narrow corridor. Scant light slipped in through a distant porthole, secured with iron bars. In such a cell one was completely isolated from the outside world, alone in a cement cubicle with a torn mattress and cold air. All one saw was the cement wall outside the door. At times the guard passed by and threw the prisoner a frozen look which made one's heart skip a beat. All I could do in that cell was reflect on my condition and the imminent investigation. Wilkin might not have known who I was, and had no way of linking me to the killing of Cairns and Barker. But I did know everything, and I did have a reason to worry.

My isolation did not last long. Shortly after I was locked up in that cell I heard official voices and in came a distinguished group headed by the chief of the prison, whose name I later on found out was Wilson. He looked at me for a long moment. He mumbled something to the effect that "We have finally caught those who wanted to kill us. Now they will sit here and won't do anything."

A few hours later, in early afternoon, I had a pleasant surprise. Haim Dviri came to see me. Dviri, an Irgun member, worked in the prison kitchen, and when food was brought to the Jewish inmates he gave me soup and meat which literally revived me after starving for several days. Since he was also the librarian, he also brought me a book to read. He told me everyone sent regards and everything would be all right, I had nothing to worry about. Inside the book I found a note from Yair. Dviri's friendly face and encouraging words uplifted my spirit and filled me with great joy. I knew I was not alone. I was part of a fighting body and would remain part of it to my dying day. Dviri told me he would bring me more food in the evening, and added that I could send a message back to Yair inside the book.

The next day I was taken again under heavy guard to see Wilkin. He kept looking at me as if trying to find out how I was affected by being put into that narrow cell. Perhaps he thought I was starting to buckle under.

Again he gestured as if to say I would not come out alive. But again it made no impression on me. On the contrary. I felt stronger than before and I knew he was losing the game. In a calm voice I repeated the story about my sorry condition as a new, illegal immigrant. I was sent back to my cell, and told Dviri about my investigation. He had a message for me from Yair, who assured me everything would be all right. I kept seeing Wilkin each day for ten days. Wilkin did not find out anything from me, and appeared satisfied with the story of the immigrant from Czechoslovakia named Ben-Ariyeh. The British press used that name years later, on the eve of the birth of the State of Israel, when I was linked to the bombing of British institutions in London.

After ten days and nights of intensive investigations I was taken out of that cell, and along with the Irgun high command I was transferred to Section 23 of the central prison, where Jewish prisoners were kept. Imprisonment is a common aspect of the underground struggle for national liberation. Underground fighting consists of three aspects. The first is underground work, lifestyle, training, secrecy and clandestine behavior, totally different from anything in the open. The second is underground activities. Underground struggle means, first and foremost, concrete physical action against the enemy. The national goals of the underground have been defined by many, orally and in writing, in poetry and in prose. This literary and educational process won many to the cause of the underground. But it seems that the first bullet fired at the Arabs and the British did more to advance that cause than thousands of words and tons of paper. The gun, the grenade, the bomb, those are the indispensable tools of the underground. The third aspect of underground war is the prison experience. There has hardly ever been a bona fide revolutionary who did not spend time in jail. Jails have helped revolutionaries develop and formulate their thought. The courtroom has been the arena of their ideological struggle with the enemy. The prison has served as a temporary shelter for freedom fighters, who did not surrender but rather sought to escape and resume the struggle. For us too jail and trial before military courts served as a unique tool for furthering our cause.

We were given a warm welcome at Section 23 of the central prison in Jerusalem, where the Jewish prisoners were held. Here were Irgun men who were under administrative arrest for underground activities. They were jailed because they belonged to the National Movement, especially the Revisionist Party, or because they had been turned in either by CID contacts or by the official bodies of the Yishuv, who strongly opposed the Irgun. Only Haim Dviri and Haim Buchko were there for a criminal offense, namely, an attempted robbery. This was the first time all of us who had been arrested at the apartment in Tel Aviv were put together in the same cell. We had the feeling our investigation was over, but we had no idea what they would do to us. One of the detainees I met at Section 23 was Moshe Segal, one of the activists of the National Movement in Jerusalem, who at that time was a member of the community council and an active member of the Irgun. He was the first Jew who had defied the British and blew the shofar at the Western Wall, and whenever the British wanted to arrest some National Movement activists they would include Segal. He had connections with the prison administration, who allowed him to get kosher food, and we used his food container to exchange notes with the outside world. This is how we found out from our people on the outside that we might be sent to a detention camp since there was no evidence we were linked to the execution of Cairns and Barker.

It seemed that Wilkin himself, who had replaced Cairns as head of the Jewish section of the CID, did not want to go too far in finding evidence against us. Quite simply, he feared for his life, and did not want to end up like Cairns. He must have concluded he could use devious methods and work quietly behind the scenes to beat the underground without risking his own life. Indeed, his method worked for several years, until Morton implicated him in the killing of Avraham Stern (Yair), and the underground's avenging arm reached him.

We now became detainees. We were given a one-year administrative detention. As we awaited our transfer to the Sarafand detention camp, the main base of the British army in Palestine, we had contacts with the outside world and held long talks with our imprisoned Irgun members. It was particularly interesting to hear Yair's ideological formulations.

They wanted to take us to Sarafand on Saturday, but we refused to go because of the sanctity of the Sabbath. They agreed to take us on Sunday. On Saturday we were allowed our first visit. To a person in jail, a visit is a great event. It puts one in touch with the outside world, helps the prisoner overcome loneliness and the loss of identity, as well as the fear of never seeing the outside again. Family members would come and huddle at the fence across the yard to see their loved ones, and one could witness heart-rending encounters between a son and his parents, between an inmate and his girlfriend, or see the unbearable pain of separation between husband and wife or between parents and children. The members of the high command, whose identity was known, were visited openly by their family members. But since I had to hide my identity, my parents did not come to visit me. If the British found out who I was, I could well be sent to the gallows. My parents did come to the prison, but did not go inside. They remained outside, not revealing their identity. The relatives of the command members gave them regards from me. After all the visitors left we opened all the food packages they had brought us and had a party.

The next day we were taken out under heavy guard and transferred to the Sarafand detention camp. The camp was surrounded by military barracks, a special security measure to prevent the inmates from escaping. Our chains were removed, we were duly registered, and were issued prisoner equipment. When we entered the camp we were received by our fellow Irgun members with mixed feelings. On the one hand, they were happy to see their leaders, and were relieved that no charges had been brought against us. On the other hand, they knew what a blow it was to the Irgun to have its top leaders put away at such a fateful moment of history.

At the camp we met David Raziel, our commander in chief, who had been arrested six months earlier. Before his arrest, Raziel had taken a more moderate stand than Yair and some of the other leaders in the struggle against the British. He felt that the CID might destroy the Irgun as a result of our stepped-up action. Yet, when the head of the CID in person, Colonel Giles, questioned him after his arrest, threatening him with jail term and hanging, Raziel stood up and told him: "I am the commander of the Irgun Tzvai Leumi, and I take full responsibility for all its operations. If you touch me, my men will avenge my blood and your men's blood will run like water, yours first." Giles was shaken by the warning, the like of which he had never heard before. How did a native, a Jew no less, dare speak such words to a representative of the greatest empire on earth? Overcoming his anger, he gritted his teeth and told Raziel: "If you are so sure of what you are saying, give it to me in writing." Raziel began to write, and as he was about to sign the Sabbath began. He told Giles: "I am sorry, but I will have to sign it tomorrow, on Sunday." At that point Giles lost his temper and told Raziel to get out.

The detention camp at Sarafand was located in the eastern section of the huge military base, surrounded on all sides by barracks. It was surrounded by a high barbed-wire fence. Outside the fence there were British patrols around the clock, as well as watchtowers with search-lights. As soon as we arrived I began to plan my escape, as befitted a freedom fighter. My belief was that a soldier caught by the enemy must always look for a way to escape, and there is no jail one cannot escape from if one is determined enough. I turned to Hanoch and told him that the commanders of the Irgun must escape in order to take charge again of the Irgun. If we remain in prison the Irgun would fall apart. I added that I had checked out the place and it should not be too difficult to escape.

My friends Kemara and Shabtai and I had spent several nights watching the patrols which made the rounds of the camp fence. We realized that they did a very perfunctory job. One guard would walk listlessly along the fence, and after one round he would sit down next to the watchtower for about half an hour, undoubtedly drinking beer or whiskey, and then would get up and saunter along with his rifle dangling like a broomstick. One of the guards was a tall Englishman who had a small dog. The dog would sometimes walk in front of him and some-times behind him. I once met him during the day and started talking to him in my broken English. I found out he was an Irishman, who for some reason had to leave Ireland. He joined the British police overseas, as many Irishmen did. I found out he had no love for the British. He was only doing his job for money. Once when I listened to his singing across the fence I heard him say, ''Those bloody Englishmen, my dog is better than they. Anyone who wants to escape, let him.'' I was quite astonished to hear him say that; and it encouraged me to tell Hanoch about my escape plan. Hanoch took me seriously, and even got Yair's consent. He also contacted people on the outside and told me that Yaakov Meridor had searched the surrounding area and found out there was no hindrance to our escape. I was very pleased, not only because I wanted to go back to my work, but also because the high command would soon resume its duties. One morning Hanoch told me Raziel, who in the meantime had been released, opposed the escape. I told Hanoch it was the greatest disappointment of my life, and added that if the command was not going to escape, I wanted permission to escape with two friends. The next day he gave me Raziel's answer: Absolutely not! No one is allowed to escape!

Occasionally I would hear bits of conversation among the Irgun commanders which alluded to a disagreement between them and Raziel. They told me that Raziel had ordered the Irgun to stop fighting the

British. Yair was more surprised than the rest of us and asked how it was possible to have a unilateral cease-fire? The Irgun was stopping its operations at a time when the British continued to carry out without reservations the White Paper policy, locking the gates of our country to stop wretched Jewish refugees from entering the country, throwing them back to sea, preventing Jews from settling in areas reserved for an Arab state. The British continued to work on reducing the Yishuv to a small ghetto surrounded by an Arab majority which could destroy us at any time. They incarcerated the members of the Irgun, while the Irgun proclaimed a unilateral cease-fire! Yair and the rest of the command were furious, and the first seeds of the future split were sown.

I was serving at the time as secretary to Yair, who occupied himself writing poems, formulating the Irgun philosophy, talking to fellow Irgunites, and holding meetings with the command. I helped him copy the poems and look up words in his Bible Concordance and his dictionaries as he searched for rhymes. He wrote at that time his famous poem *To Our Mothers*, which expressed the feelings of each and every one of us. It made us think of our mothers, who day and night worried about their sons, unable to sleep at night, fearing for our lives. I recall Hanoch was deeply moved by the poem. He kept quoting it to us, as we listened reverently.

Yair concluded his poem with the following verses, which symbolized the hope of our struggle:

> A mother's tear, wailing for her Isaac,
> God in His fury will avenge, in His mercy redeem;
> And Jacob will wrestle with man and God,
> And Israel will rise over Edom and Arabia,
> His foot on their neck—kings and rulers.
> Between the three seas and the two rivers
> Egypt the foundation and Assyria the roof;
> David's kingdom will be established in blood,
> And the entire nation will be saying as one,
>   Amen, amen!

The break between Yair and Raziel was unavoidable. One morning we had heard a rumor Raziel had been summoned to the main office. We saw a convoy of armored vehicles waiting near the office. Raziel was seen going to his hut and packing his belongings. He told us he was being taken away. We were quite worried about him. We thought they were taking him to the CID headquarters in Jerusalem to question him and perhaps even torture him, and put him on trial. We all gathered and decided that if anything was done to him we would declare a hunger strike until he was sent back to us. We immediately sent a communique to our men on the outside to let them know about Raziel, and to ask them to warn the British that if anything happened to him they would pay for it.

It was Friday. To our great surprise Raziel returned the next day. There was no need for a hunger strike, since, in effect, Raziel was being set free. He had been taken on Friday to Jerusalem to meet Pinchas Rutenberg, the chairman of the Vaad Leumi, at the King David Hotel. The Vaad Leumi was the Jewish body recognized by the British as the official governing body of the Yishuv. Before Raziel entered the hotel the British removed his chains. Rutenberg welcomed Raziel and said: ''We are now going to hold the meeting we were going to hold when you were arrested six months ago. In order to put the unfortunate period of your detention behind us, you have to promise me that you will stop the Irgun activities against the British.'' Rutenberg hastened to add that those activities interfered with the British war effort against Nazi Germany, and only Raziel, once freed, could order the Irgun to lay down its arms. As far as Rutenberg and the British knew, the Irgun was planning to take up arms again and fight the decrees of the White Paper. Raziel accepted Rutenberg's request, and was set free on October 24, 1939.

When Raziel came to see us on Saturday, after he had met with Rutenberg and promised him that the Irgun would lay down its arms, the British allowed him to meet with the command of the Irgun. They did not meet near the fence, as before, but in a special room, under British supervision and surveillance. The discussion was long, and apparently very heated. It is hard for me to believe that the British were so polite as to not install a microphone in the room and record the discussion. I am sure they recorded everything, and found out exactly what Yair thought, since he did not hide his thoughts from Raziel. They also received further confirmation of Raziel's own position. This helped them later on take advantage of the split in the underground and they knew how to treat the IZL and the LEHI.

Raziel was a fierce, uncompromising fighter, but did not have the statesman's vision. He generally relied on Yair's political assessments. But the outbreak of World War Two shattered his faith in the ability of the fighting Hebrew underground to operate under all conditions, and he overruled Yair and the rest of the command and agreed to stop the activities of the Irgun for the duration of the war.

Yair was categorically opposed to the agreement, and the rest of the command appeared to side with him. He argued that one does not support one's enemy unconditionally. Hitler might be the scourge of the Jews, but Great Britain was the enemy. We could work with the British, but we had to take advantage of the fact that they needed us and wanted to keep things quiet. We had to dictate to them our own conditions, namely, the transfer of power in the Land of Israel to the people of Israel.

Members of the underground learning to use various weapons.

FOURTEEN

Another Camp, Then Freedom

Early one morning the camp was surrounded by British police and armored cars, and by soldiers who took positions around the camp with machine guns. We were chained, hands and feet, and taken into the armored cars. We drove north, through the Arab towns of Ramallah, Nablus and Jenin, and after a grueling drive of several hours we arrived in Mezra, where the British at that time were building the central detention camp of the Mandate. It was actually a cluster of camps. There was one camp for the Hebrew underground, one for citizens of enemy countries, one for pro-Nazi Arabs, and one for special prisoners. Those included Haganah members (Moshe Dayan was among them), who were arrested during training at Yavniel, as well as the participants of the Irgun officers' course who were caught by the British at Mishmar Hayarden in Spring 1939. We were sent, quite naturally, to the underground prisoners' camp. There I met Ari Jabotinsky, who had been brought there a few days earlier when he brought an immigrant ship from Rumania and was intercepted by a British destroyer at high sea. We chose a supervisor for our barracks from our group, and began to plan our routine in the new camp.

An important rule for prisoners is to keep busy, pursue some course of study or other activities, learn a trade, draw, etc. One should also devote time to physical fitness, and find something to occupy one's mind with (the members of the underground had plenty to think and write about). Since we ate the bread of our enemy, His Majesty the King of England, we had to do all we could to improve our bodies and our minds. We also worked on improving the camp. We cultivated a garden and we grew flowers, and took care of the kitchen and all that was needed to live and work under the given conditions.

The day after we arrived in Mezra we had a formal parade attended by police and officers. The camp commandant made his appearance. He was a redhead named Pike. Red, as the expression goes, is not a color but a character. He showed up with a stick under his arm, in typically British manner. All he needed was Colonel Blimp's monocle and a few officers in shiny uniform standing in awe of him. The parade stood in an uneven line, dressed in rags, some of us with a curling mustache, others with a shaggy beard. Mister Pike marched back and forth in front of this ragtag company, his expression solemn, his nose in the air. After he was done marching, he turned to us and made a speech. He told us he was in charge and nothing was done without his approval. He had been told we were dangerous characters, and we endangered the British Empire and the British war effort, therefore he was appointed by the higher echelons of the Empire to guard us and make sure we behaved ourselves and did not make any problems. Anyone who tried to escape would pay with his life. As he spoke his blue eyes threw daggers at us. He left us with all the fanfare of the change of the guard at Buckingham Palace.

Needless to say, he did not make any impression on us. He got to know us better soon after and did not bother us, in spite of all his threats. It seems that he feared us more than we feared him. After we were told about his cruelty to prisoners we made it our point to let him know that if he touched us our friends on the outside would come after him and he would pay with his life.

An underground person must lead a double life, and at the same time make sure that he does not develop a split personality. To the outside world he must appear as a perfectly conventional person, while in the underground he must be a tough fighter, even cruel at times, to achieve the objectives of his cause. Underground life is based on keeping a secret and carrying the burden of the secret. It is a double life, two-faced, which is the only way to ensure the element of surprise. A real underground fighter is one who has attacked his enemy with his own hands and has spilled his blood. He cannot lead others unless he did the job himself. His experience is not complete if he does not spend some time in jail. Imprisonment is a necessary test for the person who devotes his life to free his people. Furthermore, as soon as he is imprisoned he has to look for a way to escape, to show his enemies that they cannot subdue him and to go back to fighting.

After one year at Mizrah, Avraham Stern, Hanoch Sterliz, Haim Lubinsky, Dov Haichman and I were summoned to the office of Camp Commandant Pike. He gave us his piercing look, and told us we were being transfered to the Acre jail. He did not have the decency to tell us we were being set free.

We were taken to the Acre jail, where the jail chief, Grant, told us we were being released. On June 18, 1940 we were set free.

It was a pleasant summer day and for the first time in over a year I felt the caressing warmth of the sun. A cool breeze blew in from the sea. I felt like a person being born again.

When we left the jail we hired a cab and drove to Haifa. Hanoch remained in Haifa to discuss matters with the local Irgun leaders, while the others continued to Tel Aviv. I went directly to my parents' home. My release was a total surprise to them. They were thrilled to see me, as if I had just returned to the land of the living. I was very close to my parents, especially to my mother. Both of them were quite concerned about me. My mother knew, with her mother's instinct, what kind of danger I was in all the time. When I left home in the morning or came home late at night she knew I was on my way to or from an operation, although we never spoke about it. My parents never told me to quit the underground, although they lived in constant fear. Sometimes I could see a tear sparkle in my mother's eye, but she must have known it was no use to try talking me out of doing those things. My mother had hoped I would become a lawyer or an engineer, and saved every penny to pay for my education. My parents had cut corners so I could attend the Herzliya high school in Tel Aviv, the best and most expensive in the country. And yet, after studying chemistry for two years at the Hebrew University I dropped out and became an underground activist, which, in their opinion, meant ruining my career. My parents were not politically involved. They were good Jews and good Zionists, and of course wanted to see our country become free, but they could not accept the idea that their first-born son might pay with his life for that freedom. They took comfort in my sister, three years younger than I, who was also a member of the Irgun but whose life was not in danger, and my younger brother, thirteen years my junior, who was too young to join the underground (he did later on).

While my parents rejoiced at my release, I could see a spark of fear in my mother's eyes. From some of her comments I was able to piece together what was bothering her. "Until now," she told me, "you have been locked up, you did not have your personal freedom. You must have suffered, but you were safe. We felt that at the camp your life was protected. Now, if you continue with your underground activities (she emphasized the word if), your life will be in danger again, and we will suffer."

I should have thought about my family's feelings. After they spent their last pennies on my education I should have found a job and helped them. Not only was I of no help to them, I even caused them no end of grief. I was closed to their feelings and exhortations. I was totally submerged in the work of the underground, and considered my release an opportunity to continue my fight. I was stiffnecked and insensitive. My parents, who deserve praise, did not say another word. My mother bit her lips, but did not say a word. She must have sensed that what had happened until now was nothing compared to what was yet to come.

Pistols used by the underground.

FIFTEEN

The Irgun Splits

Immediately after the release from Mizrah in June 1940, the members of the command became active again. They were first briefed by the field commanders, who had been waiting impatiently for Yair's return, since they opposed the line adopted by Raziel and his supporters, which the command considered defeatist. They now realized how low the Irgun had sunk under the command of our revered Raziel. As soon as operations stopped, training was discontinued. There was a tremendous decline in morale, and many of the men were compelled to enlist in the British armed forces, where they sought an outlet for their frustration and their need for action.

All the senior commanders, the city commanders and the section heads demanded that Yair head the command. It was clear to them Raziel had to step down. Indeed, in one of the stormy meetings Raziel announced he was resigning and quitting. He accompanied his announcement with a typical symbolic act: he broke a glass and said that the command was like the broken glass. It could not be repaired. The command accepted Raziel's resignation on the spot, and proceeded to appoint Yair the new head. But the commanders' joy did not last long. In less than twenty-four hours Raziel changed his mind.

During the early months of World War Two, a theory circulated among the members of the Revisionist Party, according to which the

Labor Party (Mapai) ruled the Yishuv and had great economical power because it did the bidding of the government. If the Revisionists, for their own reasons, could now accommodate the British, they could rival Mapai and take its place. Moreover, if the Revisionists could grow economically, they could also grow politically, and when the time came to fight they would be stronger and better prepared.

The Irgun command, with the exception of Raziel, rejected this theory. Yair had spoken about it many times back at the Sarafand camp. He pointed out that if there was a need to cooperate with the authorities, it was enough to have the Jewish Agency do it. Someone had to continue fighting the British White Paper and land law, which threatened the existence of Zionism. Some group had to continue the struggle, even if at the moment that group did not have the power to do it. It had to continue propagandizing, regrouping and organizing, amassing material, and be ready when the time arrived to resume the fight.

The leadership of the Revisionist Party, headed by Dr. Altman, did not accept Raziel's resignation, since it was able to dominate the Irgun through Raziel, and manipulate it at will. A chasm lay between that leadership and Yair, whom it considered totally unacceptable for the job. Altman had gone to see Raziel and handed him a telegram from Jabotinsky. It is not known to this day if the telegram was real or forged. In any case, it was clear that Altman had given Jabotinsky half-truths about the state of affairs in the Irgun, which could easily have led Jabotinsky to draw inaccurate conclusions, used by Altman against Yair, whom he considered a relentless enemy of the Revisionist Party, its interests and principles. Yair, in effect, maintained that the party, as an open and legal body, was limited to political action and propaganda. It could not be a movement which pursued all means in the fight for national liberation. Therefore, he concluded, the Irgun had to remain independent of the party and free to act on its own. Betar, the party's youth organization, Yair asserted, should remain a social and educational body, and only after a Betar member completed his or her education, he or she would decide whether to join the Irgun, thereby severing all ties with the party so as not to harm the underground. The Revisionist leadership, on the other hand, argued that the Irgun must only serve the party and its goals, and follow its instructions. If, for example, it was determined that Irgun actions against the Arabs or the British jeopardized the party or its reputation, or might result in the arrest of its leaders, the actions had to stop or at least be scaled down.

It should be pointed out that the Revisionists of the Jabotinsky school supported the British Mandate rule and considered Great Britain the steward appointed by the League of Nations to help establish a "national home" for the Jews in the Land of Israel. The Revisionists might have been somewhat more radical than the Zionist establishment in the demands they made on the Mandatory government, but they shared the belief of the establishment that the British had to fulfill their mandate in order to help achieve Zionist aspirations. Politically, the difference between the two camps was in form, not in essence. Yair, for his part, simply considered the British an enemy that had to be removed from the homeland once and for all. A good Englishman is an Englishman who is outside the Land of Israel. In light of the political reality in the world at that time, Yair insisted that the Irgun present itself before the British and the world as a Hebrew government in the making, and declare it was prepared to join the Allies if it were recognized as the temporary government of the Land of Israel, and if an agreement were reached to establish a Hebrew state in the liberated Land of Israel as soon as the war ended, the way the Allies recognized the temporary governments of Poland, Czechoslovakia, Holland, etc., most of whom took residence in London while their countries were occupied by the Nazis. Yair sought negotiations and an open pact between the temporary Jewish government and the Allies, and until his demands were met he would not consider stopping the campaign against the foreign occupier. Although he agreed to limit the operations of the Irgun in order not to interfere with the war effort, he insisted that the Irgun had to continue holding a Damocles sword over the heads of the British and their allies. He ruled out any blind submission to the interests of the British rule, and saw the need for establishing a deeper underground which could undertake any action that would bring about national liberation, inevitably leading to the rescue of European Jewry.

Yair broke away from Irgun and formed the Irgun Tzvai Leumi b'Israel, later known as Lohamey Herut Israel (LEHI), Hebrew for Fighters for the Freedom of Israel. Most of the senior commanders, myself included, joined him. The World War had put the Irgun to a test it was not equal to. Subjective reasons were added to questions of principle. Events beyond the Irgun's control deepened the disagreements on tactics and strategy. The rift could no longer be bridged. At a time when the Jewish people was undergoing the most tragic period in its entire history, it was more urgent than ever before to create a totally committed and uncompromising fighting organization. Avraham Stern, under his *nom de guerre,* Yair, faithful to the vision of national rebirth, left the Irgun and formed the new underground of which I became one of the founders.

Debris from the explosion in the courtyard below.

The assassin's view of the scene.

SIXTEEN

My New Beginning

When I was first released from my year-long imprisonment I was sent back by the Irgun to Jerusalem. I now became the commander of the Jerusalem branch of the new underground. I was well known in Jerusalem, especially among my former Irgun comrades, and so I had to go into deeper hiding. This time I disguised myself as an artist. I rented a room with a special entrance near Meah Shearim, and let the landlord know I was a painter. I assumed he would not consider it strange that his tenant was home all day and only went out at night. I had bought drawings and paintings and put my name (a pseudonym, of course) on them. I bought artist supplies, and always had a half finished picture on my easel. I became friendly with my landlord, especially with his wife, with whom I played the role of a starving artist. She felt sorry for me and one day she told me I was dear to her like her own son, which was exactly what I wanted to hear.

Our branch was small, but it had an outstanding nucleus of highly committed men, who had to be properly trained. They included Moshe Bar-Giora (fell in 1946 in the attack on the Haifa Oil Refinery), Israel Tevuah (later wounded in action and sentenced to 7 years in jail), Imanuel Hanegbi, Shlomo Yaakobi and Yosef Perlman, who became pillars of our organization, and Shaul Haglili, a fearless warrior (murdered by the British at the Eritrea camp). We also had the backing of a small number of dedicated sympathizers, invariably family men, who were willing to give us shelter and places for training. Some of our supporters were willing to help us with distributing propaganda material. In addition, the local community was congenial to our struggle for national liberation. I was determined to turn the branch into a hard-hitting fighting force that would go into action immediately.

After the split we began to reorganize. Our new cells were made up of three or four members, each cell maintaining strict conspiracy with the others. We were extremely careful in recruiting members. Before a candidate could join the organization, the sponsor would interview him personally, talk to him, get to know him, present our ideas to him, and only after a certain period of ideological training we would admit him into the cell. Here the person was trained individually. Sometimes he was tested by performing a certain task (transferring arms, spying), but the objective was to train each member as a combat soldier on the basis of four principles: knowledge, character, use of arms, and the action itself.

Training with arms underwent a profound change. The emphasis was put on personal attack: quick draw, disappearance after the attack, cover, etc., and on the use of grenades, bombs, mines, infernal machines and booby traps.

My training program was based on many practical exercises which helped develop independent thinking. If, for example, we trained in carrying arms, we told the trainee that he had to transfer a suitcase with arms from one point to the next, and we gave him a map indicating the places where he had to look out for the secret police. One of our experienced men would follow him and make sure he was taking the route marked on the map, and would observe how he went about handling the suitcase, which in effect did not contain any arms. Similarly, some of our men would dress up as British police and show up at a training place to see how the trainees reacted in time of danger. We would also simulate an attack, and find out how the trainees would behave during a real attack. Only those who passed all the tests (they were the majority) were sent on attack missions. The others were given other chores. At the same time, we taught our trainees how to maintain secrecy, which is an art with unlimited possibilities for invention, improvisation and skill. We did everything we could in that area to confuse the enemy and multiply the opportunities of surprising him.

We had acquired a sixth sense of knowing when we were being followed, or sensing that danger was near. We would suddenly feel we should not go into a certain place, and sure enough we would find out the place had been searched and some men had been caught. The fear of the secret police helped us develop irrational feelings which saved us from being arrested and put in jail.

We tried to make our training with arms as close to actual operation of arms as possible. Whenever a trainee pulled his gun he simulated facing the enemy, and had to be quicker than his opponent and take a better fire position to be the first to strike out and shoot to kill. We would train by drawing our guns at each other, or at our own image in the mirror, until we learned how to do a fast draw from the belt, from the inside pocket, or from the back pocket. We learned how to cock the gun as we drew it so we could fire immediately. We bought any kind of handgun we could find. Our trainees learned how to use guns from all over the world, became experts in fixing them when they jammed, and could draw and fire them at a high speed. Our favorite was the revolver, followed by the automatic. We always carried one of each, because of the reliability of the first and the fire-power of the second. In using submachine guns we also trained in instinctive firing, since we always had to be prepared to act instinctively. We tried to make the submachine gun as short as possible, like the paratroopers. We would remove the butt and looked for easy-to-carry magazines. We tied a pouch to the weapon to collect the empty cartridges in order not to leave any traces.

We put special emphasis on ideological training, which was based on the National Revival (Tehiya) teachings of Yair, as enunciated by the National Revival Principles. This doctrine was developed and expounded in the *Bamahteret* paper which was distributed among the members and in pamphlets and syllabi, which were used by the instructors as learning aids for recruits. The trainees had to learn the principles of Yair's doctrine, which became the foundation of their spiritual outlook.

In what way was the LEHI's fighting doctrine different from the Irgun's? In the Irgun a new recruit would immediately join a group of 10-15 men and would start group training. In LEHI, on the other hand, the training was individual. Only about a year after joining would the newcomer be put in a cell of three or four members, and no more. The training of LEHI recruits continued to be purely personal, and all efforts were centered on the individual in order to develop an ideological conviction, a strong character, expertise in the use of arms, and the capability of acting alone. Each member, if he were to become the sole survivor of the organization, could start the organization all over again, like the phoenix rising from its ashes. While in the Irgun the individual was only one of a group, and the group was the first unit of the rest of the organization, in the LEHI the individual was the cornerstone of the organizational structure. The first thing we taught in LEHI was ideology. We put a great deal of effort into it. We maintained that a member could not fight and offer his life unless he was ideologically committed and was never going to compromise his principles. In the Irgun ideology was based on years of education, especially within the framework of the Betar youth movement. It centered around a general national and universal outlook. LEHI came into being through a conviction that unless the British occupier was forced to leave our country, our people would not become a free nation. The Irgun was working on short-range problems, such as British decrees, instead of fighting the British rule per se. Only later on, before the Mandate ended, the Irgun realized that not the decrees but rather the British themselves were stopping our people from having their independence, and, in effect, adopted to a large extent the basic position of LEHI, and started a direct campaign against the British.

LEHI taught its members the tactics of terror, since it maintained that the first objective is the liquidation of the leadership of the enemy, namely, the heads of the British government, the army and the police, as well as British policemen and soldiers. LEHI believed that the enemy is most sensitive when it came to the welfare of its leaders, commanders, soldiers and policemen, and only by going after them one could put an end to the British rule.

Under my command, the Jerusalem branch became the first operational branch of LEHI, and at Yair's request I launched several operations aimed at funding the new underground.

I worked out a plan to confiscate funds from the Yefet Bank in Jerusalem. We rehearsed every detail of the plan. On the morning of the operation we received a coded message from our member who worked at the bank, letting us know that an employee of a certain company was coming to collect a sum of money. We followed him as he entered the narrow courtyard leading to the entrance of the bank, taking advantage of the high stone wall to hide from view. The members of our team deployed in the area. One took a seat in a nearby restaurant. Another stood by, talking to his girlfriend. Another sat behind the wheel of a car waiting to dash away with the loot. A fourth one was having his shoes shined on Jaffa Road across the street from the bank. The signal was given, and everyone took his position. I had picked Israel, one of my bravest men, as the lead man. He wore a hat which hid part of his face. His mouth was stuffed with chewing gum, keeping his jaws working. He wore makeup which made it hard to identify him.

Israel waited for the company employee in the corridor leading to the bank. He could see the man go to the cashier who attended him. The man came out with the money in his briefcase and went down the stairs, as Israel began to follow him, walking casually, his rubber-soles muffling his steps. As the two of them approached the exit door, Israel looked around. The courtyard, fortunately, was empty. He took the sand-filled staff out of his coat and struck the man over his head, knocking him unconscious. He dashed across the yard to the stone wall, where one of us let down a rope. In a second Israel came over the wall with the money bag. We each went away in a different direction. Israel spat out his chewing gum, removed his makeup with wet cotton, took out the rags stuffed on his back to make him look like a hunchback, and discarded his hat and dark glasses, hiding them in a prearranged cache. Someone waited for him at the next street corner, took the briefcase from him, wrapped it in a cloth and disappeared. Israel walked slowly toward the car waiting for him up the street with the engine running. The operation was a success. We had added several thousand pounds to our attenuated coffers.

We were not always so successful. We attempted a similar action, this time headed by Shlomo Yaakobi, but failed. Yaakobi and Shaul Haglili, another one of our members, lived at the time in the Old City, and were known to the police as right-wing nationalists. After the failed robbery attempt the CID came to their apartment at night and arrested them. I found out about the arrest that same night. I was facing a serious problem: Yaakobi had clear identification marks, and I was almost certain the victim would identify him at the police station. This meant years in jail for Yaakobi, and potential trouble for our entire organization. I knew the police would go through the identification parade the next morning and I had to act immediately. I did something unprecedented. I decided to warn the assault victim not to identify Yaakobi, or else his life and the life of his wife and children would be in grave danger. I instructed Moshe Bar-Giora to use a public phone near the Nablus Gate and call the victim. He called him early in the morning. It worked. A few hours later the man was asked to identify his assailant, but did not point at Yaakobi. Our member was saved from long years in jail. He was put under administrative arrest, but no charges were brought against him.

SEVENTEEN

The Tel Aviv Bank Robbery

One day I received an urgent message from Yair to come to Tel Aviv. He looked somber when we met. "Raziel's people have taken the treasury," he said. "We have no money. It would take us a long time to raise funds, and we are not even sure we can get what we need, now that we have split. We are practically destitute, and we cannot run the organization. Your confiscation of small amounts in Jerusalem is just not enough. We have no choice but to go after big money. That means a major bank robbery, so we can keep going."

He paused and then added: "I know that a bank robbery, even for a good cause, is something our men find very difficult to bring themselves to do. It is not our usual way of operating. But we have no choice. So I decided to enlist the help of our top commanders. I have put the "farmer" (Y. Zettler) in charge of the operation, and he insisted that you take part in it or he won't do it. The plans were drawn up by Zeroni, who, as you know, is one of our most gifted leaders. He says that we cannot afford to fail this time, since the future of our organization depends on it."

I assured Yair everything would be all right. I was certain we would succeed and we would be able to go on to bigger and better things.

Yair smiled and shook my hand. In my heart I cursed the "farmer" for picking me for this robbery, which was not my kind of operation. In addition, I was upset because we had that rule at the time according to which the Tel Aviv people did their own work without enlisting the help of other branches.

I kept it all to myself and said I would do it. That same day I called the "farmer" and Zeroni and we met to go over the plan. I found it to be workable, except for the retreat. According to Zeroni's plan, the escape car was going to wait near the entrance to the bank on Ben-Yehuda Street. Since one had to walk through a narrow alley off Ben-Yehuda to get to the bank's entrance, I suggested that our men, instead of going back to Ben-Yehuda, cross a fence in the alley and take the back way to Shivtey Israel Street, which ran parallel to Ben-Yehuda, where the getaway car would wait for them. My suggestion was accepted, and the plan was completed. We picked the day and we selected our team.

One of our men had opened an account at that bank, and told us that most of the time the safe was open and the cashier kept a gun in an upper shelf of the safe. We also found out that on a certain day—payday, no doubt—there was a large amount of cash at the bank, and we chose that day for our assault.

The day we picked was September 16, 1940. The entire team gathered that morning at the apartment of Miriam Robovitz, on Pinsker Street, where we could assemble without being seen by the neighbors. The assault group included the "farmer," operation commander; I, his second-in-command; and Eliyahu Giladi. Moshe Moldavsky was picked to stand guard at the entrance to the bank, prevent customers from going in during the operation, and provide cover during the retreat. Avraham Amper and Zelig Jacques were assigned to go up on nearby rooftops and be ready to provide hand grenade cover for the operation and the retreat. Max Goldman was instructed to ride a motorcycle and carry away the money after it was taken out of the bank, in order to confuse the pursuers. We also picked two drivers: Shmuel Kaplan, who would drive us after we left the bank, and Gabriel Messeri, who would take us there.

The "farmer" was caught a few months later and was sentenced to 15 years in jail. Eliyahu Giladi, after escaping from the detention camp in Mezra along with Yitzhak Shamir (later Prime Minister of Israel), was subsequently executed by LEHI for behavior that could have brought disaster on the organization, according to the executioners. Amper and Jacques were killed by the CID in 1942 in a raid on an apartment where I myself narrowly escaped death.

At Miriam's place we were thoroughly briefed by the "farmer." We had to walk into the bank at 12:25, a few moments before closing, to minimize the chance of additional customers arriving after we went in. A getaway car would wait for us outside. It was a Mercedes-Benz, stolen the night before from the owner of the ABG Men's Wear Store. The car had been left unlocked with the key in the ignition, which we considered to be a good omen. Shmuel, the getaway driver, had hidden the car on the municipal garbage truck lot, where he worked as a watchman. We knew the police would not find it there before the operation was completed.

Our weapons consisted of two handguns per person—a revolver with dumdum-type bullets, and a semi-automatic. Amper and Jacques were equipeed with noise bombs, to be thrown down from the rooftops in order to divert attention from the robbery and chase away the curious.

Each team was given a different time to arrive at its destination. Amper and Jacques went first and took their positions on the roofs. Shmuel went down to the parking lot to drive the car to our post-attack meeting point. Gabriel, whose task was to drive the attack-team to the bank, remained with us until 12 o'clock, when we left on our mission.

Before we went out we checked the masks we were going to wear during the operation. The masks, invented by Zeroni, were hidden under our hats. There were small lead weights attached to the masks, and when we raised our hats the masks fell down over our faces. We checked the masks, the weapons, and the camouflage kit we carried with us, and we left the house and proceeded toward Gabriel's car, parked around the corner.

We pretended to be a high spirited group of friends going on a picnic. As we got into the car some of our friends were hiding in the back, not to arouse any suspicion. We arrived at the bank at 12:20. Slowly, one at a time, we got out of the car and walked toward the bank like ordinary customers. I followed the "farmer" in order to be close to him during the holdup. I could see Amper and Jacques on the nearby roofs, awaiting their turn. At a distance I saw Shmuel, who hurried to the getaway car to wait for us in the car, on the next street.

When we reached the bank entrance, the "farmer" and I stopped and let the others catch up with us. We pretended to walk into the bank as individuals who happened to arrive at the same time. We did not arouse any suspicion. The employees kept doing their work. The safe was open as usual. The cashier leisurely counted the bills. There were several customers in the bank, standing at the counters. We tipped our hats as we entered, as if we were greeting those inside, and the masks fell over our faces. Instinctively we drew our guns and the "farmer" announced in a deep, steady voice: "We are confiscating funds for the Hebrew underground, to fight for national liberation. Stand up quietly and raise your hands, turn to the wall and lean against it, and follow my orders. Anyone who interferes with the Hebrew underground is risking his life."

Giladi stood in the corner and aimed his gun at the employees behind the counter. Moshe blocked the entrance and shut the door. At the moment the bombs began to explode outside, and the street became deserted. The bank staff and the customers followed the "farmer's" orders. At that moment I jumped on the counter. The cashier bent down, and I skipped over him toward the safe.

The safe was open. I took a thin cloth bag out of my pocket and began to throw in the money. I only took paper money as I emptied out the safe. Next I started to empty the chashier's drawers. He shrunk next to me, and I paid no attention to him. As I wore gloves, I was not concerned about leaving fingerprints, and I searched all the drawers.

As I finished collecting money I noticed the gun in the upper drawer of the safe. I had no interest in taking it, but I wanted to neutralize it. I took out the magazine and hid it in a drawer to prevent the cashier from using the gun during our retreat. I took a leap over the counter, holding my gun, and told the "farmer" everything was all right and we could leave. We turned to a side door, leading to the backyard, designated for our retreat. Moshe walked first, to protect the loot from the front, I followed behind him, next came Giladi, and the "farmer" was last, guarding the rear. Before he went out he hung a package on the doorknob and said: "This is a bomb which can blow up the bank. If anyone opens the door he would detonate the bomb." He closed the door behind him and joined us outside in the backyard. We crossed the fence, which we had cut the night before. It led to another yard. From there we were going to come out to the main road.

We moved rapidly, our guns drawn inside our jackets in order not to attract attention. Shmuel was waiting for us in the car. The "farmer," Giladi and I entered the back seat while Moshe sat next to the driver. The three men in the back would provide cover while Moshe was going to put the money in a satchel, dash out of the car and give the money to our motorcyclist who would be riding alongside the car at a certain point. After the money was transferred the motorcycle and the getaway car would go in opposite directions as the money was quickly brought to a safe place.

Shmuel steered the car with a sure hand as we clung against one another. We put away our guns and caught our breath. As we kept going Moshe suddenly took out his gun and started shooting at a youth walking outside, nearly killing him. We all shouted at Moshe to stop. The youth was not harmed, as he quickly dropped and lay flat on the ground. But the shots drew attention and a car began to follow us. I am not sure why Moshe opened fire. He might have been so tense he became scared and had to do something to relieve his tension. He almost brought disaster on us. At that time, in 1940, the public was not too familiar with underground operations, and had not yet learned not to interfere when someone started opening fire. We quickly assessed the situation and decided we had to stop the chasing car no matter what, or else we might not be able to transfer the money to our motorcyclist as more cars might be joining the chase, including the police. We also decided not to give Moshe the money to do the transfer. I was going to do it myself.

The chasing car was coming closer. The "farmer" took the initiative. He took aim and shot at it. He hit the windshield next to the driver, without hitting anyone. The car slowed down. We were able to get away and meet the motorcyclist. I barely had time to close the satchel after I transferred the money. I jumped out of the car as it kept moving, nearly falling flat on my face, as some bills dropped out of the bag. Max, the motorcyclist, ordered me not to pick them up but sit behind him and get going. Reluctantly, I obeyed him. We took a roundabout way, and arrived at Max's apartment, our first hideout. A young woman, Yair's liaison, was waiting for us with one of our members, who was guarding her and was going to transfer the money. We hid the bills inside the mat of a large framed picture and the two took it back to Yair, who was going to use the money to fund the underground.

The night before the operation I had slept at my parents' house. Before I left in the morning I could see my mother's face had turned to white. She gave me a strange look. I avoided her stare and hurried to our meeting place. After the operation I sent a message to my mother with a courier to let her know I could not come home. The courier told me my mother had let out a sigh of relief and returned to her housework.

When my job was done around 2 o'clock, I went to get a haircut. I relaxed in the chair and entrusted my head to the barber. The radio was on, and I could hear the Voice of Jerusalem news, announcing the holdup at the Anglo-Palestine Bank in Tel Aviv. Some 5000 pounds were taken from the bank and the robbers had disappeared. This was the first time I found out how much we had taken. I also learned that my comrades in the stolen car reached safety after I had mounted the motorcycle.

The barber joked: "Well, now Tel Aviv is no different from Chicago, and we are not different from other nations. But the difference is that in Chicago they are plain gangsters, while here we have underground fighters. May God watch over them."

My heart was filled with joy at his words. Suddenly I realized the people were with us. They approved of our struggle. They knew we were fighting for them.

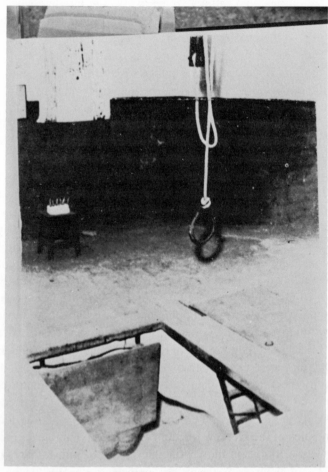

Execution (hanging) room in the Acre jail.

EIGHTEEN

The Haifa Command

After the robbery it was decided to transfer me to Haifa, to get the police off my tracks. Shortly after I arrived in Haifa the local commander, Broshi, left, and I took his place. I began to reorganize the Haifa branch almost completely.

In his second Order of the Day issued after the split, Yair proclaimed that the organization was becoming a fighting underground. This necessitated a revision of the training doctrine, which I sought to introduce to my officers' course in Haifa. Later on, when I became the head of the training section of LEHI, I applied the revision to the general training doctrine of the organization.

I maintained a personal contact with the headquarters in Tel Aviv. I would go there from time to time to meet with Yair, our head of command. We would discuss political and ideological questions. The other two members of the command were Kalay and Zeroni. With the former I discussed manpower and morale problems, and with the latter technical questions related to training.

In my meetings with Yair I demanded two things. First, I pointed out that we did not have written ideological principles. I argued that it was his duty to formulate and circulate among the members the ideological principles of the Hebrew freedom movement. Yair agreed, and told me he was working on those principles. I urged him to hurry up and finish the job, since we were in constant danger of being captured by the

British, and it would be a tragedy if we did not leave written principles for those who would follow us. In one of our meetings Yair told me I would be glad to know he had finished writing the National Revival Principles, and was going to include them in our next edition of the underground paper. Those principles, which in time became the ideological foundation of the LEHI, were:

NATIONAL REVIVAL PRINCIPLES

1. THE NATION

The Jewish people is a covenanted people, originator of monotheism, formulator of the prophetic teachings, standard-bearer of human culture, guardian of a glorious patrimony. The Jewish people is schooled in self-sacrifice and suffering; its vision, survivability and faith in redemption are indestructible.

2. THE HOMELAND

The homeland is the Land of Israel within the borders delineated in the Bible. (To your descendants I shall give this land, from the River of Egypt to the great Euphrates River. Genesis 15:18.) This is the land of the living, where the entire nation shall live in safety.

3. THE NATION AND ITS LAND

Israel conquered the land with the sword. There it became a nation and only there it will be reborn. Hence Israel alone has a right to that land. This is an absolute right. It has never expired and never will.

4. THE GOALS

1. Redemption of the land. 2. Establishment of sovereignty. 3. Revival of the nation. There is no sovereignty without the redemption of the land, and there is no national revival without sovereignty.

These are the tasks of the organization during the period of war and conquest:

5. EDUCATION

Educate the nation to love freedom and zealously guard Israel's eternal patrimony. Inculcate the idea that the nation is master to its own fate. Revive the doctrine that "The sword and the book came bound together from heaven" (Midrash Vayikra Rabba 35:8).

6. UNITY   The unification of the entire nation around the banner of the Hebrew freedom movement. The use of the genius, status and resources of individuals and the channeling of the energy, devotion and revolutionary fervor of the masses for the war of liberation.

7. PACTS   Make pacts with all those who are willing to help the struggle of the organization and provide direct support.

8. FORCE   Consolidate and increase the fighting force in the homeland and in the diaspora, in the underground and in the barracks, to become the Hebrew army of liberation with its flag, arms and commanders.

9. WAR   Constant war against those who stand in the way of fulfilling the goals.

10. CONQUEST
   The conquest of the homeland from foreign rule and its eternal possession.

These are the tasks of the movement during the period of sovereignty and redemption:

11. SOVEREIGNTY
   Renewal of Hebrew sovereignty over the redeemed land.

12. RULE OF JUSTICE
   The establishment of a social order in the spirit of Jewish morality and prophetic justice. Under such an order no one will go hungry or unemployed. All will live in harmony, mutual respect and friendship as an example to the world.

13. REVIVING THE WILDERNESS
   Build the ruins and revive the wilderness for mass immigration and population increase.

14. ALIENS   Solve the problem of alien population by exchange of population.

15. INGATHERING OF EXILES
   Total ingathering of the exiles to their sovereign state.

16. POWER   The Hebrew nation shall become a first-rate military, political, cultural and economical entity in the Middle East and around the Mediterranean Sea.

17. REVIVAL

> The revival of the Hebrew language as a language spoken by the entire nation, the renewal of the historical and spiritual might of Israel. The purification of the national character in the fire of revival.

18. THE TEMPLE

> The building of the Third Temple as a symbol of the new era of total redemption.

In one of my talks with Yair prior to the publication of the above principles, I had given him a pamphlet which I had written in Haifa, titled *The Revolutionary Tract*. In that pamphlet I proposed some guiding principles for the underground. Yair read the pamphlet and told me he had found some interesting things in it, which might help him in composing his "principles." His remark had made me extremely proud.

My second demand of the command had to do with operations. The Haifa branch was ready for action. I proposed that we use it against those elements in the British administration which prevented Jewish refugees from entering the country. After long consideration it was decided that the Haifa group attack the government immigration office in that city. It was our only operation during that period.

The immigration office of the Mandatory government determined how many Jews were allowed to enter the country and how many would be deported. It was commonly held in the Yishuv that some of the worst British anti-Semites worked in that office. Most of the staff were Arabs, and only a few Jews were employed. The Jewish community often demonstrated against that office, which prevented Jews from reaching our shores and sent them back to the Nazi beast. The main office was in Jerusalem. The Haifa branch was downtown near the German Colony. The office occupied five rooms on the second floor of a building in an Arab neighborhood. The building itself was owned by Arabs. It was necessary, therefore, to be disguised as Arabs for the purpose of this operation.

First I had to gather information. I chose an elderly couple from among our sympathizers, who went over there with the excuse of applying for their relatives to come over. They scouted the place and brought us back a detailed floor plan, with a description of windows and doors to help us determine whether to climb in by rope from the roof or climb up from the ground. On the basis of this information we drew up a plan for blowing up the office and burning the files which included data about Jewish immigrants.

I found out that the entrance door was secured with a Yale lock. After I checked the locks on the back doors, I realized it would be no problem to enter from the back. But since I did not want to run the risk of being discovered on the way in, I decided to use the staircase and open the entrance door with our own key, having our men pose as a night cleaning crew.

In order to make the key fit the lock of the main door I modified the lock, in a way that the employees who unlocked the door would not notice the change, and when our men went there to place the bombs they could use their key without any difficulties. First I bought a Yale lock similar to the one on the door. I took out the inner cylinder and then I removed the small cylinders inside it, held by special springs. A Yale lock consists of small cylinders of varying lengths, each one adjusted to the depression in the key. The cylinder is pushed down by a tiny spring, and raised by the key, releasing the inner cylinder from the outer one, and then the lock opens. When all the cylinders are filed down, any Yale key can open the lock.

We proceeded to modify the lock I had bought, and sent our break-in expert to replace the lock at the immigration office. He used a gutter to climb to a second-floor balcony, opened the balcony door with a jimmy, went into the office and removed the lock from the door as we kept guard outside and in the staircase. He had no trouble putting the modified lock in place of the old one.

I decided to use letter bombs, for two reasons. I was able to use official government envelopes large enough to hold several pounds of explosives. Those envelopes provided good camouflage. If the carrier was stopped by the British, he or she could produce a fake official ID and pretend to be on a government errand. I had used the same exploding envelopes in 1939 for blowing up the central post office and the government radio station in Jerusalem. I used four separate envelopes to be placed in each of the four rooms of the immigration office where there were files we wished to destroy. I set the timers at 15-minute intervals, so that the explosions would occur over a period of ¾ of an hour. After the first explosion the police would rush in and would be caught in the subsequent explosions. In each envelope I put several pounds of explosives, enough to blow up several persons standing nearby. Inside the explosives I placed electric detonators wired to small batteries connected to a timer used effectively in the past.

I chose one of our men who spoke Arabic, and dressed him as a messenger of a government office, equipped with the necessary documents, I gave him a messenger briefcase. Early that night he went to the immigration office, after we had checked the place to make sure no one was there. I sent some men to follow him and protect him if anything unexpected happened. He went into the building, walked up the stairs, took out the key and unlocked the door. He went inside and quickly placed the envelopes in the assigned places. He had been there before, since I had previously given him the key to go there and steal some documents. At the time he did not know he had been chosen for that mission, as it was our habit not to let those sent on a mission know about their assignment until the last moment. When I summoned him shortly before the operation I did not have to explain too many things. He knew the place and all he had to do was go there and place the envelopes in the assigned spots. I set the timers and sealed the envelopes. He had to go directly to the office and get rid of those bombs which could blow him to smithereens if he did not dispose of them in time. If for any reason he were delayed on his way, he had to leave them anywhere and get away as far as he could.

Before he left I shook his hand as usual and gave him the blessing, "God guards his warriors." He took the envelopes and went out. Two guards and I followed him with concealed weapons. He walked briskly without looking around, as if he were in a hurry, and did not arouse any suspicion. He went into the building as we stood outside, fearing for his safety. Ten mintues later he came out, holding his briefcase. I could tell the briefcase was empty. We all dispersed. I joined my female escort, who took my gun and hid it on her person. We walked up to Hadar Hacarmel. I kept looking at my watch and as we approached the city hall of Haifa I heard a powerful explosion. We approached the edge of the park in front of city hall, overlooking downtown, and we saw fire and billows of smoke rising from the direction of the immigration office. The envelopes had destroyed the offices and all the files inside them. It was our only operation during late 1940. The official reason given was the deportation of the illegal immigrants of the *Atlantic*. Because of the serious nature of the attack, the censorship did not allow any reports in the media.

This operation was important for several reasons. The British were under the impression that after the split in the Irgun they had silenced the underground. Now they found out that a new underground, which they called the Stern Gang, came to life, and turned out to be the most extreme and the most dangerous, striking at the British in a most sensitive area, namely, immigration. Since the Yishuv was unified in its demand to allow immigration and save the remnants of European Jewry, the operation was favorably received by the public, even by world Jewry. Moreover, this operation gave our faction a morale boost and created discontent in Raziel's ranks. Some of his men even joined us as a result.

Like any successful operation, it strengthened the local branch of the organization. Our men felt that the long and difficult training had paid off. Shortly afterwards, in one of our periodical meetings. Yair told me that in light of the success of my methods in Haifa he wanted me to teach those methods to the rest of the organization, and asked me if I would agree to head the national training and operations section. I agreed without hesitation, and thanked Yair for the promotion and for the confidence he had in me. I passed the command of the Haifa branch on to Zvi Frunin, my chief assistant. I said goodbye to my comrades in Haifa and moved to Tel Aviv.

NINETEEN

The Agent Provocateur

While I was still in Haifa I was in on an important political affair because of my part in Naftali Lubentchik's trip to Beirut, where he was sent by LEHI to make contact with Axis representatives in order to try to save European Jewry.

One day I was ordered to look into the possibility of sending a representative of the organization to Beirut. At the time we had contacts in Haifa with a group of smugglers who operated between Haifa and Beirut. Among them there were Jews and Arabs who smuggled men and merchandise between the two cities. Those men helped us bring in arms from Beirut for our underground activities. Beirut was then under the control of the Vichy Government, and the real power in the city were the German and Italian military delegations. Under such confused conditions it was easy to obtain arms even from the official French sources who wanted to be paid in hard currency, since they did not know what the future would bring. Those sources gladly supplied us with arms of all kinds, knowing that they were intended to attack their British enemy, thus combining French patriotism with profit-making, typical of the French colonial rule in the region.

I arranged for Lubentchik documents of a Maronite agent who came to Haifa to buy merchandise, in case of any problem at the border, although he was in the good hands of professional smugglers. Lubentchik was fluent in French and had no problem passing for a Maronite. He crossed the Lebanese border without any difficulty and reached his destination.

The idea of making contact with the Axis came up in the Irgun before World War Two, when Raziel was head of command, as a result of Yair's successful experience with the Polish authorities. In light of that pact with the Poles, the command considered a similar pact with the Germans and the Italians, in order to save the lives of the Jews of Europe. The first contact was going to be made with the Italians, and if it succeeded, the Germans would be next. In this atmosphere of a burning desire to do something for the doomed Jews of Europe, Moshe Rotstein, the agent provocateur, appeared on the scene.

It appears that Rotstein was planted in the National Movement back in the early thirties by the British intelligence, in Rosh Pina, where some members of the Irgun later became leaders of the organization. When he moved to Haifa, Rotstein gained the confidence of Moshe, who was a senior commander of the Irgun in Haifa and for a while the head of intelligence in that town. Although we knew Rotstein had contacts with the British intelligence, Moshe persuaded the Irgun command that Rotstein was one of us, and we could make use of his contacts with the British. Later on we found out that Rotstein was also a member of the Haganah, ergo, a genuine double agent. Back in 1939 Rotstein contacted Raziel and told him he could get in touch with the Italians and make a pact which would help the Irgun's struggle. The command was suspicious of Rotstein, and did not give him a definitive answer. In the meantime Raziel was arrested, the command was apprehended, World War Two broke out, and the matter was frozen. But Rotstein did not give up. After the split he turned to Moshe with an urgent offer to put Yair in touch with Italian agents to make a pact. It was known at that time that European Jewry was doomed. There were also rumors of German plans to send the Jews of Europe to Madagascar. There was reason to believe that it was possible to talk to the Axis countries about letting the Jews emigrate illegally to the Land of Israel while fighting the British. Against this backdrop, despite all the suspicions, Yair and his command agreed to listen to Rotstein. The latter came back with an ostensible Italian offer for Yair to draft an agreement.

Yair's command drafted the document known as the Jerusalem Agreement, according to which the Italians would bring the Jews of Europe to the Land of Israel, provide ships, set up transit camps in Italy, and provide arms for the Irgun to forcibly bring the refugees into the country. The Irgun, in return, would collaborate with Italy, and after its victory in the liberated Land of Israel, would help Italy expand its influence in the Middle East. At the top of that document Yair wrote the letter Aleph, which in Hebrew could stand for either Italians or English.

Yair was indeed concerned that Rotstein was a provocateur sent by the British intelligence, and wanted the British to know what his conditions were for making the pact. Yair did not care who would save the Jews of Europe, the British or the Italians. To achieve this goal he was willing to make a pact with either side.

Yair's concern was not unfounded. Later on it was established beyond a doubt that Rotstein was an agent of the CID and the intelligence. He had been sent to the Irgun command in order to expose it as a fifth column, a group of people willing to deal with the Italian and Nazi enemy for money. Rotstein said that the Italians wanted Yair to personally sign the agreement draft. This demand made Yair even more suspicious and he refused to sign. The command decided to discontinue its dealings with Rotstein and give up the entire project.

The provocation, however, was quite successful. The British, and Rotstein himself, passed the word to the Haganah and to Raziel that indeed there were negotiations between us and the Italians and we had signed some kind of an agreement. The word got out that Yair was a German agent and that his group was a fifth column against the British and against the Yishuv. This sealed the fate of Yair and his men. They were put outside the law, and anyone could kill them with official approval.

Rotstein did not stop there. About a year after he failed to make Yair sign his bogus document, he tried again, for money, to do the bidding of the British, and turn our command one against the other. This time he went to visit Moshe, who was a prisoner at Mizrah, and told him in secret that Zeroni, a member of Yair's command, was an agent of the police. He explained that back in 1939, when Zeroni was arrested and tortured in the basement of the CID in Jerusalem, the British actually helped him escape in order to use him as a provocateur inside the command of the Irgun. Moshe decided to bring this matter to Yair's attention. Yair began to have some second thoughts about Zeroni. He did not trust Rotstein, but wanted to check out the allegation.

We met to discuss the matter. Zeroni in the meantime had quit our organization, and we did not wish to deal with the past. We did come to the conclusion that Rostein was a full-fledged provocateur, and decided to liquidate him. I was given the task, since Rotstein was a resident of Haifa, where I had been in command until recently.

I went to Haifa, found his address, and planned the operation. He was afraid for his life, and kept changing his lodgings, rarely coming home, although he was married and had children. Once we almost caught him at home, but the house was full of relatives, and since we did not wish to harm any innocent people, we cancelled the operation. At that point Rotstein disappeared and we never heard from him again. The execution was never carried out.

Since LEHI was the deepest underground and its members were highly dedicated people, the authorities could not harm us by bribing any of our members. In LEHI we did not have any traitors, unlike other undergrounds. This was the reason why the British had to use an outside agent, like Rotstein. This man played a double game. Sometimes he would bring us useless information about the British, probably with their approval, in order to prove his loyalty to us. He posed as a Haganah person as well, to make us think that if we wanted to harm him, the Haganah would come after us. He was a master agent provocateur, always quick to find a weak link in any organization in order to use it against the whole.

This weak link was LEHI's head of intelligence. Rotstein gained his confidence and was able to manipulate him. It was a serious mistake on the command's part to let Rotstein be our go-between with the Italians. This man knew about our pact with the Poles, and realized that if he posed as the spokesman of the Italians, rather than the Germans, the command would believe him. The command was willing to make a pact with anyone in order to save the Jews of Europe, even with the devil himself. The command accepted without reservations the assessment of the head of intelligence, and was caught in the trap laid down by the British intelligence. Rotstein's success began the moment he made contact with the command, without the command realizing it. The command's willingness to deal with the Italians was a mistake. It gave British agents the opportunity to spread the rumor that LEHI was a fifth column. Later, when Rotstein put the idea in our head of intelligence's head that Zeroni was a CID plant, the very fact that our man passed it on to the command helped Rotstein achieve his purpose.

Let us return now to the adventures of Naftali Lubentchik. He was able to meet with an official of the German Foreign Ministry, Otto von

Hentig, who had been sent by the Nazi foreign minister, von Ribbentrop, to obtain information about the Middle East. Several months after Lubentchik left for Beirut we received a letter from him relating his accomplishments until that moment. He told us about his meeting with the head of the German delegation, with whom he discussed the plan. The German delegation head told him that there were two schools of thought among the German leadership. One pursued *realpolitik*, while the other preferred *idealpolitik*. The first school proposed to expel the Jews from Europe, possibly to Madagascar, or somewhere else. The second group was committed to the total annihilation of European Jewry. The delegation head added that he personally, as a member of the old school, sided with the *realpolitik* school. But since the solution of the Jewish question through expulsion did not seem to work out, he thought that the chances of the *idealpolitik* school were much better. In any case, he told Lubentchik he would pass on his memo to his superiors.

This was the only and the last letter we received from Lubentchik. In his memoirs, von Hentig writes about his meeting with the Jewish delegation, headed by a man "with the pleasant appearance of an officer," who brought him the proposal of cooperating with the Nazis against his orthodox Zionist compatriots, if Hitler guaranteed the independence of Jewish Palestine. The German responded to this offer with reservations, but agreed to pass on to his superiors a memo called "Outline of the Irgun in Palestine Re the Jewish Question in Europe and Its Solution through Evacuation" to the Land of Israel, where "a Jewish state would be established within its historical borders. The Irgun in the Land of Israel, proposes to provide military training for the manpower in Europe in order to organize it under the guidance and leadership of the Irgun into military units which would participate in military operations aimed at the conquest of the Land of Israel."

The memo reached the archives of the German foreign ministry and was shelved. The answer from Germany did not come in time, and meanwhile the Allies invaded Syria and Lebanon and occupied them. The British secret police had no trouble finding Lubentchik. He was arrested and sent to the Mizrah detention camp, where other underground prisoners were kept, and later on he was exiled with other underground men to Africa where he became sick and died.

TWENTY

Purge and Change

Before my transfer from Haifa in 1942, I found out about some differences in opinion between Yair and the other two members of the command, Hanoch Sterlitz (Kalay) and Binyamin Zeroni. I was told that the two disagreed with Yair's views and saw no point in fighting the British while World War Two was at its peak. They were in favor of helping the British war effort against Nazi Germany and waiting to see how things turned out after the war.

Although the two command members referred to the disagreement as "tactical," in reality it was a deep ideological rift. Yair argued that although Hitler was the archenemy, the British were the ones who deprived the Yishuv of any expression of independence, and through the White Paper sought to put an end to any Zionist aspirations in the Land of Israel. The British, therefore, were an enemy whom we had to fight. Only by fighting them could we hope to force them to change their position in regard to the Yishuv and its national aspirations. He went on to say that only if the British recognized the leadership of the Yishuv as a temporary government that would establish an independent state at the end of the war, and would recognize that state, would he agree to collaborate with them. In the absence of such agreement, any collaboration with the foreign occupier was an act of treason.

The disagreement among the command members affected the senior commanders in the field. The organization was reaching a point of paralysis. Internal disputes prevented us from planning new operations and building up the organization. We had to examine each issue and come to a decision about the future course of the organization: Would we follow the thinking of Kalay and Zeroni, which in effect meant returning to the Irgun, or would we go with Yair?

Yair called a meeting of all the senior commanders. The meeting was crucial for the future of the organization, as it set forth the question of what would be the future course of action of the Hebrew underground for national liberation. Yair opened the meeting by explaining his own views, referring to his writings and to the National Revival Principles. Kalay and Zeroni followed him, taking issue with him. They argued that it was time to rejoin the Irgun and begin to cooperate with the British.

It turned out, to the surprise of the members of the high command, that the senior commanders were even more radical than Yair. Not only did they fully support Yair's position, but went on to demand immediate action against the British in order to force the Mandatory government to open the gates for European refugees and to accept the Yishuv as a national entity seeking to gain independence at the end of the war. The disagreements between the senior commanders and the two command members were sharp. The strongest criticism was directed at Kalay. I went so far as to say that "he deserves to be shot in the head" for his views. It should be pointed out that Kalay had always been more radical than Yair, and even helped him compose the Principles. And here he made a complete turnabout and was willing to rejoin the Irgun and work with the British. To us, the senior commanders, Kalay was a broken man who had outlived his usefulness.

During one of the heated discussions Kalay got up and left the meeting. Since the British were looking for him at that time, we feared for his life, and after he left the apartment we sent emissaries after him to talk him into coming back. Our emissary found him wandering aimlessly on the beach and brought him back to the meeting. But a few days later, I believe it was the fifth day of the meeting, it became clear that neither Kalay nor Zeroni were able to continue in the organization. They left the meeting, and right then and there Yair stood up and proceeded to announce the formation of a new command.

That meeting, which lasted ten days, was the event that gave birth to the Lohamey Herut Israel (LEHI) organization, Hebrew for Fighters for the Freedom of Israel. Our discussions resulted in a reformulation of our ideology, our organizational structure, our educational method, training and operations, as well as our minimum and maximum plan of action in the fight for the freedom of Israel. We also adopted the new name of the organization, which was proposed by Yair. The meeting raised our morale, deepened our conviction that we had chosen the right way in our struggle for national liberation, and restored our faith in our leadership.

During that brief period our organization in effect became consolidated. The main factor in this consolidation process were the views and ideas of Yair. His articles in our paper, *Bamahteret*, and his National Revival Principles, as well as his speeches, became the doctrine of our movement and our practical political plan of action.

We were few in number at that time. Haifa and Jerusalem had about 20-30 members each (including sympathizers); Tel Aviv had 30-50; Kfar Saba, Herzliya, Ramataim and Rehovot, a total of 30. These numbers may be about 15-20 percent higher than the actual ones. But our morale was very high. We were a tightly-knit body, and we had gotten rid of the waverers and the compromisers. We stepped up our training and propaganda and sought new members. We also decided to take on the CID, which we did not consider to be in conflict with the war effort.

Our financial situation was deplorable. We could not solicit funds, since the incitement against us grew each day. The Revisionists looked upon us as enemies of the movement and its founder, Zeev Jabotinsky. The Jewish Agency and the Haganah, needless to say, were totally opposed to us. The full impact of the Holocaust had not yet become known at that time, and the Yishuv believed the only way to fight the Nazis was through enlisting in the British army. Our anti-British position made us a complete anomaly.

Our penury prompted us to resort to robberies. We attempted a bank robbery in Tel Aviv on March 1, 1942. This time the public was not scared away by our guns, and our men were forced to shoot and kill two innocent bystanders.

This action caused a public outcry against us, and gave the police an excuse to step up its action against us. Zetler, the "farmer," was caught by a CID ambush at his Tel Aviv apartment along with some of the command members and the Tel Aviv activists. Among the arrested were Yitzhak Yezernitzky (Shamir), Avshalom Broshi and Siman Tov. After the arrest a new command was formed, headed by Yair, with Yitzhak Zelnik as head of command, Moshe Svorai (who had escaped from Mizrah at that time) head of the Tel Aviv branch, and I, head of the Jerusalem branch and national head of planning, training and operations. Frunin remained the head of the Haifa branch.

TWENTY-ONE

Fighting the CID

After Kalay and Zeroni left the organization, the new command adopted Yair's three-point plan: 1. Raising funds to finance our arm purchases, caches, hiding places and general operation. 2. Liquidate our direct enemy, the CID, in order to go on to the next, more important point. 3. The operational and political action necessary to further our goals. After we raised some funds, Yair decided to move on to the second stage, namely, deal the CID a decisive blow in order to be able to move on to the third stage.

Before we broke away from the Irgun, in 1939, we liquidated Cairns and Barker, the CID officers who specialized in anti-underground work, by blowing them up with a mine in Jerusalem. This stopped police action against us. There were no more arrests and torture after the incident, although the Jewish section of the CID was now headed by Officer Wilkin a top expert in anti-underground work. The police, however, soon recovered, and appointed a senior officer named Morton to head the anti-Jewish operation, with Wilkin serving under him. Morton and Wilkin issued a circular letter to the British police, which stated that any policeman could shoot to kill any LEHI member or anyone suspected of being a LEHI member, without investigation and without due process of law. Even Jewish police commanders instructed their men to find and kill LEHI members, above all their commander, Stern. They even promised a high reward for it. It became clear to us that only he who shot first would survive. We met to discuss this issue, and decided to go after our chief enemies, Morton and Wilkin, and their aides, as we had done in the case of Cairns and Barker. I, who headed the Cairns and Barker operation, was now put in charge of eliminating Morton and Wilkin.

Wilkin was the most cunning of the lot. He was thoroughly familiar with the Yishuv and its problems, spoke Hebrew well, had lived for a long time among Jews, and had a Jewish girlfriend, the daughter of Borochov, one of the founding fathers of socialist Zionism. Morton was Wilkin's superior. He was highly decorated by the British Empire, mainly because of his cold-blooded murderous traits of character. He used to murder his victims without bringing them to trail. He had killed several Arabs in this manner, and more than once during his searches for arms in the kibbutzim some kibbutz members were murdered.

Morton knew LEHI would do all it could to liquidate him. He might have also been tipped off about our decision to kill him the first chance we had. After he started his activities against the Haganah and the kibbutzim he became the main enemy of the entire Yishuv, and was very cautious about his moves. He kept changing his habits and his lodgings, although his permanent residence was inside a fortified British camp in the German colony of Sharona near Tel Aviv. He was always surrounded by bodyguards, wore a bullet-proof vest and kept his hand on his gun. Wilkin was also extremely cautious, but preferred to resort to deception. He always portrayed himself as someone opposed to torture, a subordinate who took orders. He told people he was sympathetic to our national aspirations, and was serving in the Jewish section in order to help the Haganah. In reality he was Morton's right-arm man, his brain and his memory, without whom the damage done by Morton might not have been so great.

During that time we kept getting reports the police were prepared to do anything to destroy us. We heard that Officer Schiff had ordered his men at a parade in Rehovot to catch Yair dead or alive. Shortly afterwards Yair and Svorai went out to meet Shlomo Posner, who had headed the 38 prisoners of the Mishmar Hayarden course, and was recently released. They walked together along a dark street when a police armored car came by and turned a searchlight on them. They began to walk away when the car opened fire and they barely managed to escape. It was clear to us the police was out to get us. We knew that unless we intimidated the police they would liquidate us. Since Wilkin and Morton led the operation against us, we decided to eliminate them. As was mentioned before, I was put in charge of the operation.

I started with the assumption that Morton's desire to capture LEHI members outweighed any considerations of personal safety on his part. Besides, I knew that he used to get personally involved in his operations. Based on this, I proceeded to draw the following plan: one of our men would explode a small bomb in his apartment so the neighbors could hear it. He would leave blood stains inside the apartment and on the stairs outside, as if one of our men had been wounded in an accident. I knew the news would immediately reach Morton at the CID headquarters in Tel Aviv, and he would come over to apprehend the wounded person and use him to find out about the rest of the organization. I wanted to blow up Morton and his entire crew. I decided to hide a large bomb in the apartment with a remote control mechanism, so that we could avoid blowing up the wrong people.

The Tel Aviv branch soon found the right apartment, occupied by two dedicated members, and the right person to do the job. This person was Siomka (Shimon Ziv) an old commander of the underground, a fearless warrior. I knew he would do a thorough job.

I moved to Tel Aviv for a few days to work on the bomb. I rested during the day, and at night I would go out to 8 Yael Street, where I was going to lay the trap for the British brutes. The place was a roof apartment. Inside the apartment next to the door there was a chest, where I hid 55 pounds of blasting gelatin, the best explosive we had at that time. I put it inside a well-sealed tin box. Inside the explosives I attached five detonators connected in a row, each inside primer made of exploding cotton or TNT, to increase the explosion. The large number of detonators was needed to ensure the explosion and the uniformity of the burning. Around the explosives I put 33 pounds of nails of all kinds, soaked in salicylic and sulphatic acid, to aggravate the wounds. The inside and outside tin containers were welded thoroughly in order to increase the compression during the explosion, thus increasing the impact.

I pulled a wire from the bomb and tied it to two poles on the roof of the apartment, to make it look like a radio antenna. From there I continued the wire to the roof of the fourth house down the block, somewhat higher than the roof of the apartment, affording an excellent view. From there the operator could easily do his job and then go down to an exit leading to another street and walk away without drawing any attention. The wire ended in a socket which I concealed on the roof of that house. The operator was going to have a triple battery with a switch and a plug to be attached to the wire to detonate the bomb. I now proceeded to manufacture the second trap.

I decided to make two traps, so that in case Morton and Wilkin survived the bomb on the roof, they would be trapped by the one I was going to put on the walk from the street to the door of the building. I had no doubt those two would come over after the initial, attention-getting explosion. If by remote chance they did not, they would surely come after the main bomb on the roof went off. If by luck the roof bomb did not finish them off, when they reached the walk outside the building—where they must pass—they would be blown to pieces by the same type of mine that killed Cairns and Barker.

In the middle of the night I began to place the Fugaz mine I had learned how to make in Poland underneath the walk leading into the building on Yael Street. It took three hours of extremely strenuous work. This type of night work had its own special problems. First, there was always the chance of being detected when one worked outside. Second, electric work required great expertise with one's hands and eyes, since one was handling small wires and screws and was not able to use a light but had to rely on one's sense of touch and good eyesight.

I was surrounded by guards who used several kinds of disguise: a couple of lovers inside a cab, another couple on the street corner, and someone else on a rooftop. Nevertheless, I had to do my utmost not to arouse any suspicions in the neighborhood. I finally had the mine ready for concealment. It was similar to the one I had used three years earlier against Cairns and Barker in Jerusalem. It was a cone made of tin, 1.5 feet high, 1 foot across the base. Inside it I had put 33 pounds of blasting gelatin. Above the explosives I put a tin partition, well attached to the cone, and above the partition I put 22 pounds of nails and bits of iron, soaked in acid, and above those another tin partition. Everything was tightly welded to maximize the explosion and the destruction of those who stepped on the mine.

The soil on the walk was soft, and I had no trouble digging a hole for the mine. Next to the walk there was a three-story building which stood next to the building with the roof apartment, where the bomb was hidden. I pulled a wire to the roof of that building. The operator on that roof had a similar detonating mechanism as the one on the second roof.

In order to avoid any breakdowns, I tested the circuits. I used low voltage which would not set off the detonators, only show that the

current was going through. Such test is crucial for the success of this type
of operation.

The two traps were now ready for their prey. Siomka had a few
hours to rest and toss in bed. I finished my work around 4:30 in the
morning. We were going to set off the bait at 9:30. By then Morton and
Wilkin should be sitting in their office and receive the news we were so
anxious for them to receive. I had posted guards to keep an eye on the
traps. The time between the installation of a bomb and its detonation is
most critical. If the plot is uncovered, the police could lay in wait for the
operators and arrest them, catching them in their own trap. This kind of
thing happened more than once.

Before dawn I went to the home of some trusted supporters, who
lived in the neighborhood, and knew nothing about the operation. The
person in charge of securing the operation had instructions to go there
and alert me if anything went wrong. The two bomb operators also were
instructed to go there before the operation. Since this mission was crucial
to the future of our organization, the operators had to be extremely
dedicated, even tempered, and fearless. I had picked two of our best
men. One was Baruch, an old and devoted member, who later took part
in the famous escape from Latrun, and had all the qualifications for the
job. The other was Yehoshua, who from the day he joined the underground as a child became a legend of self-sacrifice, devotion and
courage. I had the feeling both would do their job without a hitch.

Baruch came over at 8, and Yehoshua at 8:45, taking all the
precautions of the underground. I gave them their last minute instructions. I told them in no uncertain terms that the trap was intended for
Morton and Wilkin, and if those two did not show up it was not to be
used. We would sooner get caught than use it on anyone other than those
two. Baruch said he knew Morton and Wilkin well, since they had
questioned him before he was sent to jail, and he had also seen them at
the Mizrah and Latrun camps. There was no way he could fail to identify
them. He also pointed out that he trusted his good eyesight, especially in
daylight, in spite of the fact that his position was at some distance from
the target.

Yehoshua had the reverse problem. His position was atop a three-
story building, directly above the walk where the mine was hidden. He
could easily see who was walking over the mine and activate it. I
assumed it would be easy for him to escape in the crowd that would come
up to the roof to look at the view after the explosion. I knew from

experience that if one acted in cold blood and adapted his behavior to those around him, one could easily escape. We had had cases in which our man, pursued by a crowd shouting, "Catch the thief," began to shout the same thing and was able to escape from the police. Yehoshua had another problem, which he brought up during the briefing. During the explosion there might be other people near the mine, besides Morton and Wilkin. I asserted that, based on my experience, the police would immediately quarantine the building and not let any civilians come near, since they might interfere with the investigation, especially since everyone would know it was a political problem, and one never knew who in the crowd was sympathetic to the perpetrators. One, on the other hand, could assume that along with Morton and Wilkin there would be other British detectives. Even if a Jewish detective were among them, so be it, since that person was a traitor to his own people. If along with Morton and Wilkin some other British detectives, as well as a Jewish one, were killed, it would not conflict with the objective of destroying the Jewish section of the CID.

I said to Yehoshua: "Your task of setting off that mine is of utmost importance to the command and to Yair. You have to do it no matter what, even if innocent passersby are killed. The liquidation of the Jewish section of the CID is the guarantee for the survival of LEHI and its founder. You must do it, even if you endanger your life."

I did not have to say this to him. We all knew that he valued his work for the underground more than his own life. He did not bat an eyelash as he listened to me speak in such a harsh tone. He was a boy, albeit he had had several years of underground activities behind him. He accepted my instructions without reservations, shook my hand, and set out on his way.

Baruch and Yehoshua had to take their positions on the roofs as soon as Siomka's attention-getting explosion was heard. At that moment, we estimated, the neighbors would call the police, and the trap would be set. Around 9 o'clock the person in charge of securing the operation came to tell me everything was in place. When the explosion occurred, the securing team would take positions on the operators' route of escape and be ready to help them if they ran into any difficulties. Our Tel Aviv head of intelligence also informed me that Morton and Wilkin did go into their office at 8:30. Had they not, we could have postponed the operation. Everything was ready, and I gave Siomka the sign to proceed.

Siomka had slaughtered a chicken and had put its blood in a plastic container, and when I gave the sign he put a match to a 1.5 foot long fuse in the apartment, went out, closed the door, and ran down the steps sprinkling the blood on the stairway. He did not get too far from the building when the explosion was heard on the roof of the house on 8 Yael Street. The neighbors rushed to the stairwell. One of them must have seen the blood, and phoned the police. The call reached Morton's office at the Tel Aviv destrict police headquarters. Morton and Wilkin were attending at that moment an important meeting in the next office. When Morton got the message he asked Major Schiff, the commander of the Tel Aviv district police, to take along a few officers and detectives and rush to the site of the explosion, in order not to waste any time. Morton assured Schiff he and Wilkin would be there in a little while.

Schiff, along with Goldman, his second-in-command, and his aides, did his master's bidding and went to 8 Yael Street. Morton also sent along Officer Turton, who had hanged Shlomo Ben-Yosef, the first underground fighter to be hanged by the British. Turton's task was to keep an eye on the Jewish chief of police. The entire party hurried to Yael Street, without Morton and Wilkin, as we had hoped. They came and identified the blood on the steps as the blood of the escaped young man. They went up to the apartment on the roof, headed by Major Schiff, who was eager to personally apprehend wounded terrorists. He was followed by Officer Goldman, his close associate, with Turton close behind, to see what the Jewish officers were doing. Baruch saw them come up on the roof. Schiff was tall and broad-shouldered, and from the back looked like Morton. Also his uniform was similar. Turton resembled Wilkin, and Baruch had no doubts who the two were. He put his finger on the button and watched the group. Schiff dashed across the roof and reached the door of the trapped apartment. All three men had drawn their guns. Baruch was ready. He pushed the button and the bomb went off. The apartment went up in the air. Its debris landed over an area hundreds of yards in radius. Along with the debris went the smashed limbs of the three officers. It was January 20, 1942.

Baruch removed his gloves and his hat, straightened his clothes and went down to the street, where he signalled the securing team to let them know he was proceeding to his last destination.

Following the explosion, several neighbors went up on the roofs to take a look at what had happened. Most men had gone to work by now, and the crowd consisted mainly of women and old people. Some people must have gone up on Yehoshua's roof as well. He pretended to be one of them and asked them, "What happened, what happened?" They were not sure themselves. All they could see were the clouds of smoke rising above the next house. Yehoshua stood there, hiding the switch to the mine with his body, waiting to see if he had to do his own part in the operation. Everything was ready. People stood around him, not suspecting anything. Yehoshua had seen Schiff, Goldman and Turton entering the building. He had seen the explosion, and he knew Baruch had misidentified Morton and Wilkin. He realized that now the success of the entire operation depended on him, that, indeed, the fate of the organization was in his hands. If he did not kill Morton and Wilkin now they would liquidate the organization and destroy its leaders one by one, first and foremost the founder of LEHI, Yair.

Things moved fast. As Morton was leaving the police headquarters on his way to 8 Yael Street, he got the message about the explosion on the roof. He did not wait for additional information, and sped to the scene, both he and Wilkin in one car, with several detectives in two additional cars. From the roof Yehoshua saw the three cars screech to a stop in front of the house. The moment Yehoshua had to push the button in order to rid the Hebrew underground of its most dangerous enemies, he hesitated and did not push. He decided to retreat. When he saw me he was pale and shaken. I felt as though the ground had swallowed me up.

ANNOUNCEMENT

We would like to clarify the following in regard to the explosion on Yael Street:

The political background: For sixty generations millions of Jews have been persecuted throughout the world, spat upon and humiliated. Here in the Land of Israel fifty myriad Jews are living under foreign rule, which has taken everything away from them and not given them what is their by right. The refugees from the death camps are not allowed in. The *Patria* atrocity. The cruel expulsion of the *Atlantic* immigrants, resulting in 54 dead. Official proclamations about annexing the Land of Israel to Syria, reducing us to a ghetto surrounded by Arab savages out to annihilate us. It should be clear to all by now: The Mandate government is the *enemy* of Zionism, and will not save us. Only Hebrew rule, and none other, will provide a haven to the exiles, freedom to the enslaved, bread to the hungry. But no Hebrew government will be established without first *defeating* the existing government. Since the police is guarding the foreign rule and the anti-Zionist regime, we must fight it.

The police in this land is staffed by Arabs, British and Jews. The Arabs have little to do with Jewish affairs. The British are doing their duty. But a Jew who hands his fellow Jews who fight for the freedom of their people over to the enemy, is betraying his national duty. He is a traitor and an enemy of Israel.

The background of the operation: When we started our fight against Arab terror, we had to defend ourselves and we shot and killed Detectives Braverman, Beck, Polonsky. During our fight against the White Paper we blew up Officer Cairns, the head murderer. In addition, we executed Detective Tzufyuf in Rehovot. In a statement following his execution, we cautioned that his death should serve as an example for all detectives, both professional and amateurs. But the police did not pay attention. We therefore decided to strike out not against the emissaries, but those who send them. We carried out our decision.

The casualties: British Officer Turton, the executioner of Shlomo Ben-Yosef. Major Schiff is the man who served the foreign rule with his club. He bathed his club with the blood of hungry workers in Petah Tikva, and with the blood of the National Youth during the demonstration against the hunting of the "illegals." He said he broke his club on the backs of our prisoners. He then dedicated himself to handing the Fighters for the Freedom of Israel to his British masters. Officer Goldman was Schiff's trusted assistant.

The lesson: Jewish officers and policemen and the entire Yishuv are asked to do their national duty and stand beside us, for the establishment of Hebrew sovereignty in Zion. Once again we warn all the informers who serve the *foreign* rule. If they do not desist from their actions, we will continue to fight them to the end. We will reach them anywhere, and nothing will spare them from us.

THE IRGUN TZVAI LEUMI B'ISRAEL (LEHI)

TWENTY-TWO

The CID Strikes Back

The police officers who were killed at Yael Street were not the ones for whom the trap had been laid. Nevertheless, the elimination of Schiff, who had made it known he was determined to kill Yair, and of Turton, the executioner of Shlomo Ben-Yosef, the first underground fighter to be hanged by the British, helped our cause. LEHI issued the above announcement justifying this action, albeit it was originally directed against Morton. This operation lifted the spirit of the organization, and we dedicated ourselves to strengthening our ranks, recruiting new members, and intensifying our training program.

I returned to Jerusalem to resume my duties as district commander, and devote myself to expanding the activities of our group. During that time something happened to me that has changed my life to this day. As part of my new work with the Jerusalem branch, I organized a course for cell leaders in preparation for our operational activities. One of the participants of the course was a 17-year-old woman, tall, attractive, agile, with burning black eyes.

I must confess that until that time I had no special relations with the opposite sex. The underground left us little time for personal feelings, either in relation to our parents or to the opposite sex. I recall, for instance, the time I met my parents on Balfour Street in Tel Aviv. It was one week after the operation on Yael Street. My mother seemed to be quite worried about me (and as the reader will soon find out, she had good reason to worry). My mother supported the underground, but her maternal feelings were equally strong, if not stronger. This time she implored me to quit the underground. She spoke with great emotion. My father was shocked when I failed to say anything to her. I got up to leave when suddenly my mother fainted and collapsed. I did not say a word. I passed by her inert body, and walked away, letting father take care of her.

Now something inside of me began to stir. For a moment, as I looked into Hannah's big black eyes I forgot my mission. I was conquered. I knew the good Lord had intended for her to become my life's companion. I had seen her once before, from a distance, standing next to one of my friends. Back then, at first sight, I knew fate would bind us together. Hannah was a dedicated, highly trusted member of the underground, who had been put in charge of our arsenal in Jerusalem.

LEHI considered its female members totally equal to the men. Women were judged by their capability and courage, not by their sex. We expected the women to be as self-sacrificing and tough as the men. The women, however, had to consider the danger awaiting them if they fell into the hands of the British. In some instances, as had happened with Cairns, women were subjected to torture. In the basements of the CID, a captured underground woman was not in an enviable position. Nevertheless, we attracted courageous women who worked efficiently and made a major contribution to the underground. We saw to it that the women were treated as total equals, and if anyone violated this rule, he or she would be put on trial. Still, it was only in the nature of things that more than once our common work created a closeness between two members of the opposite sex. If the relationship lasted, the couple was officially pronounced an underground couple. Those couples knew they would have to live under severe conditions. It was extremely difficult to lead a normal family life in the underground, let alone raise children. A couple was often kept separate, and for obvious reasons was never allowed to go out on a mission together.

Against this backdrop my relations with Hannah began to blossom. I made it clear to her I could not consider normal family life, since I realized that sooner or later something would happen to me. To be perfectly honest, I never dreamed I would live so long, and I certainly did not expect to have a family and raise children.

On January 27, 1942 I went to Tel Aviv to conduct a short course for our local branch commanders. Early in the morning, when the streets were still dormant, I arrived at a rented apartment at 30 Dizengoff Street. Moshe Svorai, the newly appointed Tel Aviv commander, Avraham Amper, commander of the local fighting unit, and Zelig Jacques, one of our outstanding local commanders, were there waiting for me. The place was chosen because it was considered one of the safest places in Tel Aviv. It was recently rented by Jacques and the police could not possibly know who was using it. Besides, it had a back door which enabled Jacques, who only went out at night, to slip out without being noticed.

However, the Tel Aviv contingent did not take several things into consideration. First, since the attack on Yael Street, a witch hunt had been unleashed against LEHI. The British knew it was the right time to liquidate the fighting underground. Public leaders, the press, and even the man on the street, were caught up in the British propaganda and preached the elimination of LEHI. Second, the police had announced a reward of 2000 pounds for anyone who provided information which would lead to the arrest of those who had put the bombs at 8 Yael Street. Morton later wrote in his memoirs that a Jewish bus driver had tipped the police about the hideout at 30 Dizengoff Street, and was duly rewarded. Third, Jacques had rented the apartment from a family unknown to us, a cardinal sin in the underground. Fourth, only a week earlier Jacques had escaped from the police. The police had posted his picture everywhere, and quite possibly someone had recognized him and reported him to the police.

I proceeded to the third floor and knocked on the door according to our agreed code. I was let in and immediately started our training session.

Amper had brought a dummy grenade and electric accessories for class demonstration. I used sketches and drawings to illustrate my lecture. It was a concentrated course, and we did not stop for lunch. I wanted to complete it in one day so I could go back to Jerusalem. At 4 o'clock I finished, but I remained in the apartment so I could leave after dark. We had two hours to kill, and we decided to make some sandwiches and talk about underground affairs. Around 5 o'clock Svorai lay on the bed in the corner of the room with a book about Russian socialist-revolutionaries. Jacques was stretched on a cot and read a newspaper, and Amper sat on a chair next to the window and told me about his adventures when he escaped from Poland through Russia and Turkey and entered the country with false documents. I stood next to the window, and, in retrospect, I can say I felt suspicious of someone outside, a Jew, who stood across the street and looked up at our window, perhaps a detective, or an informer. I had an uneasy feeling, but I reminded myself I would soon be on my way to Jerusalem.

I went to the bathroom, when I heard a faint knock on the outside, door, across the hall. My sixth sense told me to be prepared. I heard the landlady open the door. She let out a muffled cry and retreated into her apartment. I felt like a cornered animal. All my muscles were taut. I heard the slow steps of detectives, and I knew we were trapped. Suddenly I heard shots. There were three or four bursts of automatic fire, a pause, and then another burst. I was stunned. It was the first time the police opened fire at us without stopping for identification. They were shooting to kill. The shots were accompanied by the familiar British curses: "Bloody Jews! Filthy Jews!" I now realized the British were killing my defenseless friends.

Svorai and Jacques, it turned out, had been lying down, unaware of what went on, when the detectives arrived. When the door opened they did not pay attention, since they thought it was me coming back from the bathroom. As soon as they saw the detectives they jumped to their feet. Three brutes stood at the door: Morton in the middle, with Sergeant Woodward on his right and Sergeant Day on his left. Their guns were drawn. The men raised their hands.

Morton walked in, stood in the middle of the room, his face twisted and his eyes darting. Suddenly he aimed his gun at Amper and shot him three times in his stomach. He then turned to Jacques and shot him three times. Next he turned to Svorai and shot him twice. After Svorai fell, Morton approached him and shot him in the head at one-yard range.

A pack of British detectives stormed the room, led by Wilkin. They kicked the wounded men who were writhing on the floor, turned them from side to side, spat in their faces and laughed raucously. They cursed the wounded and their entire race.

It was clear to me that after they finished off my friends, they would start searching the rest of the apartment. When they found out the bathroom door was locked, they would shoot through the door.

I was right. As my three comrades lay in pools of blood, Morton, Woodward and Day began to search the apartment. They tried the bathroom door, and when they found it to be locked they perforated it with eight bullets. At that moment I was on my way out the window, going down a pipe. I was going to let myself into the second floor window and hide there.

As soon as I reached the pipe outside the bathroom window I heard shots. I looked down and saw British detectives shooting at me from the street and shouting profanities. I shouted back at them to hold their fire since I was coming down. My words only made them intensify their fire. As I reached the second floor I suddenly felt the lower part of my body go numb. I touched my hip and felt blood running down my thighs. With my remaining strength I slid down the pipe and the ivy and fell on the ground bleeding profusely. The British attacked me with their boots and the butts of their guns. They dragged me to the back of the house and dropped me to the ground, and started beating me from head to foot.

I was dazed. The lower part of my body was paralyzed. I felt I was about to die. They tortured me for about half an hour. I kept losing consciousness and coming to. I decided to make them pay dearly for my life. I struggled and rose up on my shaky feet and shouted at them: "You British, you are shooting people without checking their identity and without trial. We, the freedom fighters, will make you pay for it. Our friends will kill all of you!" I steeled myself and called out: "Long live the Hebrew war of liberation!"

Since I thought I was about to die, I was going to try and snatch a gun from one of the British, shoot at them and try to run away. I made a threatening gesture. They drew back and watched me from a safe distance. At that point I felt dizzy from the loss of blood. My eyes dimmed and I collapsed.

When I opened my eyes the British were standing around me, ready to shoot if I made any suspicious move. All around me, on roofs, balconies and windows, I saw men, women and children looking at the scene. The crowd must have saved my life, since the British did not dare murder me in full view of the public. Somewhere in the crowd I saw a pair of burning black eyes, enchanted eyes, which pierced my heart like an arrow of fire and reminded me of my girlfriend, Hannah, whom I so yearned to see at that moment. I was swept by waves of great love, and I knew my life had a purpose.

I lay there for about an hour and a half, bleeding, helpless. My two old friends, Morton and Wilkin, came down to see me at one point. Morton, the butcher, seemed deathly afraid of his own victims. Wilkin came down with a picture spread but failed to identify me. He went back into the building. As I later found out, he placed a grenade and a gun in the apartment. Since we had been unarmed, the British had to fabricate a reason for shooting us.

Finally the ambulance came. Three men in white with a red Star of David on their arm bands laid me on a stretcher. One of them, who seemed to be the doctor, examined my wounds and whispered in my ear: "You are lucky. The bullet went through your buttock and came out. You will be all right." He then added in a lower voice: "Be strong! Those bastards will pay for it!" I knew the doctors of *Magen David Adom* were secret members of the Haganah. When I heard the doctor's opinion of the British I felt much better.

After they dressed my wound they went upstairs. Here their job was much more difficult. Svorai had been shot three times—in the shoulder, in the leg and in the chin. When Morton had aimed his gun at Svorai's head he turned his head instinctively and was shot in the chin. His wounds were not mortal. Amper and Jacques, on the other hand, had been shot in the stomach and in the liver. Their condition was critical. The doctor wanted to inject them with morphine, to ease their pain, but the British would not let him. They wanted to see us suffer, and expected us to die. The doctor protested, arguing that they had no right to stop him from doing his work, but they wouldn't budge.

As I lay on the stretcher I thought about the future of the organization. What would happen now, with four senior commanders captured by the enemy? I was suddenly surrounded by top commanders of the police: Giles, the head of the CID; Ford, the head of the Jaffa police; Herrington, head of the Tel Aviv police; and Hackett. All four stood there, their eyes shooting darts at me, as Wilkin came by and joined them. Again he checked his picture spread but could not identify me. At that moment I decided to reveal my identity. I was certain the British would not dare kill me at that place and time, since I had been given medical attention and was surrounded by a large crowd. I also knew that as soon as I revealed my identity the police would rush to my parents' house to conduct a search. Once my parents found out about my arrest they would contact a lawyer who would see to it that the British did not kill me before I was brought to trial. I had made this arrangement with my parents beforehand, as a security measure. As the four stood around me, accompanied by Wilkin, I smiled and told them I did not want to make their work more difficult than it was, and wished to reveal my identity. I was not Birnbaum, as my ID card stated. My name was Yaakov Levstein.

When they heard my name they were stunned. I could see a murderous glint in their eyes. Hackett, clenching his teeth, muttered:

"We have finally caught the killer of Cairns and Barker, the one who had made the mines that killed our men. Finally!"

For hours we lay bleeding, refusing to die. It had grown dark. The British no doubt were concerned our comrades might come under the cover of dark to free us. They decided to transfer us to a secured place. They would not use the ambulance. Instead, they had ordered armored cars. They lifted us by our arms and legs and tossed us into the cars. Presently we found ourselves in the prisoners' wing of the government hospital in Jaffa.

Again I was carried by my arms and legs and thrown on a bed. Now I was in the trusted hands of hospital nurses, mostly Arab. I was greatly surprised to see a Jewish nurse among them, whom I happened to know. She recognized me, but pretended not to know me. From the way she arranged my bed I could tell she was nervous. When the Arab nurses went out I told her my parents' address and asked her to send them my regards. I gave her my watch and asked her to give it to my parents to confirm my identity. She agreed, and that same evening she went to see my parents and assured them my wounds were not serious and I would soon be back on my feet.

We had all been put in the same room. I was next to the door. Jacques was across the room. Svorai was on my left, next to the window, and Amper was across the room from him. Svorai and I were chained to our beds, since we were not seriously wounded. We had to lie all the time on our back. The hospital was heavily guarded. There were policemen with machine guns and submachine guns outside our door, and police guards with armored cars and half-tracks in the street. There were even guards on the roofs around the hospital.

Amper and Jacques were mortally wounded. They were operated on as soon as they were brought in. They were near death. In the morning they woke up from the anesthetic, and suffered in silence. Their bellies were swollen. Their eyes were glazed. At times they stopped breathing, and were injected with morphine. The effect only lasted a moment, and their condition worsened. They were fed through the vein, a drop of liquid at a time, but their stomachs were destroyed, and they kept vomiting. Despite their condition they remained conscious, and between spasms of pain they said things one could never forget: "It is good to die when it makes sense." "It is good to suffer when you know your suffering will be avenged." "Some day the Yishuv may realize we were its soldiers, not Yair's soldiers, not the organization's. We were the first secret soldiers of the Yishuv, of the nation.''

British detectives kept walking in and out of the room. Our two friends did not want them to see how much they suffered. I called the British administrator of the hospital and demanded that the two be transferred to Hadassah Hospital, or at least that Dr. Marcus (a well-known surgeon, sympathizer of the underground) be allowed to see them. She told me she would talk to her superiors and let me know as soon as possible.

Early in the morning Morton came into our room. He seemed quite pleased with himself. His murderous expression remained unchanged. He first looked at my three comrades and then turned to me and said: ''You, filthy Jew, you are lucky.'' I reciprocated with an appropriate curse. He kept coming every morning to see who died and who was still alive. Each time he left the room he cursed me, and I replied as best I could.

The hospital swarmed with dozens of guards, policemen and detectives. Senior police officers kept visiting our room. The place looked like an army camp under alert.

The administrator did not appear too interested in helping our dying friends. We waited in vain for her reply. On the third day Moshe Svorai and I proclaimed a hunger strike. We told the administrator we refused to eat until she brought over Dr. Marcus. She assured us she would bring him, but we told her we did not trust her and were not afraid of the police. We fasted for one day when Amper and Jacques seemed to be doing better. Jacques woke up and said that he felt strengthened by his wounds. Jokingly, he added he was now bullet-proof. Amper also seemed to be in good spirits and sent regards to his friends and relatives. The next day they seemed to improve, but when they woke up they were pale and listless. At noon Jacques suddenly collapsed, and by the time the nurse came in he was dead. About an hour later Amper also took a turn for the worse and expired.

As the two lay dead the administrator came in to see them. She did not look at me. I couldn't hold back and said to her: ''Aren't you proud of yourself?'' She quickly left the room. Moments later Morton came in, his eyes bulging as he looked at the dead, and he then turned to us. I clenched my teeth and held the pain inside of me.

Years later my friend, Binyamin Gefner, a LEHI veteran and an underground historian, went to London to tape some testimonies of former British police officers who had served in our country during that period. One of them, Officer Ternant, asked him: "What is Yaakov Levstein, that British-killer, doing these days? I should have killed him when he came down that pipe from the third floor instead of wounding him."

Gefner told him Levstein, now known by his Hebrew name, Eliav, was a respectable citizen in the free State of Israel. Ternant was amazed. He got up and mumbled to himself, "And here I thought he was a murderer." He went into the next room and came back with my photograph, lying wounded at the government hospital in Jaffa.

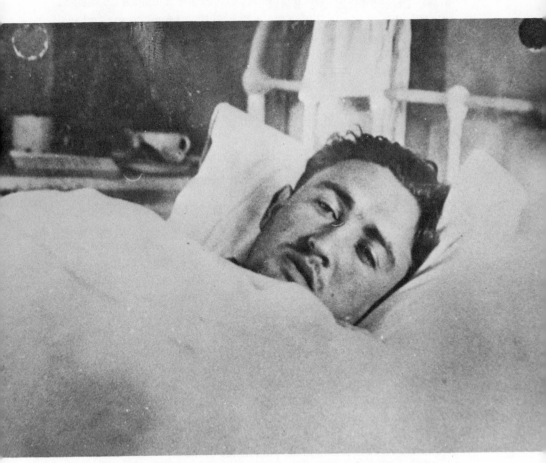

The author lying wounded in the Jaffa hospital under British surveillance.

TWENTY-THREE

The Slaying of Yair

In addition to the heavy guards in and around the hospital, the British had assigned a policeman to accompany us in our room, ostensibly in order to attend to our needs. It was clear to me the policeman, an Arab, knew Hebrew, and was listening in on our conversations. I alerted my friends, and we all began to watch what we were saying. Back in those days there were no bugging devices, and one could easily guard oneself against monitoring.

After Amper and Jacques died the Arab policeman was replaced by an English sergeant named Dailey. As soon as he arrived he told us he was Irish, and had Jewish friends. He kept talking about his friends in Petah Tikva, where he had served for a long time on the local police force. Dailey did his best to befriend us and put us at ease. Svorai and I were chained to our beds and had to speak across the room with Dailey listening to every word. At one point Dailey asked me if I wanted him to give any message to my parents. Since I had been completely cut off from the world, I jumped at the opportunity. I knew how worried they were, and how much better they would feel if they got a direct message from me.

I wrote my parents a letter. I knew the CID would read it, so I wrote it in Russian with Hebrew letters, to make the translation work more difficult. Svorai also used the opportunity to write to his wife and let her know he was well. Tova, Svorai's wife, was an old member of the underground. Svorai wrote in Hebrew and asked his wife how the "guest" at her apartment was doing, and added regards to him. He put his letter inside mine.

Svorai must have assumed my parents would deliver his letter to his wife. In reality, my parents had no idea where his wife lived. It appears that after the CID went over the letter, Morton must have suspected that the "guest" was Yair. My parents' house was surrounded by detectives who waited around the clock, hoping to find Tova Svorai's hideout. My parents, however, kept Svorai's letter, since they had no idea where to send it.

A few days later Dailey came to us with a new proposal. He told me: "You will soon be transferred to the central prison in Jerusalem. Before you go away you may want to see your mother." By then Dailey had become quite friendly with my parents. He would stop to see them, chat with them, enjoy my mother's home-made cookies, and even received a shaving kit in return for his good offices. I was quite glad to accept Dailey's offer. I told him I would be happy to see my mother.

It was a beautiful spring day, full of sun and the singing of birds. I was happy to be recovering and looked forward to seeing my mother. I knew she would feel much better once she saw me. After all, she had once said that a prison was a safe place for me, since she did not have to worry constantly something was going to happen to me.

Dailey, who had been sitting between Svorai's bed and mine, got up and told me my mother was outside, near the window. A few yards separated me from the window, where Svorai's bed was. Dailey stood by like a panther ready to pounce on his prey. When I saw my mother I told her in Russian I was well, the bullet had hit me in the hip but came out without leaving a mark. I had regained the full use of my body, and was waiting to be transferred to the central prison in Jerusalem, until they brought me before a military court.

Dailey interfered and demanded that we speak in Hebrew. We switched to Hebrew, and I knew Dailey understood every word. Needless to say, he did not hear me say anything useful.

Once he realized he did not stand to gain anything from my mother's visit, he motioned to her it was time to leave. As my mother was about to leave Svorai turned to her and said in a clear voice: "Perhaps you can give my regards to my wife who lives at 8 Mizrahi B Street."

Dailey lunged across the room as if bitten by a snake. He went to the phone outside our door and called someone. I fell back on my bed, my heart pounding violently. I knew something terrible was going to happen, and I was helpless to do anything. I could barely breathe. I looked at Svorai. He was as pale as his sheets. It was too late. He had spoken the forbidden words and he realized what a catastrophe was awaiting us.

My fear was confirmed sooner than I thought. As I was lying there, motionless, staring at the ceiling, two top British detectives stopped near my bed. In the past they always looked at me as if about to shoot me. This time they were at ease, acting almost like real English gentlemen. Carefully they removed my chains, inviting me politely to come along with them. Their manner and their tone of voice made it clear to me something very bad had happened to the underground, which they were about to show me.

I got out of bed in my pajamas and hospital gown, and almost fell on the floor. I had been off my feet for eight days and this was the first time I stood up. The two detectives propped me gently under my arms, and proceeded to handcuff me, my right hand to one detective's left hand, and my left hand to the other's right one. Slowly they led me to the courtyard where I saw the morgue. It was a low cement room without windows, only an entrance door. When I went in my eyes were blinded by strong lights flooding the room.

In the middle of the room I saw a high cement platform with a dead body lying on top, covered with an old military blanket. Two feet protruded at one end, wearing shiny shoes with evenly tied shoelaces. The shoes dripped blood and water. Around the body stood senior officers of the British police, with Morton at the head. They all wore uniforms, officers' hats, and a gun, as if taking part in a formal ceremony. I stood out among them in my pajamas and hospital gown. I stood erect and sombre, waiting for the next move. They all seemed tense. With a nervous gesture, Morton removed the blanket from the dead person's head and shouted like a possessed person: "Look at your leader!" It was Thursday, February 12, 1942.

I froze. Yair lay before me. A bullet had smashed his temple. There was still a trickle of blood oozing from the wound. His eyes were shut. I could still see vital signs in his face. It appeared he had just been shot. I looked at him for a long time without turning to those around me. I did not say a word. After I bowed my head before my fallen leader I glanced at the police officers (who also bowed their heads, as if before an important enemy). I turned away and left the morgue.

Slowly I paced back to my room. The two detectives treated me with deference. Courteously they chained me back to my bed. Svorai way lying in his bed. They had taken him to the morgue before me. We lay for hours without touching our lunch. We were allowed for the first time to go out for a short stroll in the fenced yard, overlooking the beach. The police guarded us. We did not speak to each other. Suddenly Svorai said to me: "Yashka, I want to commit suicide." I told him he had a lot to offer to the underground, and he would atone for his sin. It was hard for me to see him suffer so much, and I wanted to lift his spirits and prevent him from doing anything out of despair. I told him he had to live not only for the underground but also for his wife and little daughter. I had a feeling I was getting through to him, but his silence told me he was in deep pain.

Tova Svorai, in whose apartment Yair had hidden and was killed, tells the following about what happened on the day of the murder:

"Around 9:30 there was a knock on the door. It was a gentle knock, not the way the police usually knocked. Yair immediately went into the closet to hide, and I opened the door.

"My old friend, Detective Wilkin, stood at the door, followed by two others. They searched the beds and looked in every corner, and then went to the closet. I stood next to the couch, facing the closet. A tall Englishman opened the closet. He did not see Yair. He thrust his hands into the closet and checked, when he touched Yair, and began to pull him out. At that moment he put his right hand in his back pocket and took out a gun. I rushed across the room and stood between him and Yair and said: "Don't shoot, or you will have to shoot me." Wilkin went over to this man, gently removed the gun from his hand, and told him something. I was innocent enough to believe I had saved Yair's life. I thought they would only shoot Yair in a moment of excitement. Oh, how wrong I was!

"They ordered him to sit on his bed, which was next to the entrance door. The detective sat across from him, aiming his gun at him. Next to the door stood Sergeant Day (I knew him from the search in my apartment on Keren Kayemet Avenue), aiming his gun at Yair as well. A moment later more detectives came and handcuffed Yair.

"The apartment was now filled with tall, strong British detectives ... They told me to get dressed and go downstairs. On my way down I was surprised to see they were rudely pushing women out of the house."

After Tova Svorai left the room, Yair was left with Morton and Ternant (the officer who had shot me at 30 Dizengoff Street in Tel Aviv). Morton pushed Yair against the window and shot him several times in his back and in the back of his head. He then turned to Ternant and said: "You saw how he tried to escape through the window." Later on Ternant testified as Morton had instructed him to do. Thus, one of the great sons of the Jewish people was gone. David Ben-Gurion said about him later on: "I have no doubt, that Avraham Stern (Yair) was one of the greatest personalities that arose during the British Mandate period. I respect and admire with all my heart both the poetry and the steel of his soul."

The answer of LEHI appeared one morning on walls and fences and billboards throughout the country in the form of the following poster:

THIS IS THE ANSWER OF THE FIGHTERS
FOR THE FREEDOM OF ISRAEL:

When the Yishuv remained silent after the murders at 30 Dizengoff Street and at 8 Mizrahi B Street, when the Yishuv was quick to forget the blood of women and children beaten in Atlit by British murderers, when the Yishuv responded with a stupid sit-down strike to the murder of 700 of our brothers on board the *Struma*, when it responded to the provocative speech of the secretary of the colonies with idle prattle in the assembly and more recruitment to the British Army—When all this went on, the Fighters for the Freedom of Israel prepared their own answer. Theirs is the answer of the ancient and pround Hebrew race, the race of Joshua and Samson, of Judah Maccabee and Bar Kokhba and the supreme commander, Yair. The foreign rule has rejoiced in vain when it thought it had liquidated the only fighting force which stood in its way, thwarting its evil designs. The Jewish lackeys of the foreign rule thought they could breathe more easily, now that they had silenced the voice and the force that shook them from their complacency and nailed their servile ear to the doorpost of the British landlord.

WE CONTINUE.

We have erected a memorial of blood and fire on the tomb of our commander YAIR, founder of the Hebrew Revolution and its first leader. We erect a memorial of blood and fire on the grave of our holy brothers murdered on the *Struma*.

The Fighters for the Freedom of Israel will not lay down their arms and will continue to fight the foreign oppressor to the end.

THUS commanded the Lord of vengeance.
THUS commanded the heroes of Israel in all generations.
THUS commanded the supreme commander Yair, the memory of a hero be blessed.

IRGUN TZVAI LEUMI B'ISRAEL

TWENTY-FOUR

The Trial

A few hours after Yair was murdered I was taken to the administrative office of the hospital and told to sit across the desk from Officer Rosenstein of the Tel Aviv police. Rosenstein told me I was accused of carrying arms and making an attempt on the lives of His Majesty's security officers, and I had to stand trial before a military court. He asked me if I pleaded guilty, and told me that anything I said could be used against me later on in court. He spoke softly, as if he was reading the charges against his will. He had been told about the killing of Yair, and must have known how we felt. He told me that I would be transferred to the central prison in Jerusalem in the afternoon. I was consumed with helpless fury over the murder of Yair, and I despised Rosenstein as a stooge of the British. I shouted at him: "You will pay dearly for this." And I walked away.

In the afternoon the hospital was surrounded by army and police. We were told to get dressed. We were bound, legs and hands in crossed, interlocked chains. With difficulty we climbed into the armored cars, each one in a different car. We drove to Jerusalem in a long convoy with armored cars behind us and in front of us, and an airplane flying overhead. I was pleased to see how scared of us they were, and to what length they had to go because of us. I thought with pride that even as prisoners we continued our war against them.

After I was duly registered I was taken into the cell of the underground prisoners. A hush fell on the cell when I walked in. They all stared at me in silence, refusing to believe their eyes. A moment later they were all hugging and kissing me. I had tears in my eyes. It turned out that my comrades had thought the British had killed me as well. They had mourned me, and my friend Yaakov Orenstein had even eulogized me. Now I came back from the dead, and they were jubilant.

I spent three months in the central prison waiting for my trial. The CID asked Svorai and me to talk to our friends on the outside and persuade them to stop their activities against the British in return for our release, or at least our transfer to a detention camp. We categorically refused. We told them we would consider political negotiations, but no unilateral halt of activities.

After a short stay at Cell 23 with our underground comrades, we were put in solitary cells at Section 18. Special British guards, belonging to the special anti-LEHI unit, were posted outside our cells, an unprecendented measure in the history of the prison. Obviously, the British did not trust the maximum security arrangements of the prison when it came to the two of us.

Our solitary cells had their advantages. The special security arrangements earned us the special attention of the prison administration and the respect of Arab prisoners. We did not lack food, had comfortable accommodations, and books to read. In addition, we had good communications with the outside world through notes smuggled in and out of jail in the bread and fresh fruit and vegetables we received.

On the morning of April 27, 1942, Svorai and I were told we were being taken before the military court. We put on our suits and ties, polished our shoes and looked like bridegrooms going to their wedding. It was customary for our men to appear before the British judges in high spirits, as if we were the judges and they were the accused. Our trial took place during the three-month period when the British had forgone capital punishment, which might be the reason why we were not given the death sentence.

The court used to meet at the building of the former Italian Consulate, near the present-day residence of the president of Israel. This time, however, it was held at the Allenby Army Camp near Talpiyot. The police said they were afraid an attempt might be made to free the defendants by force, which necessitated a secure place. We were taken into an armored car, our hands and legs in chains, and were shackled to the inside wall of the car. Through the cracks I could see the views and people of Jerusalem. The car stopped at the gate of the camp, and I could see my parents and my girlfriend, Hannah Mussayeff, waiting for us. I waved to them, and they noticed me and waved back. I was now ready to face my judges.

Morton was there, checking all the security arrangements, concerned about a counterattack. We were taken into a large hall, converted into a courtroom. At 9 o'clock the judges walked in. At the defense table sat Attorney Gluckman, Svorai's lawyer, and Goitein, my lawyer. In the other corner was the prosecutor and his assistant. Next to the bench sat the official interpreter. The prosecutor stood up and said: "For reasons I cannot specify I respectfully request a closed trial. I therefore demand that my distinguished colleagues' assistants leave the court, and that the interpreter only come in when his services are needed."

The chief judge granted the request without hesitation. Only the judges, the two defense attorneys and the prosecutors remained, as well as the accused and six armed British policemen. The charges were read: "Moshe Svorai and Yaakov Levstein were apprehended on 27 January 1942, when two grenades, a detonator, a pistol and bullets were found in their room at 30 Dizengoff Street in Tel Aviv."

At first I was going to start out by announcing the goals of the organization and the purpose of its activities, but when the judges decided to try us behind closed doors I decided not to recognize the authority of the court and refused to take part in the trial.

Officer Morton took the witness stand, was sworn in, and said in answer to the questions of the prosecutor: "On Tuesday, January 27, 1942, at 15:30, we were informed by a Jewish source that four young Jewish men were at the apartment on the third floor at 30 Dizengoff Street. The source added they only went out at night, and were visited by suspicious types.

"We did not have concrete evidence that those men belonged to the Stern Gang, but the unusual circumstances made me certain they were the men we had been looking for. The great interest the informer showed in the 2000-pound reward we had offered did not leave any doubt in my mind about the identity of those men, and dispelled my suspicion the whole thing was a death trap for me and my men. I took along several detectives and policemen and drove over there. We arrived there at 4 p.m. We surrounded the house with a chain of police and I went up to the third floor with two British sergeants, to the apartment of the Messer family, where the marked room was. I forced the door and saw three suspicious looking men. I ordered them in Hebrew not to stand up, but they did not hear my order and stood up. Hence, in order to protect my men, I opened fire. Those three men were Zelig Jacques, Avraham Amper and Moshe Svorai. I then found the bathroom door locked, and shot at it five or six times."

Detective Alex Ternant picked up the thread of the story at this point: "I stood behind the building, on its right corner, and guarded the entrance door. I heard shots on the upper floors. Suddenly I saw a young man (he pointed at me) coming out the third floor window and sliding down the water pipe. I noticed he made suspicious motions toward his pants, and I shot him. He kept coming down. We captured him on the ground, took him behind the building, and kept an eye on him."

A few witnesses spoke, and then the defense attorney spoke. He said, among other things: "A senior officer of the police, accompanied by British detectives, followed the orders of the rulers of this land and murdered Jews without a trial and without justification. After the murder they placed a pistol in the room, in order to be able to arrest their victims. They were not concerned about the act itself, since the police is the government, who is going to challenge it? But they were concerned about the publicity which their despicable act might arouse. This is why they fabricated the statement about the clash between the police and 'suspicious' men. All of this makes it clear why the trial must be conducted behind closed doors. In my cross-examination I have proven that this is a mistrial, and I ask that the court free the accused."

The judges adjourned and came back with their verdict: "We find Moshe Svorai and Yaakov Levstein guilty of possession of arms. We sentence them to life imprisonment."

After the trial our lawyers shook our hands. Goitein promised us he would appeal the sentence since it was far more severe than the charges. He must have failed to realize at the time that the sentence was based on information about us the court must have received from the CID rather than the official charges.

Inside the armored car on the way out of the camp, I once again saw my parents and my girlfriend through the cracks. When I saw them they had already learned about the sentence. They were angry and sad I was going to jail, but they were also proud of my role in the war for our national independence. Deep inside they did not believe I would spend my whole life in prison. They took comfort in the thought that behind bars I could not risk my life. I took comfort in the thought I was still alive, ready for new operations, in our fight for freedom. As soon as I arrived in jail I wrote my parents the following letter:

Dear Father and Mother,
I received my sentence with perfect calm, as if nothing has changed, and I am as strong as ever. Life imprisonment is better than 15 years in view of the conditions here. There is no point in your trying to do anything for me at this time, since you would be wasting your energies. I will start my studies after Shavuot, and will decide about everything. Don't worry about Sarah, it won't help, she should only take care of herself. I will always remember your concern about me, my dear parents, and you will always be the ones I love the most. I thank you again with all my heart. You have to go home and take care of your affairs. I do not lack anything. Please give my regards to Glossman as well as my thanks, and also to my dear teacher.

Yours,
Yaakov

The British continued to keep us isolated, under special guard, as befitted highly dangerous prisoners. Our special status raised our prestige among the inmates, especially after the trial, which helped me later in planning my escape. Despite the security arrangements, I began to study ways to escape the moment we entered the central prison. Through our jail cook, Haim Dviri, I informed Israel Tevuah, who was in charge at that time of the Jerusalem branch, that on a certain day I had an appointment at the dentist on Jaffa Road. We had a general practitioner who visited the prison once a week, but for special problems we were taken to the clinic in the city. On the day of my appointment I was taken in chains by armored car to the dentist's office. Tevuah was waiting for me there, a large bandage covering half of his face. I sat next to him in the waiting room. He mumbled: "Too bad it failed. But they won't get away with it. As for your escape, we will do it next time." I muttered: "Attack from the roof. Retreat from the back balcony, through the yard." I said no more. I was sure he understood. According to my instructions, the men would hide on the roof, where they could see the arrival of the armored car. I would come out of the car and enter the building. They would not have to confront the guards, who would be armed with submachine guns. From the head of the stairs on the roof they could see me come up to the third floor, where the clinic was. The roof was on the fourth floor, and its access and egress were from the back yard, where I would retreat after my release. Thus my friends could take positions without being seen, be well prepared for the attack, and then retreat without ever coming in contact with the armored car in the front of the building. If the guards on the armored car noticed anything or heard shots, they could be easily neutralized from the roof and stopped from coming up to the third floor.

Everything was ready for escape. At that time, after the murder of Yair, the command was shaky, and it was of utmost importance for LEHI that I return to my duties. Unfortunately, shortly before my second visit to the dentist the practice of taking prisoners outside the prison to see specialists was discontinued, and I had to wait for two more years for my chance to escape. Moreover, the two comrades who were going to free me were arrested several weeks later by the British. One, Moshe Bar-Giora, also had to wait for two years until the two of us escaped together. He was killed in 1945 in the blowing up of the oil refinery in Haifa.

The capture of Bar-Giora and Tevuah is a special page in the history of the underground. We were going to retaliate as forcefully as we could for the murder of Yair and the attack at 30 Dizengoff. Since I could not take active part, those two men were going to plan the reprisal. They planned the assassination of a senior British official. Then, before the state funeral for that official took place in Jerusalem, they were going to mine the road to the cemetery on Mount Zion. The funeral would be attended by the high commissioner and the top British officials, who would be blown up as they arrived at the cemetery, and the British leadership in the Land of Israel would be liquidated. Our initial victim, the one for whom the funeral would have been arranged, was going to be Commander McConnell, an Irishman who had escaped from Ireland after he was sentenced to death by the Irish Republican Army. We would have achieved a double goal by killing him—paying back the British for their murders, and helping the Irish Republican Army. He was the one who had ordered Morton to kill Yair as well as Jacques and Amper. This plan was originally discussed with me before my arrest, and we even did some preliminary work, including the new invention of blowing up a car. It was always my objective to go after the head, knowing that the body could not function without it.

One night Bar-Giora went to McConnell's house and crawled under his car which stood under guard in the garage. He attached a bomb with a wire tied to the back wheels, so that when the car moved the wire would wind around and close the circuit, detonating the bomb. Here we had made a mistake. We did not realize the first person who started the car and drove it out of the garage was the Arab chauffeur. And so it was that the chauffeur, rather than McConnell, went to an early grave.

No state funeral was planned for the chauffeur, and now we faced the serious problem of dismantling the mines we had hidden in the stone fences on both sides of the road leading to the Mount Zion cemetery. Here something inexplicable happened, over which I have been puzzling to this day. When our men approached the place where they had hidden the mines, they realized the area was surrounded by British police and detectives. They were able to get away, but no one knows how the mines had been discovered, since they were well hidden and hard to discover.

Tevuah and Bar-Giora did not remain free for long. The British did all they could to catch them, alive or dead. They knew the two would not stop at anything in seeking revenge. They surprised them at a hideout in Givat Shaul, and after a shootout in which Tevuah was wounded in his side, the two were captured. They were sentenced to seven years in jail for belonging to an illegal organization.

TWENTY-FIVE

Jail

As we entered the jail, the other inmates who had found out about our sentence, received us with applause. The status of a prisoner is determined by the severity of his sentence. The stricter the sentence, the higher the status of the prisoner among his inmates.

We soon became full-fledged life-prisoners. Our civilian clothes were taken away and we were dressed in life-prisoner uniform. We wore a black beret, unlike the other prisoners who wore a brown one. Our fellow-prisoners treated those who wore a black beret with special respect.

Life in jail was quite different from life in a detention camp. At camp the guards only came to check you in the morning and in the evening, leaving you the rest of the day to your devices. It was also much easier to escape from a camp, as many of our members at home and abroad did. Escape from jail was always extremely dangerous, and often ended in death. Moreover, at camp one was allowed to preserve one's identity, while in prison the authorities did everything they could to deprive one of his identity and personality. The British authorities did not distinguish between political prisoners and common criminals, and threw them all together in the same jail.

We slept on a mattress stuffed with rags, known as *Bursh*. We had a bucket in our cell to relieve ourselves, called *Kardal*. At 5 in the morning we had to get up for roll-call, known as *Taamam*. The guard would touch each one of us as he counted us to make sure we were there in person, and check our name on a list.

We would then receive some water to wash ourselves with. We were not allowed to have razors to shave ourselves with, for obvious reasons. We did, however, manage to smuggle in some razors and hide them in our cells, and we learned how to shave quickly, before they could discover us.

After the clean-up we would straighten our cell, pick up everything so they could wash the floors of the cells. We usually had additional mattresses, which we bought from the quartermaster for a high price, so we would not have to sleep on the cold floor. The cleaning was done by the "temporaries," those who were only serving a one-year sentence. They were made to do all the hard menial jobs. They were supervised by Arab policemen with whips and reminded me of slaves in ancient Egyptian murals, with taskmasters standing over them with whips. Each morning the prison was assailed by the smell of Lysol, and to this day that smell makes me think of prison.

We would then be let out into the high-walled yard for our morning walk, marching in pairs round and round for about half an hour. We would then be served breakfast: *pitta* bread, at times dry, at times even mouldy, never well-baked. Aluminium cans with date jelly, barely edible. Sometimes on the way to the yard the baker would slip us a fresh baked *pitta* or some other delicacy. During the walks and meals we were able to talk with our comrades and discuss the affairs of the underground. We held those discussions three times a day, during each of the three walks.

The two issues we seemed to discuss most often in those days were a political issue and a moral one. The political issue was the future of LEHI after independence. Some members maintained that LEHI should end its work after the establishment of the state. The moral issue was the eternal question of idealists-activists: does the end justify the means? I personally maintained that after the birth of the state LEHI should seize power, which was our supreme goal. Eliyahu Amiqam, my old comrade who was serving five years for taking part in the holdup of the Arab bank in Jerusalem, totally disagreed with me.

LEHI prisoners were treated well by the imprisoned Arab gangleaders. Most of them were villagers who had experience in countryside guerrilla warfare. I had many discussions with them about their tactics, and told them about our ideology and objectives.

The prison courtyard was the arena of prison politics. Here too, as they did on the outside, the British pursued the ancient policy of divide and rule. They always set one group against another. Among the prisoners they appointed block heads and supervisors. The latter would pick some of their own to be responsible for the hospital, workshops, baths, kitchen, etc. All those appointments were made from the same group, usually an Arab community from the same town, exploiting the traditional rivalries among the various towns. Thus, Hebron was always a rival of Nablus, and the two were always rivals of Jaffa. The group in charge was always more privileged, and controlled a vast network which smuggled cigarettes, drugs, and food into the prison, with the tacit approval of the guards.

After a certain group had been in charge for a while, the British would suddenly decide it had become too powerful, and it was time for another group to take over. This would result in mass brawls among the groups, and much blood was spilled. I once witnessed one of those transfers of power. It was a beautiful Jerusalem morning. Early that morning one could feel tension in the air. Some groups began to provoke one another. Suddenly, as if by order, a huge fight started. The Hebronites, armed with clubs, iron bars and knives, began to attack the Jaffaites. The guards did not interfere. They were obviously on the side of the former, who soon took control of the situation. Now the Hebronites were in control. Later on, the same scene was repeated and the Nablusites took power. We stood by and enjoyed the spectacle. We found out that the Arabs hated one another more than they hated us.

At exactly 8 o'clock the bell rang, and it was time to go to work. We went to the prison workshops, where we worked mostly for the British administration. Some of us worked in the print shop, where we printed government publications. On the sly we also printed underground posters and fliers, which were smuggled out by Jewish policemen. This was a relatively safe underground press. We also worked in the locksmith shop, where we made tools for breaking out of jail.

Sabbaths and holidays were special occasions. We would scrub our cells, wash up and gather in the prison chapel, where we said the prayer over the wine and the *hallah* bread. On such occasions we were visited by Rabbi Aryeh Levin, the prisoners' rabbi, who always radiated joy and love and lifted our spirits.

Rabbi Levin was an institution. To us he embodied the spirit of our Jewish faith and traditions. We would wait for him early in the morning of the holy day at the door of the synagogue. He was first greeted by the *gabai*, the person in charge of the service. As he arrived, the rabbi would shake our hand with his right hand as he caressed it with his left. While he caressed our hand he would slip us a note from the outside world. He always looked at us with wonderment in his eyes, almost child-like. He would always seem to marvel at the wonders of creation as he looked around himself. His entire philosophy was summed up in his look: life is not happy or tragic, but a mixture of both.

He never refused a prisoner's requests to get in touch with his family. He made no distinctions between a political and a criminal inmate. After he shook the many hands extended to him, he would go up on the *bimah*, and begin to pray. His voice always moved us to the core of our being. After the prayer he would always speak words of Torah.

After the service the rabbi would circulate among us and shake hands as we slipped him messages for our friends and relatives. Sometimes he even brought us money, which was a serious violation of prison rules. Around noon he would leave.

On holy days we were also permitted to go out to the barbed-wire fence to receive visitors. Our visitors would stand on a ramp behind the fence, and we had to look up and shout at them to be heard, 20 or 30 of us all at once. My parents always came, sometimes accompanied by my sister and little brother. They always brought me a little present. Hannah, my girlfriend, also came. She remained faithful to me. Later on when I became block supervisor, I was allowed to receive additional visits. At this point Hannah could meet me at closer quarters, across an iron grill.

One aspect of prison life always struck fear in our heart. Those were the hangings that took place in the central prison. Whenever someone was sentenced to death, the person was dressed in a red uniform and was weighed. Death row was separated from th rest of the jail by a heavy iron door, and faced the gallows room. The prisoner on death row awaited execution or pardon from the British high commissioner. A guard, invariably British, was there all the time, taking care of the prisoner's needs. The light in the cell was on day and night. However, the prisoner could have unlimited food and cigarettes. A small window in the cell enabled the prisoner to look out on the inner courtyard, where the other inmates took their walks. Arab gang-leaders sentenced to death would often talk to their comrades through that window. They would speak against the British and declare their commitment to the Arab nation and their aim to expel the British from the Middle East. They never mentioned the Land of Israel in their speeches, not even in passing, or, for that matter, the Palestinian people and its homeland. They kept talking about their struggle against the British as representatives of the entire Arab nation.

Those speeches would often elicit the attention of the Arab inmates. The speaker would always end with verses from the Koran and with the call "Allah is great, and Muhammad is His prophet," and the listeners would respond in chorus. It was different with common criminals, who would spend their time praying for their own soul, or would talk about themselves and insist they were innocent. Although the Muslim religion respects anyone who is about to depart from this world, those prisoners did not get too much attention from their coreligionists.

One day before the execution the condemned was taken to the special prison bath where one could purify one's body before going to heaven. Forty-eight hours before the hanging the gallows were tested with a weight equal to the prisoner's to check the strength of the rope. The law mandated that if the rope tore during the execution, the condemned person's life was spared.

On the day of the execution all the prisoners remained in their cells and did not go to work, to prevent disturbances. This rule was closely adhered to during political hangings. A hush fell on the prison, until the last cry of the condemned was heard, "Allah is great, and Muhammad is His prophet." At that point the inmates began to bang on their cell bars, and the rhythmic noise reverberating throughout the prison did not stop until the execution ended.

The execution was conducted as follows: between 9 and 10 in the morning (the executioners obviously did not want to miss their breakfast), the prison commander, the prisoner's clergyman, and all ranking officers, all British (Arab and Jewish staff were not allowed to witness executions), would gather in the gallows room. The condemned person was brought in, wearing the clothes in which he was arrested. The prison chief would read the sentence, and the clergyman would offer an appropriate prayer. The condemned was made to stand on a wooden platform. A bag was placed over his head and the noose was put around his neck, well tightened. The prison chief, who acted as executioner, would open the wooden trap door on which the convicted stood. With a thud, the person dropped into the gaping hole. His neck bone broke, and the head was severed from the spine. The prison doctor would then administer an injection to complete the death process. At this point the body was taken down, put on a stretcher along with all the personal belongings, and taken to the outside gate. Before the body was let out it was stamped with the word FREE. The body was delivered to the family of the deceased, who paid for the cost of the execution. Some of the money was given to the prison chief.

The inmates always knew when the execution was over. The *muazzin* would begin to chant verses from the Koran in a loud voice, and they kept responding for a long time, until the body was removed from the prison. While in jail in Jerusalem, I witnessed four executions. The first to be hanged was a 30-year-old journalist from Damascus, a tall, good-looking, well-educated person. The British had captured him in Nablus, where he had headed an Arab gang. After a battle with British armor, he was taken prisoner, brought to trial and sentenced to death. Before his sentencing he used to walk around in the courtyard, and we got to know each other. He was a member of the Baath Party which was active in the Near East and also in Iraq. During our walks in the courtyards we talked a great deal about cooperation in our struggle against British imperialism in the Middle East. After he was sentenced to death he would hold speeches from his cell window, overlooking the courtyard. I saw him one day before he was executed. He was calm. He knew what he was dying for. He told me others would achieve the goals of Pan-Arabism. He was certain that because of the fight of his move-ment the British would be expelled and the Arab nation would become independent. I wished him well and gave him my last blessing. He walked to the gallows with his head high and put the noose on his neck with his own hands. With a call to victory over the British oppressors he gave up his soul. The Arab inmates kept talking about him for a long time. They must have felt that with leaders like him they were sure to win.

Around that time one of our own men was sentenced to death. His name was Yehoshua Becker (Israeli). He and Nisim Reuven, known as Nitchko, were arrested after a failed attempt to rob a bank in Tel Aviv. During their retreat they were forced to open fire, and Becker was accused of killing a man and sentenced to death, while Nitchko was given 14 years in jail. Both were tragic victims of acts the underground was forced to undertake. An underground needs money for its very existence. It needs to pay for hideouts for its members, support the families of those in jail, buy weapons and equipment, conduct propagan-da, maintain clandestine hospitals, etc. The robbery of the Anglo-

Palestine Bank in Tel Aviv, in which I took part in 1940, helped support LEHI for two years. Our men were never happy to engage in those robberies. Therefore we always picked old members who were able to overcome their moral conflicts. Yair himself always hesitated for a long time before approving any such acts and only agreed to them when our situation became desperate. We knew, for example, that during the great robbery of the Anglo-Palestine Bank he recited Psalms during the entire operation.

The operation undertaken by Becker and Reuven was poorly planned and ended in the death of innocent persons and the capture of the perpetrators. Becker was sentenced to death for shooting and killing one of his pursuers. As he sat on death row in his red uniform, we did all we could to strengthen his spirit, but instead he strengthened ours. After a long period of an agonizing wait, his sentence was commuted to life imprisonment. I recall the morning he came back to us, in his red uniform, radiating joy. Our cooks prepared a feast that day for Block 18, where the underground prisoners lived.

During my stay in prison we began to receive Haganah prisoners. The British at that time thought they had liquidated LEHI, and decided to go after the Haganah, despite the fact that the Haganah did not engage in terrorism and even accepted the British rule and cooperated with it. The Haganah even helped the British maintain internal security around the country. Nevertheless, the British started to make arrests among Haganah members. In one instance a British soldier was sent to kibbutz Givat Brenner and offered to sell Haganah members weapons from the British arsenal. The Haganah fell for it and agreed. Subsequently, the British police laid a trap for the purchasers, arrested them and sentenced them to jail terms of 5 to 12 years. One of the Haganah members who joined us in jail at that time was Eliyahu Sakharov, a senior Haganah commander, who was found to be in possession of one pistol bullet, and was sentenced to 7 years in jail.

Before long a rather large group of Haganah members assembled in the central prison in Jerusalem. They were given their own block, and soon we began to cultivate close relations. I became particularly close to them because of my job as Jewish prison librarian. The police treated them like underground prisoners, and proceeded to pressure them in order to obtain information, especially about the arms caches in the kibbutzim. Haganah members had not been taught to regard prison life as a phase in their struggle, and they considered it a misfortune, something they did not deserve. The moment they came in they knew the role of their leaders was to intercede with the authorities in their behalf and set them free. We, for our part, had no doubt in our minds sooner or later the Haganah would have to join us in our common struggle against the British enemy. We therefore did everything we could to raise the morale of the Haganah prisoners.

One example of the above was the case of Haganah commander Yeshaayahu Yarkoni. He had joined the British Royal Navy, and was arrested in Alexandria, Egypt, on charges of stealing arms from the navy and transferring them to the Haganah. He was sent to the prison in Jerusalem where he was put in solitary confinement in order to confess and cooperate with the police. This technique sometimes worked, and when I saw Yarkoni taken in and out of his solitary cell, haggard and unshaven, I arranged with the prison cook to have good food sent to him. I also bribed the Arab quartermaster to give him a good mattress and blankets. As a librarian, I was allowed to bring him religious books. I used the opportunity to talk to him, and found out he was accused of fourteen counts of possession of arms, smuggling arms, bribing British soldiers and more. He was facing a long jail term. I immediately explained to him his rights as a prisoner and emphasized the three no's: no talking, no admission and no signing. If he disregarded those rules, he would be in deep trouble.

I recall Yarkoni's expression when I began speaking Hebrew to him. He did not know me, and since I was dressed as a prisoner he thought I was an Arab. After I told him in Hebrew who I was he began to trust me. A few days later Yarkoni was taken to the prison office. I happened to be there because of my daily chores, when, lo and behold, who came in if not my old friend Wilkin, carrying a heavy dossier under his arm. He sat at the special desk of the secret police, pretending not to know me, although he knew exactly who I was. Yarkoni walked in and we exchanged looks. I knew he would play his part the way I expected him to.

Wilkin read Yarkoni the fourteen counts and expected him to sign on the dotted line. He said that the investigation was over, and he was not sure what the court's verdict would be, but he expected things to go well because of the intervention of Jewish institutions. The army, Wilkin added, did not want to see its soldiers in jail, and so all Yarkoni had to do to get out of that mess was to sign the documents.

For a moment I thought Wilkin would trap Yarkoni, as he did

so many other members of the underground. Yarkoni sat up in his chair and said he refused to confess, sign or talk. Wilkin's face turned white. He tried to persuade Yarkoni, but the latter repeated his refusal and got up to leave. Wilkin kept sitting there, visibly shocked, and looked at me furiously. He then got up and left the room. A few days later Yarkoni was transferred to a detention camp, where he only spent one year until he was released. Thus he was spared long years in prison.

TWENTY-SIX

Escape

Some of the Haganah prisoners who had been put in the block next to ours in the central prison in Jerusalem showed interest in our ideology and tactics. Their arrest made it clear to them the fight against the British was a serious matter. Many of the Haganah members on the outside, especially those who belonged to the operational units, such as the Palmach and the Hish, sided with the LEHI fighting doctrine. I had long talks with such Haganah members while in prison and often found them to be quite sympathetic. Some of them insisted that several of their friends on the outside were even more radical and anxious to act than they.

This fact brought about a change in my way of thinking and acting. The change also had to do with internal LEHI problems during that period. After the murder of Yair and the arrest of most of the senior commanders of the organization, I began to feel we needed to reorganize. At that time Menahem Begin assumed the command of the Irgun because of his leadership qualities, his courage and his great personal example of self-sacrifice. He revolutionized the Irgun, pulled it out of its paralysis and made it the leader of the struggle for Israel's independence. Among the ranks of the Palmach there was a clamoring for action against the British. Under such circumstances, I gradually became convinced it would be possible to achieve cooperation among the three organizations in the war against the foreign occupier. I was willing to cooperate with the Haganah, even follow its operational orders, as long as they were directed against the British. Both the Irgun and the Haganah were going to adopt not only LEHI's mode of operation, but also its ideology. I expressed those ideas to the Haganah commanders I met in prison and I became interested in what the commanders on the outside thought about them. I sent a message to my cousin, Nehemia Brosh, to visit me in jail. Nehemia was a top commander of the Haganah, a member of the high command, and could talk directly to the top leaders. In addition, he had special feelings for us, since his sister, Roni, was Yair's widow, and despite all the differences of opinion between him and Yair, Nehemia had the highest opinion of the fallen head of LEHI. Because of my special privileges in the prison as block leader, I could speak to him intimately.

After several meetings with Brosh, he told me that Eliyahu Golomb, who headed the Haganah at that time, said that there was basis to talk to LEHI, since it was not a political party but rather a fighting organization which had its admirers among the rank and file of the Haganah. The Irgun, on the other hand, was considered by the Haganah, the Histadrut and the Jewish Agency an arm of the Revisionist Party, and therefore there was no basis for discussion with that organization.

After I carefully considered this development, I decided I had to do all I could to escape from prison and help bring about cooperation among the three fighting organizations. It took me a whole year to plan my escape. I knew that the preparations were the guarantee for success. First, I had to make contact with our people on the outside. Outside help was indispensable for an escape. It could save the escapee from a certain death during the escape and facilitate the escape itself and the subsequent hiding. While in jail we had lost contact with members on the outside. When I began to make contacts I was shocked to find out that the response was not forthcoming. I decided, therefore, to escape without help from the outside. I planned the escape all by myself with my personal resources. The escape was an inner command which I had to obey no matter what.

The central prison in Jerusalem was a veritable fortress. The inner walls were at least three feet thick. The heavy iron doors were bolted and shut with heavy locks. At each corner there was a guard. The cells and the offices were in the center of the building. That was the most difficult part of the prison to escape from. However, the workshop where funeral accessories and grave markers were made was an annex of the prison, a less guarded area. Here the more privileged prisoners and the staff could go into a large back yard and take a walk. Behind that yard, across the fence on an elevated area, was the home of Mr. Wilson, the prison director.

My plan took into account the layout of the prison. First I had to go to the office area, where security was less strict than inside the prisoners' area. From there I had to proceed to the cemetery workshop. My old friend, Rafael Saban, worked in that shop. He had been my superior in the Irgun back in 1937-40. He was captured during an unsuccessful bank robbery in Jerusalem, and sentenced to 5 years in prison. Now, in 1942, he was about to be released. I asked Saban to bequeath me his job at the shop when he left the jail. He was able to arrange for me to become his assistant, and possible successor. A few months later when Saban was set free I took his place. Now I needed a position of responsibility among the prisoners, which would provide me with greater freedom of movement around the prison. I became friendly with two prison officers, a Jew named Rubin and an Egyptian named Ahmed, and after presenting each one of them with a fountain pen (which my girlfriend Hannah smuggled into the jail), they recommended me to Mr. Wilson, the prison director, for promotion. I was soon promoted to block foreman.

My new promotion enabled me to go out each day at 4 p.m., stay at the back yard of the prison for an hour, and smoke one cigarette. It also showed my jailers that I was trustworthy and responsible, and in the end facilitated my escape. I now had to gain the trust of Mr. Wilson, a rather friendly English gentleman, who had the personality of a bookstore owner rather than a warden. He lived in a frame house outside the fence of the prison's back yard, behind the Russian Orthodox church. His house was the second stage of my escape. I realized that without outside help, my only route of escape was through his house. To get to his house, I had to befriend him and cultivate close relations with him.

I started building my relationship with Mr. Wilson brick by brick, putting each brick in place with great care. Fortunately, the director looked upon me as a prisoner rather than a dangerous terrorist who had to be kept under maximum security. The cemetery workshop was adjacent to the director's office, and soon I began to exchange pleasantries with him in English, and I could tell he took a liking to me. I also noticed Mr. Wilson was a sentimental fellow, and each time he looked at the grave markers I was making he would remark to himself, "Here is someone who died doing his duty. . . too bad this young life had to be snuffed out in the Holy Land.'' I shared his sadness, expressing my own sympathy. I did not add that the poor victim would still be alive if he stayed in England and did not come here to oppress us. I think our sharing of such sentiments is what first brought us close together.

Wilson was a bird lover. I told him I was an expert in making bird cages and would be glad to make him some. He gladly accepted, and I began to learn a new trade of making cages. I ordered them from the prison carpentry, and would paint them in bright colors and install an electric light. Electricity is something I had learned when I manufactured bombs and mines.

While I was installing electric connections in the bird cages I had a new idea. I decided to acquire an assistant, who would become my fellow escapee. Our men in Section 18 were divided on the question of escape. Some of us, especially the old-timers, argued that this was not the time to escape, since we had hardly a place to go or an organization we could do much with. Since the war against Nazi Germany was at its peak, it was not the time to fight the British, and the best place to be was the prison. It was better to wait until the organization recovered, and the world conflict resolved. Others disagreed and said that any underground person locked in jail had to do everything possible to escape and become active again. If the organization was small and weakened, so much more the reason to escape and help rebuild it. I sided, of course, with the latter.

One of those who supported me was Moshe Bar-Giora, one of our youngest and most capable and interpid commanders. He was one of my trainees at my course in Jerusalem immediately after the split with the Irgun. He had commanded several operations under my supervision and proved to be daring and effective. When he told me he wanted to join me on my escape, I did not hesitate. In addition, he was an expert electrician. I could use him in making the cages for Mr. Wilson.

I told the prison director I needed an assistant to make the cages. He readily agreed. Thus Bar-Giora became my assistant not only with the cages but also at the cemetery workshop.

After cultivating my relations with Mr. Wilson for a whole year, I decided it was time to offer my services at his home, from whence I would stage my escape. At that time I had completed a correspondence course in chemical engineering, and received my degree. I knew I could use my knowledge in manufacturing explosives for LEHI. I also completed a translation from Russian of the book *Life of a Terrorist*, which narrated underground activities against the Czarist regime. I felt I had put my two years in prison to good use for my organization, and now the time had arrived to leave and carry on the fight on the outside.

It was about a month before Christmas 1943. I saw Wilson and wished him a happy holiday. I told him I was sure he had a sparkling Christmas tree at home. He replied that, unfortunately, he was not able to get the kind of a Christmas tree he would have liked to have for his wife and children. This was my turn to act. Very delicately I told him that if it was a question of money, I was willing to decorate a tree for him without charging anything. He asked me, "What about the decorations? Who would pay for them?" I told him I would take care of everything. It would not cost him a penny. As soon as he told me to go ahead, I started making preparations.

Bar-Giora and I began to collect electric wires, sockets and small lightbulbs for Mr. Wilson's tree. We obtained all those items from the prison's electric shop. Now we needed a transformer to reduce the voltage for the tiny bulbs. I contacted a Jewish prison guard who was sympathetic to the underground, and arranged for him to buy a transformer in town. We now had all the parts we needed for the tree, and we began to look for the accessories we needed for our escape. I assumed that while we worked at the Wilson residence we would be guarded by two Arab policemen armed with shotguns loaded with one bullet, used for hunting. They used those guns because they were easy to operate and could kill an escaping prisoner on the spot. I decided that the thing to do was to make those guards drowsy, or put them to sleep altogether. I turned again to the Jewish prison guard, and told him that some of us could not sleep at night because of family problems, and we needed some strong sleeping pills. The guard had a warm Jewish heart and complied with my request. My friend Becker made a tin mould, into which I poured melted chocolate and mixed it with the sleeping powder. That was the Christmas candy I prepared for our guards, to sweeten their duty of guarding us and make up for the trouble we would cause them with our escape.

Bar-Giora and I had prepared some ordinary clothes for ourselves with the help of Jewish inmates who were expert tailors, not telling them of course what the purpose of those clothes was. In addition, we started to let our hair grow (we had our heads shaved while in prison) and hid it under our berets. We then borrowed 12 pounds from our friends, so we could pay for a place to stay after our escape.

Two days before Christmas I told the director my friend and I were ready to go over to his home to install the electricity on his tree. I added that I did not wish to do private work during official work hours, and would go after 4 o'clock, when the prison work hours ended.

A few days before my escape date Hannah came to visit me. As I looked into her eyes I wondered if that was the last time I was going to see her, or would I soon—as I dearly hoped—see her on the outside and clutch her to my heart. I did not say anything, only kept looking at her. After the meeting I told her: "Let's pray to God things will get better." She must have sensed something, and I could see fear in her eyes. She must have known there was no point in talking me out of doing what I was about to do. She went to the Western Wall that day and left a note between the stones, asking God to save me from all my enemies.

TWENTY-SEVEN

Freedom

The date I had picked for my escape was December 23, 1943, the day before Christmas Eve, the fourth day of Hanukkah. I came back early to my cell that day to prepare for the coming events. Bar-Giora and I got dressed, packed the candy, then each of us hid 6 liras in his shoes. We looked at each other. Our silent question meant, Are we going to be brought back here again, this time with smashed limbs?

Around 4 o'clock I heard the Arab sergeant calling: "*Ya'ub, Ya'ub, Musah, illa la'bab*" (Yaakov and Moshe to the gate). I took it to mean our call to freedom.

I took along all the electric accessories and tools. The Arab policeman was armed with that scary shotgun. We were escorted to the Wilson residence, where the green Christmas tree stood in the living room, ready to be decorated with colorful electric lights.

No one was home. Mrs. Wilson and her daughters must have been at church. Mr. Wilson was busy inspecting some pigs he bred on the prison grounds. Bar-Giora and I first toured the house, ostensibly looking for electric outlets, as we drew up our plan of escape. We decided to escape through the porch, climb a water pipe reaching the top of the ramp in the backyard, go over the fence and reach the back of the Russian Orthodox church at the Russian Compound.

After we completed the tour to our satisfaction, we offered the guard some chocolate. We encircled the tree with electric wires and attached the bulbs. The guard sat in an armchair across the room and began to nod at us, visibly drowsy. We worked slowly, so we could leave under the cover of night.

Another Arab guard armed with the same murderous shotgun joined the first one at dusk. He had to keep an eye on us until we finished the job. I gave him a generous portion of chocolate. Soon he too became sluggish like the first one. Then, after we had worked in the dark for half an hour, I told Bar-Giora, "Now is the time to escape." I turned to the guards and told them we had to attach the wire in the bedroom, and from there pull it to the Christmas tree. "It is very complicated work," I added. If they did not help me, I could not finish it on time, and the director would blame them for it.

The guards were frightened, and told me they would help us finish the job. I placed two chairs in the bedroom and told them to stand on the chairs. I attached the wire to the barrels of their guns and told them to hold their guns against the ceiling so I could pull the wire to the tree. As Bar-Giora and I unwound the wire, we walked back to the living room and I kept calling at the guards to hold their guns steady. We walked out the door and I tied the wire to a post on the porch so the guards would not notice that I had let go of it. I kept yelling at them not to move, we would come right back.

At that moment I crossed the yard with Bar-Giora following close behind, and we climbed the fence and found ourselves behind the Russian church. We kept walking fast, almost running, as if escaping from the drizzle that had started at that moment. We saw the director's wife and two daughters coming back from church. I hid my face with my hand. They did not notice us. Even if they had, they would not have imagined we were in the process of escaping from jail. We kept running at a moderate pace, and I turned my face upward and drank the raindrops of freedom. Near the state hospital at the Russian Compound I turned left and crossed an alley with houses on the right and a prison fence on the left. I knew there were no guards along that fence, and in the dark I could walk next to it without being seen. I went down to Shivtey Israel Street and entered the Arab neighborhood of Musrarah, knowing that there were no British patrols in Arab neighborhoods. Because of the rain and the dark the streets were deserted. I advanced carefully toward my meeting point with Bar-Giora, near Bermann Bakery in Meah Shearim. Here, in this ultra-orthodox neighborhood, the British seldom showed their faces, so I felt safe. I went into a courtyard and took off the sweater I wore under my shirt, and put it over my shirt to improve my appearance. I went back into the street, feeling less like an escaped prisoner. As soon as I started to walk I ran into someone in the dark. The person switched on a strong flashlight and held it to my face. He yelled like a madman, "*Hada Ya'ub*" (this is Yaakov). It was the guard from whom I escaped less than an hour ago.

The two guards, who had stood on the chairs in the bedroom as I had told them to do, finally realized something was fishy. They went outside to look and found out we had deceived them. They immediately alerted the officer of the guard, and a patrol of some fifteen men with rifles, flashlights and dogs went after us. They charged in military formation toward the closest Jewish neighborhood, thinking it must be our escape route. Thus, they were pursuing Bar-Giora. They did not catch him. He was able to arrive at our meeting point near Bermann Bakery at 8:30, and waited for me. The patrol continued its search along Habashim Street, and ran into me, who had taken the roundabout route.

I turned around as the policeman dropped the flashlight and grasped his gun. I hurled myself on the smooth stones of the sidewalk and lay flat. He shot at me in the dark and missed. The members of the patrol heard the shot and thought the policeman was being attacked by underground members. They began to shoot in all directions. The dogs were barking and flashlights were aimed in all directions. After the first shot I realized the policeman wasted no time reloading his gun. The sparks from the first shots must have revealed my place, and now he would surely hit me. I lunged and dove again on the pavement. He fired again and missed. Without waiting a second I made a dash to the nearest stone fence and skipped over it, running into the dark yard.

I heard shots and barking and saw the flashes of searchlights, but I could tell they had lost my tracks. Inside the yard I ran into a stone wall with barbed wire on top. I scaled the wall and jumped over the barbed wire. On the way down the barbs scratched my knees. I reached the ground and examined myself. I was not seriously wounded. Nearby, about twenty yards from that fence, I knew a family whose daughter was a member of the underground. I knew her parents. I did not hesitate and walked into the apartment, without knocking on the door.

She was not home. Her parents were sitting in the dining room with their other daughter. When the sister saw me, bedraggled and begrimed, she let out a cry: "You must have escaped from jail. Go away. We don't want to see you." She said this in spite of the fact that they knew me well. I did not hesitate and told them that indeed I had escaped from jail and the British were after me. If they did not give me clothes and let me stay the British would catch me and I would spend many years in jail.

My words, or the way I said them, must have had an effect on them. The head of the family suddenly got up and opened a closet and began to throw clothes at me. I took the hint, and started to put on the clothes he had given me. In one moment I became a yeshiva student, with the dark garb and the *kapota*. I even put on the fur hat known as *shtreiml*. I could now circulate in the streets of Meah Shearim without being detected. Later on I learned that yeshiva students only wear the *shtreiml* on the Sabbath.

I left the apartment and went up on the roof to survey the neighborhood. I could hear orders in English from the direction I had taken. I saw flashes of light and heard an occasional shot. I knew they had lost my trail and were continuing down the street I had left. It finally dawned on me I had been saved from a certain death and I was now free again to resume my underground activities. I came down from the roof and my first thought was to get back in touch with Bar-Giora, who was supposed to wait for me at the Bermann Bakery. I assumed that Bar-Giora had given up on me and had gone away to look for his own hiding place. It was 9:30. We had arranged to meet at 8:30. If there were any problems, we said we would meet at 10:30.

I proceeded to the house of Moshe Segal, who lived nearby in the Even Yehoshua section. Even before we escaped I targeted Segal's house as my refuge. I did not know at this point if he belonged to LEHI or the Irgun, but I knew he would welcome me, offer me his home and put me in touch with the underground.

I had known Segal while serving as operations officer of the Irgun in Jerusalem. He was active in the Irgun as a civilian member, and led a religious youth movement called Brit Hahashmonaim, whose leaders belonged to the Irgun and recruited members for the organization from among its youth. During that period we had worked closely and had high regard for each other. Segal admired Yair and fully agreed with his doctrine. After the split he joined LEHI and accepted all the risks involved, albeit he was married and had children and was endangering his family. Several times he was arrested and released. When I commanded the LEHI in Jerusalem in 1942, shortly before my capture by the police in Tel Aviv, Segal was active in LEHI and helped me in Jerusalem. But when Yair was murdered and the LEHI command collapsed, Segal decided it was time to reunite the two factions in order to bolster the fighting underground. But although he strove to unite the groups, and might have returned to the Irgun, I knew he would not turn me down if I went to him.

I was right. Exhausted, my knees bleeding, disguised as a yeshiva student, I went to Segal's house near Meah Shearim. I was afraid I might not find him at home, but I was pleasantly surprised. After my first knock the door opened and there stood Segal. He was surprised to see me. When he saw my face running with sweat he realized what was going on. He took me inside and locked the door. His face glowed as he hugged and kissed me. He called his wife and told her to dress my wounds. They treated me with firm and loving hands. I felt better. I washed up and sat at the table like a human being. Segal's wife prepared a wonderful omelette. I can still taste it. I must have dreamed of it during my two years in jail.

It was almost 10:30, time for me to meet Bar-Giora at Bermann Bakery. I was quite concerned about him, fearing he might not find a shelter as I did. It turned out that he did wait for me near the bakery. He heard the shots of the patrol, and after waiting for half an hour he concluded something had happened to me and he went to look for shelter. The only person he trusted in those days was Rabbi Levin, the prisoners' rabbi. He immediately proceeded to Levin's house, near Mahaneh Yehuda. The rabbi welcomed him, but he could not stay in the rabbi's modest apartment, since the British detectives were sure to search the place. The rabbi put on his raincoat and went out with Bar-Giora to look for a hiding place. He could not find any safe place. The rabbi then asked his daughter Ettil, who was engaged to Rabbi Elazar Palchinsky, to accompany Bar-Giora on his way back to our meeting place near the bakery, so he should not attract the attention of the police. Bar-Giora went back with a glimmer of hope that he might still run into me. I had asked Segal to go out and look for Bar-Giora, which he gladly did. Moments later the two came back. We fell into each other's arms and embraced for a long time.

I began to consider my next move. First I wanted to see Hannah, who, unconsciously, might have been the one because of whom I wanted to escape. Besides, she was in charge of LEHI's arms caches in Jerusalem, and since she belonged to the large and wealthy Mussayeff family, who owned many buildings, many of those caches were on her family's premises. The CID must have known about our relationship, because of Hannah's frequent visits to jail, so I had to caution her about it. I asked Segal to go and see Hannah and bring her to me. He went over to her house and told her father he was the tutor of one of his sons. Hannah had eleven brothers and sisters, and one of them was always being tutored in something. Her father let him in, and when he saw Hannah he told her she had to come to his home to meet a LEHI commander. Taking a roundabout way, she came to Segal's apartment, and when she saw who the LEHI commander was she was stunned. I was speechless when I saw her. I put my arms around her, and she drew back and asked me: "Why did you escape?" I told her: "In order to kiss you and to die."

After we both calmed down I told Hannah the British might lay a trap for us. We could not see each other too often, and we had to use the greatest precaution. I also warned her about the arms caches, which the British might be searching for very soon. She had to contact our men right away and start transferring the arms to a safer place. Hannah left and proceeded immediately to take care of the matter.

I was now determined to get in touch through Brosh, my cousin, with the command of the Haganah, and offer my plan for cooperation among the three underground organizations, in order to form a united front against the foreign occupier. I had known Brosh's address, since he gave it to me during one of his visits to the prison. It was midnight, and I went to sleep at Segal's house. After two years of sleeping on rags on the prison floor, the bed and the clean sheets, soft mattress and warm blankets were heavenly.

I woke up early in the morning. When I woke up Mrs. Segal was busy making breakfast. Segal was outside, assessing the searches of the British police and wondering how safe we were at his apartment. He came back and told us Jerusalem was practically under siege with police and army forces everywhere. There were orders from the high commissioner to capture the escapees. Segal added that the British appeared certain that I would try to leave the city, and the heaviest guards were on the roads leading out of the city. He had also gotten in contact with the LEHI center and told them about my escape. They instructed him to keep me for a few days until they could arrange a safe place for me to hide. I decided to proceed with my plan. I assumed that in the first stage of my negotiations with the Haganah I would be under their protection thus releasing Segal from the great risk he was undertaking by hiding me. I was going to see Brosh.

I told Segal I had an important meeting which I couldn't miss. In order to reach my destination I had to cross several main streets swarming with British police, soldiers and detectives. I had to come up with a convincing disguise. Mrs. Segal provided me with woman's clothes and I became a bona fide woman. To be even safer, we arranged for a man to accompany me, as we would walk with our arms around each other. An old friend, Meir Medan, now the scientific secretary of the Academy of the Hebrew Language, volunteered to be my suitor. He did not get into trouble with the British on my account, but inadvertently, he almost did get into deep personal trouble, for, as we walked down the street embracing like two lovers, his future bride happened to see us. She ran home crying bitterly. As far as she was concerned, the marriage was off. It took a gread deal of persuasion on Medan's part to convince his fiancee his new girlfriend was a man, whose life was in danger.

I walked next to Medan on high heels. It was a pleasure to be able to stroll nonchalantly along a main street of Jerusalem, with British detectives everywhere, carefully eyeing the passersby. They must have had my photograph, but the rouged and mascaraed woman hardly matched the object of their search.

We soon found Brosh's apartment, on the third floor of a central building in the heart of town. Only his mother-in-law was home. His wife, Esther, who had just given birth to their daughter, Ofra, was coming home from the hospital that evening. I waited with Medan for an hour until the proud parents came home with the baby. I got up on my feet and congratulated them on the birth of their daughter.

Brosh looked at me in utter disbelief. All he said was, "How?" I simply told him I had escaped. He did not say anything. I said: "Nehemia, I have something private to discuss with you." As Medan waited in the living room, I went with Brosh into the bedroom. I told him I had escaped from prison in order to pursue the idea I had mentioned to him before, namely, the cooperation among the three organizations. He told me he had made some inquiries, but had not yet received a definite answer. I begged him to bring the matter up to the attention of the Haganah command without any delays. He said he would attend to it right away, and since the matter was so urgent and involved great risks, we should set two alternate meetings. We arranged to meet the next evening at the corner of Haneviim and Habashim, and if Brosh did not show up we would meet the next day. If he failed to show up the next day

I would take it to mean the answer was negative. I would then go back to LEHI without any further dealings with the Haganah.

Medan and I went back to Segal's apartment. The next day I went to meet Brosh, dressed in the same outfit as the day before. An ambulance stopped next to me. Brosh came out and helped me climb into the ambulance, like a woman having pregnancy problems. As soon as we were inside the vehicle he turned on the flashing red light and the siren and sped across town. All the British patrols waved him through and all the traffic stopped as he went by. He turned to kibbutz Ramat Rahel outside Jerusalem, one of the Haganah's secret headquarters. On the way he told me he had contacted his command and after an urgent meeting they decided they wanted to see me. They chose Ramat Rahel as a safe place to meet.

The person in charge of kibbutz security, Moshe Katz, came out of one of the small kibbutz homes. He took me inside and I quickly changed back into man's clothes. I now looked like a kibbutznik in work clothes. Brosh told me I would remain under Katz's supervision. In a day or two someone from the Haganah command would come to talk to me. I stayed with the Katz family, to whom I was introduced as a member of a kibbutz up north who had come for a visit. I played briefly with Katz's children, and for a moment I was transported to better times. But soon I had to stop playing. Katz came back and told me he had orders to transfer me to a safer place. He gave me warm clothes against the Jerusalem winter, and took me to the watch tower on the edge of the kibbutz. As I sat there I realized that the kibbutz secretariat had decided to hide me outside the perimeter of the kibbutz so that in case I was caught they could wash their hands of any complicity, and say I had hid there without their knowledge. I was not angry at them. After all, I was the only one who had to take responsibility for my escape.

I had climbed up the tower to the upper platform where I found a cot to lie on. Katz had left me some food and told me he would personally bring me my meals. I had to play the part of night watchman, which, in effect, was his own duty. He shook my hand and left. I was not allowed to make any light. I lay in the dark and listened to the sounds of the night. A clear moon swam through the star studded sky. I checked the tower, its access and egress, and took a short tour of the surrounding area, in case I had to escape. After I satisfied myself with the prevailing situation, I went up again and got into my cot. Next to my cot I found crates with fresh picked apples. I ate an apple and thought about the sweeter future.

Katz came in the morning and brought me a hot cup of coffee and some fresh bread and jam. He had no idea who I was. He thought I was a member of the Palmach who had to hide from the authorities. After he left I surveyed my surroundings. I saw the cultivated fields all around me. Farther away I saw Jerusalem, and on the other side Bethlehem. At noon Katz brought me a basket with lunch. He told me my meeting was set for that evening. Half an hour after dark he came to escort me to the meeting. I could see he was being very cautious. As he approached the tower he looked around him, and then walked at some distance away from me. When I entered his apartment I noticed it was surrounded by guards, and for the first time it occurred to me he might have found out something about my identity.

After we waited for half an hour in the darkened apartment, Brosh came in with another man who introduced himself as a representative of the Haganah. I told him it was a historical imperative to unify the forces in the struggle against the British. The sooner it took place, the faster the White Paper would be revoked, the survivors of the Holocaust allowed into the country and an independent state would be established, as the only hope for the Jewish people in a post-Holocaust world. The Haganah person told me that my words were validated by the thinking of Haganah members. They too realized the time had come to go on the offensive against the British. He expressed great admiration for LEHI's members, dedicated idealists, and took issue with the Irgun members who served the interests of the Revisionist Party. At that point I interjected: "Let's start by having the Haganah and LEHI cooperate, and the Irgun will later accept the established conditions of cooperation." I added that if we could not find a way to cooperate, LEHI would continue to pursue its objectives with all its might. I personally hoped that the fight would reach other parts of the Jewish world, which would make the Jewish Agency lose control of the situation.

I was getting the impression he was being persuaded, although he was only a mediator between me and the Haganah. After some more friendly talk, he promised me to relay my words to his command who would give it due consideration. He was hoping that the Palmach and the Hish would pressure the command to accept cooperation, which he personally fully supported. He kept stressing the importance of exerting pressure by the lower echelons of the organization in order to take action against the British, which would accelerate the dialogue. After the meeting I was taken back to the watch tower, surrounded by security people. I was told the ambulance would be back in the morning to take me back to town.

After dark I went back to Katz's home and dressed up in my woman's clothes. The ambulance came. The driver gave me a nurse's white uniform, and I rode next to him as part of the medical team. After a short ride with emergency lights and siren going, I was back on the street corner where I had been picked up a few days earlier by Brosh. I went over to Segal's apartment, where I was given a warm welcome. I asked Segal to make contact with the LEHI command in Jerusalem. He did, and the next afternoon LEHI's Jerusalem commander, Yehoshua Cohen, came over. He told me I would be transferred in the evening to a safer place, and from there I would be taken to Tel Aviv. In the evening Cohen's aide came to take me to my new hideout. We walked through dark alleys to Yegiat Kepayim.

We went into a yard. My escort told me to stay out of the sight of the neighbors. We took off our shoes and walked slowly and cautiously to one of the entrances. He opened the door and let me in. He told me to come in without turning on the light. In the dark I would find a cot and some food. I had to keep that storage room locked in the daytime and only come out at night. I remained there in the dark and went to sleep.

In the morning when I woke up some sunlight seeped in through the cracks. To my amazement, I found out I was in an arms cache, full of firearms, explosives and mines. It didn't take me long to realize it was not only a cache but also a shop where bombs and mines were manufactured. Now I understood why I had such a splitting headache. I had been poisoned by the fumes of the explosives, which, after being stored for some time, had the tendency to emit poisonous gas. My headache indicated I was in the early stage of poisoning, and unless I did something about it I was in grave danger. As I was considering my condition and trying to decide what to do, I found an interesting occupation. As an old expert, I began to check the mines and took out some of the bugs and imperfections to make them more secure and effective.

As I was working on the mines and repacking the explosives to reduce the emission, the yard outside was coming to life. Children came out to play and mothers came to draw water out of the well and buy groceries at the nearby store. I peeked through the cracks and enjoyed the sight of Yemenite children. I could hear the guttural trill of the Yemenite women. I kept my nose next to the crack because I wanted to breathe some fresh air. As I remained in that position I suddenly saw a door open across the yard, and out came Gamliel, the Yemenite warden of the central prison, wearing his uniform and his gun as he left for work. I had no doubt the moment he sensed anything suspicious going on at the storage place he would notify the police. When Cohen came at night I told him about the modifications I had made in the mines. I added that I needed a better hideout. I did not escape from prison to be caught in an arms cache. He quickly agreed, and that night I was transferred to the home of one of our supporters, where the family welcomed me with open arms.

A few days later Shlomo Posner came disguised as a doctor along with a male and female nurses in order to transfer me to Tel Aviv. They wrapped my head with bandages, put a cast on my arm and leg, and carried me on a stretcher to the ambulance. I had to be transferred to Tel Aviv to get proper medical attention. For added security they hid a pistol and a grenade under my pillow.

That evening we arrived safely in Tel Aviv. I was delivered to the clinic of Professor Marcus, the chief surgeon of Hadassah Hospital, a great friend of the underground whose clinic took care of underground members.

Shortly after my arrival at the clinic I was visited by Michael (Yitzhak Shamir, later Prime Minister of Israel). We embraced each other, rejoicing to see each other again. I had known Yitzhak back in 1938, when he served under Aryeh Yitzhaki in a unit that became known as one of our best. He was the "farmer's" (Yehoshua Zettler) second-in-command. Shamir was a great organizer and knew how to set priorities for underground operations. After the "farmer's" arrest Shamir was also arrested and sent to detention camp at Mezra. He drew up a meticulous escape plan and was able to return to his command in Tel Aviv, where he and Eliyahu Giladi headed the organization.

After the joyful reunion, Shamir grew quiet, even sombre. He told me: "I have to tell you we have liquidated Eliyahu Giladi, who had escaped with me from prison, because we found him to be dangerous for the underground. Both Gera (Yellin-Mor) and Eldad (Dr. Israel Scheib) of the LEHI center gave their consent."

At first I was shocked. Giladi was a senior commander, a seasoned fighter. He had taken part with me, under Zettler's command, in the robbery of the Anglo-Palestine Bank in Tel Aviv in 1940, where he proved to be highly capable and helped make the action a success. My connection to Giladi must have prompted Shamir to break the news to me right away. I told Shamir I was not aware of the reasons that led to the elimination of Giladi, but since I fully trusted Shamir, I had no comments to make. Shamir only nodded and told me I had to rest for a few days to get back to myself and that the organization would be in touch with me to plan reintegration in LEHI. As soon as he finished his briefing he got up and left.

TWENTY-EIGHT

Contacts with the Haganah

A week later I decided to continue my efforts to unite the fighting forces, which I considered the only way to further our cause of national liberation. I told LEHI center members Yitzhak Shamir and Nathan Yellin-Mor I had decided to approach the Haganah with a LEHI proposal to pursue unified action. The next day Shamir informed me the center had given its approval and authorized me to speak to the Haganah as LEHI's representative. He added that Shlomo Posner was assigned as my liaison with the center, in order to monitor my activities. For added emphasis, I was given a service gun. Again I made contact with Nehemia Brosh and told him LEHI center was prepared to talk to the Haganah and had released me for this task.

After the Haganah command accepted my proposal, Brosh showed up at my hideout one morning. In his car was a female escort, who turned out to be Margot, the wife of Yitzhak Sadeh, the commander of the Palmach and member of the Haganah command. He had come to transfer me to the Valley of Jezreel, where most of the Palmach members and their commanders were concentrated. I spent nine months in five kibbutzim. There I trained Haganah and Palmach commanders in tactics to be used against the British in our war for national liberation. In the evenings I had lively discussions with kibbutz leaders, who were also national leaders, on the burning issues of the day. When I was free from instructing, training and lecturing, I would spend hours in the fields. I plowed, sowed, fertilized and worked the combine. Out in the fields I felt safer as I filled my lungs with the pure air of the homeland.

Givat Zeid was the last kibbutz I stayed in under the auspices of the Haganah. Here I was the guest of the local Haganah commander, Binyamin Blumberg, who quickly became my friend. Here also I took stock of my activities. I had been hidden by the Haganah now for nine months. It was enough time for building bridges between the Haganah and LEHI. The time had arrived to sit down and nail down an agreement. I got in touch with LEHI. They sent Posner, who nine months earlier delivered me to the Haganah, to Givat Zeid to get my report. I told him I had finished my work with the Haganah, and regardless of whether or not I was now going to meet with the upper echelons of that organization, I was ready to return to my work in LEHI. At the same time I sent a message to Brosh to put me in touch with the authorized Haganah representatives so we could come to an understanding.

The answer came quickly. Israel Galili and Eliyahu Golomb, the heads of the Haganah, came to see me. I spent hours with each one of them, showed them my plan in writing, and explained my ideas about the organization and management of our cooperation, as well as the benefits we could derive from it, and, conversely, the results of non-cooperation. A few days later I received their answer. The Haganah commander agreed in principle, but it would take several months before the proposal could be presented to the leadership of the Yishuv and the Zionist organization and be approved by them. In addition, the Haganah had to persuade several individuals and bodies who were against the idea. They told me they did not mind if in the meantime I continued to work on the kibbutz, and did not, on the other hand, consider my going back to active duty in LEHI an objectionable decision on my part. Galili added with a smile that now I could bring the teachings of the Haganah to the ranks of LEHI. I told him I did not intend to remain inside the framework of the Haganah. I felt guilty being away for so long from underground activities. I preferred to wait for further developments between LEHI and the Haganah inside the LEHI, rather than within the Haganah framework.

Eliyahu Golomb told me he understood my decision and appreciated it. But he was sorry I made it. In any case, he hoped that before long the cooperation we wished for could be achieved.

When Golomb spoke those words he did not realize he was being prophetic. Forces he had no control over had been at work, and in hindsight it turned out that they were stronger than any individual or organization. Two LEHI members, Eliyahu Bet-Tzuri and Eliyahu

Hakim, had just assassinated Lord Moyne, the British minister of state, in Cairo. The day after the assassination, during a rain storm, Golomb came to see me at Givat Zeid. There was no paved road at that time, and because of the rain and mud the kibbutz was practically isolated. Golomb could not reach the kibbutz with his car. He left the car three miles down the road at kibbutz Alonim and came to Givat Zeid on horseback, accompanied by the Alonim commander. He wanted to see me in private. We went into someone's room, and a guard was posted outside.

Golomb started out by saying that the assassination of Lord Moyne (November 6, 1944) could put an end to Zionist aspirations and the hopes of the Jewish people. He said that Churchill had announced that if LEHI was not liquidated following this deed he would have to reexamine his attitude toward Zionism, and the results of such reexamination would not be good. Therefore the institutions of the Yishuv had decided that terrorism must be eradicated before it brought an end to the Yishuv and its struggle. He spoke for about an hour and was greatly agitated. He finally paused and said to me: "Yasha, what are we going to do?"

From the way he spoke I could tell that the national institutions, in their fear of the British, might unleash a campaign against the underground which could result in a full-fledged civil war. I told Golomb that Churchill was not the father of Zionism and did not promise the Land of Israel to the people of Israel. He was not the one who would give us that land or the one who would liberate it. Moreover, Churchill was the man who bore the moral responsibility for the murder of millions of Jews who had been exterminated by Nazi Germany without any interference on the part of the Allies. Therefore, the only way we could talk to Churchill was with a gun, and blessed were the hands who had eliminated Lord Moyne. I warned Golomb not to start a civil war, and as for LEHI, I said that if anyone touched LEHI, the organization would use its arms and its first target would be the leaders of their opponents. This would eliminate the collaborators, and would shorten the road to national liberation. LEHI would not stop at anything in its fight for freeing the homeland. I clarified with all severity that if he gave an order to attack LEHI he would be risking his life.

I remember Golomb became pale. He got up, pulled his gun from his inside coat pocket and said: "I also have a gun. We shall see who wins." I told him "Eliyahu, remember what I told you. It is important who draws first, and I assure you the LEHI people draw faster." He put his gun back in his pocket and sat down. He looked into my eyes and repeated: "Okay, Yasha, what do we do?"

"In light of what you are saying," I told him, "we only have one hope. If you want the attacks on the British in the future to be better controlled and more restrained, you will have to cooperate." I added that I hoped that now, after the elimination of Lord Moyne, LEHI would be willing to cooperate and accept the authority of the Haganah in regard to future operations. But only on the condition that cooperation meant action, fighting, not sitting on one's hands. In addition, I said, during the negotiations period LEHI would agree to stop all operations, which was in the interest of the Haganah.

After we talked for two hours, before midnight, Eliyahu stood up and said: "I will pass it on to our people, and I will let you know their answer in a day or two." He embraced me, mounted his horse and rode toward kibbutz Alonim.

The next day, Saturday, I met with Posner in the woods outside Givat Zeid. I told him about my meeting with Golomb and I suggested I be transferred to Ramat Gan to start practical negotiations between LEHI and the Haganah. I asked for an answer the next day, so I could tell Golomb about it when I saw him again.

Posner came back the next day and we met in the woods. His answer was unequivocal: LEHI center was willing to meet with the Haganah command. Two or three days later the rural-guard pickup came, driven by Ben-Menahem, the Haganah commander in the Nahalal area. I was given the disguise of a rural guard, and was taken to Nahalal to meet with Golomb. Ben-Menahem knew who I was, and kept praising LEHI, especially the courage of LEHI men who stood before the military courts, where their fiery speeches made a deep impression on the operational commanders of the Haganah. He told me that many of his comrades were in favor of LEHI and its operations, and were only sorry LEHI was not under the authority of the national institutions.

Golomb had been waiting for me at Ben-Menahem's apartment. He greeted me warmly and I could tell he had a positive answer. The hostess brought us coffee and cake, which I found to be delicious. Golomb told me the answer was positive. In a few days I would be transferred to the Ramat Gan area in order to begin my mediation between LEHI and the Haganah for an agreement on cooperation between the two organizations. He added that "if we can achieve this cooperation, the things you have taught the Palmach will be put to good use on the battlefield." We spoke for about an hour and I left with the hope that in a few days everything would be put down in writing and signed.

Ad in the Haaretz daily, May 12, 1944: The British Police offers an award for information leading to the arrest of Stern Group members. (Top left) the author, Yaacov Levstein (Eliav), 500 pounds. (Top center) Yitzhak Yezernitzky (Shamir), later Israel's prime minister, 200 pounds.

The day after my meeting with Golomb I had a most unusual surprise. I was in the field plowing, when someone came to tell me I had a visitor. I was afraid it was Golomb, who came back to tell me there was a problem. I rushed back to my room at the kibbutz when I saw Shmuel Eyal and my sweetheart, Hannah. Eyal had found out through Brosh where I was hiding, and made secret arrangements to bring Hannah to see me without putting the British on my trail.

Hannah's problem with police surveillance was quite serious. A few days after my escape the CID designated a special team to hunt me down. They had searched all the buildings, warehouses and yards owned by Hannah's father, Rehavia Mussayeff. They watched Hannah day and night, hoping to find a clue leading to my capture. All British detectives had my photograph. A reward of 500 pounds was offered for any information leading to my arrest. My picture was posted on billboards all over the country along with those wanted by the police.

I spent two hours in Hannah's company, when Eyal came back and took her home. I went out and wandered in the fields and groves, unable to collect my thoughts.

Golomb came to see me one week after our meeting in Nahalal. He told me he was taking me that evening to Ramat Gan. I had known about the arrangement, and I had alerted Posner and told him to let the LEHI center know about my arrival in Ramat Gan. Golomb came over and told me to get into his car without any disguise. I hesitated, since I knew I was breaking the rules of clandestine behavior. He told me not to worry and do as he said. I took my few belongings and put them in my small suitcase and got into his car, wondering why he was being so reckless.

A few moments later we arrived in kibbutz Yagur. Golomb went out and came back with a group of friendly foreigners. They all squeezed into the car, speaking English among themselves and joking. I could tell they knew Golomb, who from time to time took part in their conversation. I soon realized I was sitting in the company of members of the British Parliament, headed by a Laborite, Barnett Janner. They had come here on a fact-finding mission, in order to bring a report from the Yishuv to the Government and Parliament of Great Britain. Golomb used the opportunity to transfer me to Ramat Gan. At one point Golomb looked at me as if to say, "I also know something about clandestine rules."

Four times we were stopped by British army and police patrols. Each time Janner told the officer who the passengers were. The officer would salute and apologize, wishing the passengers a good trip.

Golomb dropped me next to a solitary building in Ramat Gan. I thanked the delegation for being such good company, and entered the apartment. It belonged to a good friend of my family, named Meushar. He greeted me with open arms and showed me the lovely little room he had arranged for me. I told Golomb he could now reach me through Mr. Meushar.

Meushar was a senior Haganah commander whom Golomb trusted and chose to be my host. Shamir had agreed to leave me under the protection of the Haganah, since LEHI had problems arranging a safe hideout for me. I told Meushar I had to go out for a few hours and he did not have to worry about me. He showed me where the key was hidden and told me to let myself in whenever I came back.

I was going to make contact with the LEHI center at an agreed meeting point on the border of Ramat Gan and Bnai Brak. I knew the Haganah would follow me to find out where LEHI leaders were hiding, so I took a roundabout way and made sure no one was following me. After half an hour I arrived at the meeting place and saw Avraham Lieberman, Shamir's liaison. He embraced me and hugged me for a long time, clearly moved to see me back after two years in jail and another year in hiding. Some years later when I reminded Lieberman about that reunion, he asked me: "You remember how much I hugged you and kissed you?" I told him: "Yes, of course. It was a very emotional meeting." He said: "Don't think it was so emotional. What really happened was, Yitzhak told me to hug you and touch you all-around to make sure you were not armed. If you had carried a gun I might not have taken you to him." It seems that, subconsciously, Shamir was still afraid I might be setting a trap for him.

In reality the meeting with Shamir was very warm, and from the first moment he showed complete trust in me. He told me he would invite Yellin-Mor to a meeting with me the next day. He trusted me enough to let me come over to his regular residence at the Kiryat Meir section of Bnai Brak, where he was known as a bearded young rabbi who studied Torah day and night.

We had come full circle. Shamir had agreed to my mission to the Haganah, and now he agreed to have me back as a member of the center of LEHI and the operational commander. By giving me this last assignment he had put a great deal of power into my hands. He also showed himself to be a courageous, generous man of vision.

TWENTY-NINE

Training and Combat Doctrine

Until the agreement was reached I was under the protection of the Haganah. I had to keep changing my hideouts frequently. My last hiding place was in Ramat Hadar. The agreement had already been initialed, and I asked Shamir to let me organize a course for LEHI commanders, to which he agreed. A hut was found inside an orange grove, five minutes' walk from my hideout. I personally picked the best LEHI operational commanders to take part in the course, and started to train them as the new nucleus of our fighting unit.

There were twelve members in the course, which lasted for one month. I taught the trainees the combat doctrine of LEHI as a revolutionary underground. I combined partisan warfare I had learned at the Palmach camps in the Valley of Jezreel with guerrilla warfare I had been taught in Poland in 1939. The result was the combat doctrine used by LEHI from that time until the birth of the state.

When the course ended the trainees took a final test in the presence of center members. They all did well in the use of arms and showed high professionalism in planning guerrilla activities. The center gave its blessing to the graduates and told them that they were the core of our new fighting force about to be established throughout the country. Those men, indeed, became the commanders of the new LEHI fighting force which I commanded until I went abroad to organize a LEHI operations overseas. When the united resistance began its operations, LEHI had its own elite force.

I developed a revolutionary underground fighting doctrine for LEHI. This doctrine was based on four principles: ideological indoctrination, character building, thorough knowledge of and experience with weapons, and the application of the warfare doctrine of a revolutionary underground. Our doctrine was based on the individual. It sought to turn every individual into a warrior who, if need be, could start the underground movement all over again. His convictions, character, knowhow and will to fight were such, that if the enemy dealt the organization a mortal blow, that individual, like the legendary phoenix, would rise from the ashes and start all over again.

After the LEHI candidate passed all the admission tests—personal and family background, social milieu and views, medical confirmation of physical and mental health, and a personal recommendation from an old LEHI member who knew the candidate for at least five years, he would be referred to an instructor who would personally work with him on the basis of the four above principles.

The ideological education was thorough, with special emphasis on past Jewish wars for national liberation in the Land of Israel, and wars of liberation of other nations. This education was based on Yair's National Revival Principles, which the trainee soaked into the marrow of his bones. Character building was based on the realities of a LEHI member's life: clandestine existence, actual fighting, and living behind bars.

A LEHI member who devoted himself totally to underground work had the problems of deception, wearing disguises, concealment and improvisation. He had to live on little, sometimes go without food for days, hide in the most unlikely places, share everything with other members at all times. His life was always in grave danger. At any time he could be called upon to attack the occupiers of his land, with all the resulting consequences. He always faced a long jail term. This created great tension and constant psychological preparedness. The instructor had to prepare the trainee for all of this.

Our underground weapons instruction included all light arms—pistol, submachine gun and hand grenade; the use of explosives—their nature, various types of detonators and primers; the making of mines and bombs—containers, camouflage, firing devices, arrangement of explosives, assembling the firing device, concealment, traps, as well as adaptation and improvisation under changing conditions.

The basic principle underlying our training was that the more British officials, soldiers and policemen were eliminated, the sooner the foreign occupier would have to leave our land. The training with light arms, therefore, was based on quick draw under all conditions, and instinctive firing in motion. The important thing was who fired the first effective shot.

The teaching of explosives, including detonators and primers, was based on military, professional and underground literature. The emphasis was put on explosives we could obtain locally, and later on clandestine shipments from abroad. It included such high explosives as blasting gelatin, gelatin TNT, dynamite and exploding cotton, and low explosives of the gunpowder variety. Special attention was paid to home-made explosives, since at times we could not obtain any other kind. We would buy the elements from open-market sources such as drugstores or chemical supplies stores. We bought potassium chloride and mixed it in a wooden container with 50 percent sugar powder to make low explosives. We made Molotov cocktails from inflammable material, adding sulphatic acid, and pasted potassium chloride mixed with sugar on the bottle. In 1947-48 we were able to make nitroglycerin which was put to good use in the last stages of our struggle against the British. We modified the regular and the electric detonators, removing the tin cylinder. We learned about the tools and the means of detonating them. We would make a cross-cut on the head of a fuse and sprinkle potassium chloride mixed with sugar, cover it with wax paper or rubber and tie it to the fuse. At times we attached hard sulphur to the head of the fuse. Rubbing the sulphur, or touching it with a burning cigarette would light the fuse. We would fuse a detonator to ignite a detonating cord, using a safety fuse for the detonator.

We had two types of electric detonators—one using direct current and the other alternating current. We mostly used direct current derived from all sorts of batteries. We would connect the batteries and the detonators in a row. We used testing instruments to check the current.

I taught our men ways of detonating mines and time bombs. For mines they had to use an outside control, and for time bombs they would use built-in timers. The timers were basically modified wrist and pocket watches, which I introduced back in 1938. They were used by the underground ever since. We also had a variety of electric switches and chemical delaying devices which activated the time bombs. The making of mines and time bombs required a great deal of inventiveness. We had to match wits with the police and be able to outsmart its experts.

The first three principles—indoctrination, character building and technical knowhow, reached perfect harmony in the fourth principle, the fighting doctrine of the organization. Each operation was carefully planned to ensure effective strike against the enemy and safe withdrawal, so the men could go back on their next mission. It was based on the following steps: intelligence, planning, choosing arms, rehearsing, intelligence update, execution, withdrawal. Each operation was checked out beforehand on location by the commanding officer and had to be approved by the national commander, who would often visit the targeted area in person.

To keep up morale, secure the targeted area, help the attacking team in case of an emergency, monitor the operation, and learn its lessons, the supervisor would usually be in the area. After the operation the combatant would submit a detailed report. We would carefully study the report and learn how to improve our operation. A combatant who did well became a supervisor. Thus, in effect, we began the Israeli tradition of "follow me" back in our underground days.

Finally, the preparation for life in jail. This was taught in three parts: arrest, prison life, and escape. The underlying principle was that acquiescing to incarceration was tantamount to treason. LEHI members executed extremely ingenious and daring escapes from prison, thereby keeping LEHI alive and enabling it to renew the struggle for national liberation over and over again.

My course at Ramat Hadar applied the above principles which resulted in the training and combat doctrine of LEHI, recorded in special pamphlets and guides for instructors and supervisors. It was our combat lab and our tactics workshop which turned LEHi into a fighting revolutionary underground, highly daring and innovative.

THIRTY

The United Resistance

The negotiations lasted for a month. We met once a week, sometimes twice. After each meeting the LEHI center would convene to discuss the proposals of the Haganah. Yellin-Mor would sometimes report the talks had reached a dead-end, and I was asked to mollify the other side. I would meet with Golomb, sometimes with Dayan, who would report to Golomb and bring back his reply. This became an additional official meeting, which enabled us to reach an agreement on a particular point. By the end of the month the two parties reached an agreement, drank *L'chayim*, and began to organize the mechanism needed for the implementation, administration and supervision of the agreement.

During a meeting of the LEHI center prior to the signing of the agreement, I had proposed that we include the Irgun in the agreement. At the joint meeting after the cooperation between the Haganah and LEHI was finally agreed on, Yellin-Mor stood up and suggested that the Irgun be included in the agreement. The Haganah representatives were taken by surprise and said they would have to consider the matter and bring back their answer to the next meeting. In the meantime, since we had already initialed the agreement, they requested that we act according to the spirit of the agreement until the Irgun question was clarified. Based on this understanding, the LEHI center contacted the Irgun command

and obtained its consent to enter negotiations on a tripartite agreement for the establishment of the Hebrew revolt movement. During that period the Irgun suffered severely from Haganah kidnappings of its commanders and members. It needed time for reorganization, and to that end it had to demand that the Haganah stop its activities against it. Ideologically and operationally, the gap between the Irgun and the Haganah was not so great as the gap between the Haganah and LEHI. Hence the Irgun's commander, Menahem Begin, was invited to the meetings of the negotiations committee, and after several meetings it was agreed that the resistance movement would encompass the three underground organizations—the Haganah, LEHI and the Irgun—for a joint action against the foreign occupier.

The operational agreement read as follows:

1. The Haganah organization is initiating a military campaign against the British government (the "Tenuat Hameri"* is born).

2. The Irgun and LEHI will not carry out their operational plans without the approval of the command of Tenuat Hameri.

3. The Irgun and LEHI will carry out the operational plans assigned to them by the command of Tenuat Hameri.

4. The discussions of the proposed operations will not be formal. Representatives of the three fighting organizations will meet regularly, or as the need arises, in order to discuss the plan from a political and practical standpoint.

5. After the operations are approved in principle, the experts of the three organizations will discuss the details of the execution.

6. The approval of the Tenuat Hameri command is not necessary for arms acquisition (taking arms from the British). The Irgun and LEHI are allowed to pursue such operations on their own.

7. The agreement among the three fighting organizations is based on the "commandment of active action."

8. If at any time the Haganah is ordered to give up the military campaign against the British rule, the Irgun and LEHI will continue to fight.

After the three undergrounds agreed on the establishment of the united resistance, or Tenuat Hameri, the LEHI center appointed me commander of the LEHI fighting unit and member of the center. I met

---

*Resistance Movement

one more time with Golomb and thanked him for the Haganah's hospitality. Golomb said he understood my decision to go back to LEHI, and expressed the hope that the same spirit of understanding which prevailed during my contacts with him and with the Haganah would continue to guide me after I returned to LEHI's ranks. We shook hands and embraced. I left my Ramat Hadar shelter and went into a new hideout in order to resume my duties with LEHI.

My new headquarters were in Tel Aviv. My staff included a team in charge of developing munitions, a head supervisior in charge of all arms acquisitions and concealment, head operation planner, and head of operational data. All those departments operated in the Tel Aviv area and were directly accountable to me. Our operational units were located in Jerusalem, Tel Aviv, Haifa and the moshavot. In Tel Aviv the commander was Yaakov Banai (Mazal). In Jerusalem Yaakov Granek (Dov the "blond"). In Haifa Moshe Bar-Giora, my fellow-prisoner and escapee. In the moshavot Shlomo Yaakobi (Levi), who was a member of the first group of commanders I trained in Jerusalem right after the 1940 split.

The field commanders would report directly to me with their operation plans. I would not give my okay unless I could personally visit the venue and check out the details. After the operation was approved, I would bring it to the attention of the center and explain it briefly, mostly in political terms, since the center left the operational aspects to my judgment. After it was formally approved, I would issue an order to carry out the operation. Thus, for example, if we decided to place mines somewhere in order to blow up a military or police vehicle, the center would pick the appropriate time in terms of political significance, and the appropriate place in terms of the reactions of the nearest Jewish population. The operational head, however, would work out the details of the operation, the place of concealment, the vigilance, stages of operation and withdrawal.

Night of the Trains

On the night of January 11, 1945, LEHI and the Irgun demolished the railroad shops in Lod. That same night, the Haganah blew up railway lines throughout the country. The operation plan called for a massive attack on the railway lines system and on patrol boats guarding the shores against illegal Jewish immigrants. Fifty Palmach units with hundreds of men went into action that night and destroyed railway lines in 153 places. They concentrated on such vital points as junctions, bridges and culverts. That night the Palmach sunk three British patrol boats assigned to hunting immigrants, two in Haifa and one in Jaffa.

The blowing up of the railway lines by the Haganah had not been discussed by the joint command of the undergrounds. Yitzhak Sadeh had kept it a secret from the Irgun representative, Yeruham Livni, and from me. The plan for the destruction of the Haifa oil refinery, on the other hand, was brought up for discussion before the joint-action supreme committee, in which Golomb and Moshe Sneh represented the Haganah, Menahem Begin and Haim Landau represented the Irgun, and Yellin-Mor represented LEHI. The reason was the special political significance of the operation.

LEHI had discussed the refinery operation long before the united resistance came into being. We decided to do it as part of the new resistance movement. When Yellin-Mor brought it before the supreme committee, it refused to approve it. The matter was brought back to the center, and although Yellin-Mor argued it would wreck the united resistance, I insisted we go ahead with it on schedule, because of its political significance and because we should not let the Haganah think we were its patsies. Yellin-Mor stuck to his guns, but Shamir sided with me and the operation was carried out.

The attack on the railroad shops in Lod had been planned by Etan and myself. We visited the site, chose the objectives, determined how much explosives to use, studied the access and withdrawal routes, and decided on ways to secure the operation. This time Irgun units operated alongside ours. The LEHI force was commanded by Shaul Haglili, one of my Jerusalem trainees, who was later murdered by the British at the detention camp in Eritrea. His second-in-command was David Shomron. Each organization operated in its own assigned sector with good coordination. The units reached the place at 4:20 in the morning. They cut the fence and went into the shop area. They came under fire from all sides. They found two rows of locomotives, huge black monsters emitting heat and roaring with engine noise. the assault team divided into two: one put the bombs on the left row and the other on the right, inside and underneath the locomotives. A huge explosion was heard 200 yards away as the control tower went up in flames, followed by a series of explosions in which the locomotives blew up. A thick pillar of fire and smoke testified to the explosion of the fuel tank. All the charges worked well. The first Irgun-LEHI joint attack was a success. One Irgun member, Issahar Wigman (Moshe) died in action.

After that night, the railway system was paralyzed for a long time. The British authorities were aware of the cooperation among the three underground organizations. The joint operation nearly reached the dimensions of an all-out revolt against the British occupation forces.

Blowing Up the Refinery

The oil refinery in Haifa Bay was extremely vital for the British strategy in the Middle East. The destruction of the refinery, or at least part of the installations, was considered by the LEHI center a major blow to the enemy. As was mentioned before, we decided to carry out the operation against the objection of the supreme committee of Tenuat Hameri, disregarding the fact that it could wreck our partnership.

Our Haifa commander at that time was an outstanding fighter, Moshe Bar-Giora, who had escaped with me from the prison in Jerusalem. Because of the great importance of the operation, I decided to join him in preparing and commanding the operation.

Bar-Giora found out that a LEHI member, Moshe Artel, worked at the refinery. We met with him and instructed him to collect data, maps and charts, everything that had to do with the refinery layout and operation. We were looking to attack the most vital parts of the installations in order to inflict a major blow. The most vital point had to be hit first, followed by a chain of explosions and fires causing maximum damage.

A week later I had in my hands the plans of the refinery, thanks to Artel's diligence. I found out where they refined the highest octane gasoline, used for aircraft. I was also able to locate huge storage tanks for that fuel on the refinery tank farm. I pinpointed the place where the highest burning-point fuel was kept, and especially where the boiler room was, servicing the entire huge complex. After we had thoroughly studied the refinery, Bar-Giora and I infiltrated the plant dressed as two plant workers, and, guided by Artel, toured all the installations we had circled on the map. We estimated the explosion impact each item required. We measured the distances and time for the advance and withdrawal.

The British had anticipated an attack by the underground on those installations. The place was heavily guarded. On the grounds there were African soldiers. At the gates there were British policemen and detectives who thoroughly searched everyone going in and out.

After we decided on the routes for smuggling the explosives into the facilities, we determined the places for assembling the mines and the bombs, a starting point for concealing the mines, and a point of assembly in case of emergency and for the withdrawal. The bombs chosen for subverting the objectives were delayed-action bombs, time-bombs and dynamite sticks. For blowing up the tanks we prepared floating bombs. All the devices were made at our central lab under Frunin's supervision. Frunin was our bomb whiz. He was assisted by Yaakov Bentov. It took a long time to make all those things, and we checked each device over and over again.

After we finished preparing all the explosive devices, on which the success of the operation depended, we proceeded to study the question of introducing the material into the refinery. This was Artel's task. He would go to work with a false-bottom lunch box, in which we smuggled the explosives and the accessories. The police did not notice anything suspicious about a worker's lunch box. Artel would hide the stuff under a certain bridge, among the rocks, wrapped in plastic to keep it dry.

A few days before the joint actions of the united resistance began, I met with the operation team in Haifa. Bar-Giora lived on Mount Carmel, posing as a Technion student. He rented a room from a British engineer who worked at the refinery. Three men composed his team: Moshe Artel (Zvi), Avraham Yehudai (Elhanan), and Yaakov Greenberg (Dan). The latter had just left Tel Aviv where he had just been "burned out."

Dan was a cool man, level-headed and intrepid. He was a technical expert. He found lodgings with one of our supporters, and applied for a job at the refinery, which was offered to him after he was interviewd by a British engineer. He had to take a course in oil production. He showed special interest in the course, and got to know all the installations thoroughly. He then began to study the security arrangements of the plant. He was able to change shifts and was rotated to all three wings of the refinery. He learned all the production stages and knew all the passwords one needed to know in order to go in and out of the various areas.

Because of the importance of this operation, Bar-Giora insisted he wanted to take part in it in spite of his position as Haifa commander. I refused at first, but finally gave in. According to the plan, all the participants had to go in in the evening with the night shift, hide the bombs in the various locations, and leave the plant at 6 a.m. with the outgoing shift. The bombs were set to go off at 7:30 a.m. We had decided to alert the refinery management right before the explosion, in order to spare the lives of Jewish personnel. The searchlight system, the cement and barbed-wire walls, the sewage canal running around the facilities, made it clear to us there was no going back once we started. We knew we might be forced to fight with our back to the wall.

We made false ID cards for Yehudai, Bar-Giora and Artel. Each person received a double-bottom lunch box for carrying firing devices, a personal weapon, and detonators. Using deception, Greenberg was able to obtain the watchword for that night, and the four could move about freely.

On November 1, 1945, the night the three organizations were launching the united resistance by carrying out a joint strike against the British, I travelled from Tel Aviv to Haifa and walked into one of our hideouts on Mount Carmel. Bar-Giora was waiting for me with the equipment, ready for action, cool and composed. After we assembled everything, we went over all the details of the operation and considered every possible mishap. As the sun was setting it was time for me to go back to Tel Aviv. I shook Bar-Giora's hand and hugged him. He was one of our best and most beloved commanders. I did not know I was seeing him for the last time.

I went back into the cab that had brought me from Tel Aviv, dressed in my tuxedo, and sat next to my bride in her wedding gown. Next to the driver sat my bodyguard, also in tuxedo, and on my left sat the bride's sister. The cab was bedecked with flowers, as befitted a happy honeymoon couple. The British were usually taken in by this kind of a jolly sight, and did not bother to search the car.

After the operational team of four passed the inspection at the refinery gate, they went over to the bridge where the explosives had been concealed. The packages were taken out and brought over to a shelter, where Bar-Giora began to prepare the bombs. The objectives were located in three different directions. The team had to split and hide the bombs in the different spots, then regroup and wait for the night shift to finish. Bar-Giora finished assembling the first batch of explosives, intended for the refining pumps. It was a time bomb. He put the explosives in his lunch box. For some reason he shut the box too tight. An infernal explosion occurred.

The blast was terrific. Dan Greenberg was thrown back three yards and landed on his back. At first he could not see or hear anything. When he recovered his eyesight the shelter was a heap of rubble. Bar-Giora and Yehudai had remained inside and seemed to have been buried alive.

Artel, who had been standing guard, came back running, disheveled and wild-eyed. He pulled Greenberg away from the shelter entrance and tried to get inside. A fire raged inside and the smoke got into his eyes. Greenberg was bleeding and his clothes were on fire. In his pockets he had timers and detonators, which could explode any second. He tore off his clothes and remained in his underwear. Artel had not been wounded. He supported Greenberg and began to retreat from the place of the explosion. They climbed over the high fence, and swam across the 5–6-foot deep, 18-foot wide sewage canal. The cement wall on the other side was not hard to scale. They ran past the watch towers and the searchlights. In the distance they could hear explosions. It was the Haganah, blowing up railway lines. Artel carried Greenberg on his back for several miles until they reached a flour mill. Good Jews took care of them. Greenberg was taken by ambulance to Hadassah Hospital, and was whisked away the next day by our men, under the noses of the British who came to search for wounded terrorists.

During the explosion Yehudai had stood directly behind Bar-Giora. One of his eyes was torn out of its socket. He bled profusely, but did not pass out. He decided all was lost. He took out his gun and headed for the fence. He climbed over two fences and crawled under a watch tower. When the light was flashed around him he lay motionless. He crawled on until he reached the highway. Pain shot through him and his thirst became unbearable. He struggled back on his feet and looked for water, then collapsed on the sand. He made a final effort and reached the murky Kishon River, where he washed his face with a piece of cloth torn from his shirt and wiped the coagulated blood. About to pass out, he kept moving until he reached some bushes where he was able to hide. Paralyzed with pain, his teeth chattering from the cold, he lay there, barely conscious.

At dawnbreak he was somewhat revived and managed to reach a friend's house in Haifa. After he recovered he wrote the following: "I am now healthy and strong again, and I can see well enough with my remaining eye to fight the occupiers of my land."

Four men had gone out on a mission. Bar-Giora was killed. Yehudai, Artel and Greenberg had extricated themselves from the jaws of death, because they wanted to go on fighting. Artel and Yehudai were back in Haifa Bay shortly after the refinery mission, to take part in the LEHI attack on the railroad shops. They were both killed in action. Only Dan Greenberg survived.

The Attack on the CID Headquarters

In December 1945, the Irgun and LEHI, represented by Yeruham Livni and myself respectively, came before Tenuat Hameri with a plan of attack on CID headquarters in Jerusalem. Yitzhak Sadeh, chairman of the supreme command, approved the plan. He requested that we blow up the front building of the department on Jaffa Road, where files on Haganah members were kept. We readily agreed. It was exactly what we had in mind.

In those days the CID headquarters were housed in several buildings at the Russian Compound in the heart of Jerusalem. There were other central government buildings in the compound, including the high court of appeals. But the CID buildings were the most heavily guarded, since the British knew that sooner or later they would be the target of an underground attack. The headquarters had been attacked before, causing losses to the British. Consequently the area was secured with cement pillboxes, barbed-wire, high walls and mobile security units equipped with armored cars and half-tracks. One of the buildings, as was mentioned before, jutted toward Jaffa Road, a teeming Jerusalem Street, and was more vulnerable than the rest. This was the first premise of my plan of attack.

Since they could not include that building in the defense system

The British Police headquarters in Jerusalem reduced to rubble by the underground.

surrounding the rest of the complex, the British compensated by placing several gun positions on the edges of the compound around the building. My plan was based on the following elements: a) Units armed with Bren machine guns would draw the fire of the British positions, as other units attacked those positions and overran them. b) Men on the roofs of nearby buildings, especially the Generali building across the street, would open fire on buildings where special British units were quartered, keeping them at bay and preventing them from reinforcing the attacked positions. c) The access routes to the CID headquarters would be sealed off by our men to stop mobile units from coming in. d) At that moment British army camps in the Jerusalem area would come under attack to stop reinforcement from being rushed to the area. After everything was properly secured, the demolition team, headed by Dov the ''blond,'' would approach the building, blow up the gate, place the explosives and the delayed-action devices, and withdraw. The bombs would then go off and the building would go up in smoke.

Next to the place where the teams had to break into the building there was a cement pillbox with machine gun holes protecting the building. In order for the operation to succeed, this position had to be silenced. The first volley, therefore, was earmarked for this position. In addition, we had to make sure no one would reinforce that position after it came under attack. I put Dov in charge of that task, placing him across the street inside the entrance to the Feingold Building. From there he would proceed to carry on the main mission inside the CID headquarters.

Around 7:30 p.m. the neighborhood around the Russian Compound was dark. An occasional private car or armored vehicle would pass by, or a lone Jerusalemite would hurry by bundled in a long winter coat because of the cold. The moon kept peeking out of the clouds, playing hide-and-seek. Our men took their positions, ready for action. The first volley was fired around 7:45, directed at that pillbox which blocked the approach to the gate. His finger on the trigger, Dov waited for the three guards to come out of their shelter. As soon as they showed up they came under fire from three positions.

All three dropped, and the road was cleared. The three crawled for shelter. At that moment fire was opened on the more remote British positions, and the access routes to the area were blocked. Units hiding outside the perimeter of British army camps around the city began to pin down the reinforcements. The main battle, however, took place at the gate of the headquarters. As soon as Dov began to advance toward the gate, a British officer heading a security team came running down the street. Dov knew that if that officer reached the fortified position the entire operation might fail. He remained standing in the middle of the street and opened fire on the officer who was now only twenty yards away. The officer was armed with a submachine gun. The two warriors squared off, their faces illumined by the fire our men had started down the street to block the road. They fired at each other at close range, as if engaged in a prearranged gun duel. Dov stood there face to face with his rival, his shirt torn and his blond hair disheveled. The officer was mortally wounded. He collapsed in the middle of the street. Dov, also wounded and bleeding, gave the order to charge the building.

In a few minutes the gate was blown and the team went inside the building. They placed the bombs, ignited the fuses and withdrew. Dov fired a rocket to signal the withdrawal. As the road-blocking fires burned in the streets, the units withdrew in an orderly fashion and went back into hiding.

Dov was attended to by our medical team. He had a wound in his chest. The wound was not critical, but he had lost a great deal of blood and needed a blood transfusion. We were able to give him a transfusion in our makeshift clinic, and that same night we transferred him in a roundabout way to Raanana, north of Tel Aviv. The next day I went to visit him. He had rested and was in high spirits. I shook his hand and hugged him. He reminded me of an earlier operation he had commanded which had failed, and added: "You see, I have made up for Tel Litvinsky." I told him "Not only did you make up for it, with your success in Jerusalem you have given LEHI back its reputation as a fighting force. You will bring LEHI more victories and honor than anyone who preceded you." Indeed Dov went on to become a living legend until he died in action in Israel's War of Independence at Nitzana (Uja al-Hafir). In that war he served again under my command, this time as company commander in the Israel Defense Army.

The CID headquarters collapsed, and all the secret files with all the data about the Haganah and its command disappeared. The operation made a great impact throughout the country and abroad. The question was raised in the British Parliament: "How could the Hebrew underground penetrate the innermost chambers of the CID and demolish one of its strongolds?" Yitzhak Sadeh praised the planning and the execution of the plan. He called it a masterpiece of small-unit warfare. The effect on the foreign occupier was fear and dismay.

A Trap in Ramat Gan

A week after the blowing up of the CID headquarters in Jerusalem, the Irgun confiscated a large quantity of weapons from the British Army depot at the fair grounds in Tel Aviv. During the withdrawal the attackers ran into a British ambush and suffered losses. The wounded were transferred to Ramat Gan, a place congenial to the underground. I was in Ramat Gan that weekend for talks with our command, and on Friday night I went to visit the Halpern family, since I felt like spending the Sabbath with friends rather than alone.

Gamliel Halpern and his family welcomed me and I was asked to join their Sabbath meal. It was a pleasant evening, and after I retired for the night Gami Halpern woke me up and told me the British had imposed a curfew on Ramat Gan and were looking for underground members.

I looked outside and realized the town was surrounded with British soldiers and armored cars. I knew I had to get away, since I did not want to implicate my hosts. As I was trying to decide what to do there was a knock on the door. Five British soldiers broke in and ordered all the men to come with them. I knew that they could easily identify me, and I was in for trouble.

As we were taken out of the house I decided to escape. We were led in an Indian file with guards all around us. However, as we passed by a low garden hedge I managed to duck and I rolled over the hedge and disappeared on the other side. I lay in the mud, covered with twigs for a long time. Several hours later I emerged from my hiding place and walked toward a two-story house to look for a hiding place. Two women saw me, all covered with mud. One clasped her hands and cried, "Oh, my poor child, come, I will hide you."

I hid in her house until evening, when I heard her call out: "The search is over. You can come out now." She gave me a good meal and sent me on my way.

THIRTY-ONE

Going Down to Egypt

After our operational commanders had established a record of successful operations, I felt it was time for me to leave the command in their hands and go abroad to fight the British in their own backyard. It was decided that on my way to Europe I would stop in Egypt and try to organize some activities in that country. At that time Egypt was the most important British military base in the entire Middle East, from where they ruled our country as well. I maintained that if the Hebrew underground could remove the British from our land we would inspire other freedom movements throughout the British Empire to do the same. I also believed that if we carried our war against the British abroad and struck out at them in strategic centers, especially in their own capital, we might win. The LEHI center accepted my proposal and decided that after I passed the command to several experienced LEHI commanders, I would go to Egypt and from there continue to Europe and begin preparing our base of operations against the British on the continent.

In those days I would occasionally see my girlfriend, Hannah. I took many precautions in arranging our meetings in order to outwit the British who kept a constant surveillance over her. We began to discuss marriage, and when I was getting ready to go abroad, Hannah promised to wait for me and join me at the first opportunity. In order to put a fait accompli before Hannah's family, we decided to become engaged before I left. Hannah's father, a wealthy merchant, member of an old prominent Jerusalem family, did not imagine in his wildest dreams that his beloved daughter had chosen a man who had just escaped from prison, was wanted by the British who had set a reward for him, who any day could be mowed down by British bullets. On the eve of my departure we became engaged before an underground rabbi in Givat Shmuel with Hannah's father's blessing.

One sunny morning I boarded the train in Tel Aviv and travelled to Egypt disguised as a British sergeant. In Qantara, near the Suez Canal, I changed trains and continued to Alexandria. That same day I went to see my contact and, after I was given civilian clothes and the documents of a seaman, I moved into my prearranged lodgings in that city and began my activities.

The three large cities of Egypt—Alexandria, Ismailia and Cairo—were surrounded by British army barracks where a good number of my compatriots, serving under the Union Jack, were stationed. I kept shuttling to those three cities, organizing a LEHI cell in each one of them. I would hold meetings with the cell members and instruct them in accordance with the four principles of LEHI: ideological indoctrination, character building, weapons, and underground operational techniques. I concentrated mainly on this last area, since I was eager to begin local operations as soon as possible.

With the help of our members under uniform I began to collect data on important objectives in Cairo. My main objective was the British Middle East headquarters in Cairo. Aharonson, one of our members, served at headquarters, and gave me a full disclosure of the layout and inner workings of the place. After I analyzed the material I concluded it would be easy to introduce a bomb in a suitcase or a coat to the munitions depot at headquarters, and cause an explosion that would reverberate around the world. After working on the project for a whole month I came up with a detailed plan. Since the depot had a common wall with the office of the British commander in chief, I thought we had a chance not only to blow up the facility but the head man as well. To my regret, I found out the chief had gone on a Middle East tour and would not be back for two months.

After much thought I decided it was worth my while to wait for two months, and in the meantime plan another operation. I also began to look into purchasing arms and transferring them back home. There were great quantities of all sorts of war materiel abandoned in the western desert, where for several years the British fought the Italians and the Germans. During their advances and retreats, those fighting forces had left behind tons of materiel on the ground or in underground storage. The Bedouins roaming the area collected the weapons and equipment and kept it, and had started to sell it to the highest bidder. I occupied myself with arms purchases for a while, and was able to send a truckload of arms to our forces at home through the good offices of the Haganah agents who specialized in that sort of operation.

I now became interested in the idea of a bomb attack on a British destroyer. Those destroyers, docked at the Alexandria harbor, were used for intercepting Jewish immigrant boats and taking the immigrants to detention camps in Cyprus (in the case of the ship *Exodus*, they took Holocaust survivors back to Germany). I knew that some of my compatriots served on those ships and frequently sailed from Alexandria to Haifa. One such man, Peter Partosh, was a recently arrived Jewish survivor from Hungary, who had joined the Royal Navy. When he saw what the British were doing to Jewish immigrants on the Mediterranean he immediately joined LEHI and expressed his willingness to do whatever I asked of him. When I first met Partosh I knew he was a highly reliable man. I offered him the mission and he accepted immediately. After I obtained a plan of the destroyer *Chevron*, specializing in hunting immigrants in the eastern Mediterranean, I instructed Partosh on how to install a powerful bomb in his knapsack. We arranged for him to leave his knapsack near the munitions storage of the ship, so as to produce a big enough explosion to sink the ship. We put 44 pounds of high explosives in his knapsack, enough to sink the ship. He decided to detonate it when the destroyer reached Haifa harbor. He made all the necessary preparations, and seemed to have everything under control. He made, however, the mistake of letting a friend of his know about the operation, in order to have that friend provide him with cover. The friend did not have any underground training, and for some reason aroused suspicion. One of the ship officers took him in for questioning. The man yielded to pressure and told the officer about Partosh's plan. Partosh was arrested, court-martialed in Haifa and given six years in jail. Later on, when the *Chevron* came to Belgium on a courtesy and show of force visit, I tried to sink it again, this time in my capacity as LEHI commander in Europe.

After six months in Egypt I took stock of my accomplishments in that country. I had organized cells in the three large cities, with a mixture of Jewish soldiers from the British army and local Jewish youth. The cell members had become well trained. My arms purchases were successful, while the sinking of the destroyer had failed. We kept looking for ways to ship arms to our people at home and continued to work on a daring attack on the British military headquarters in Cairo. All in all, morale in our Egypt branch was high, now that the local leaders had recovered from the setback they had suffered because of the assassination of Lord Moyne.

I now felt I could transfer the command in Egypt to someone else and go to Europe to export our war of liberation to London, the nerve center of the foreign occupier. The original plan had called for my staying in Egypt for only six months, and then go to Europe to establish a fighting LEHI unit that would begin operating in London. I had complete freedom of action, and could decide on the type and time of operations in the enemy's capital. I wrote Shamir and told him about my forthcoming trip. He wrote me back a long letter in which he mentioned the fiasco of the attack on the railroad shops in Haifa, and the high number of young commanders—my former trainees—who had fallen. He did not say anything about my coming back home to take charge again of the operational command, but I could tell that he was hinting I should do it. I faced a serious dilemma. After much soul-searching I came to the conclusion that the place where I could be most effective was in London. I did not give up my plan to go to Europe.

Before I left for Europe I had to bring over my fiancee, since I had promised her I would not leave Egypt without her. Fortunately, five of our members were about to go to Jerusalem on a short leave, and they agreed to bring Hannah back with them. Hannah was given a British auxiliary corps uniform and forged documents, and joined those five soldiers on their return trip to Egypt.

We decided not to waste any more time and get married. Asher Rivlin, a chaplain of the Jewish Brigade in Egypt and a friend of mine from my Irgun days in Jerusalem, agreed to marry us. After five years of courtship, we finally became married.

I started preparing for our trip to Europe. First I arranged myself a temporary Egyptian travel document. The secretary of the Jewish community in Cairo gave me a birth certificate which stated I was born in Egypt. I took Hannah to the French consul in Alexandria and told him we wished to spend our honeymoon in France. We were young and well dressed and we must have made a good impression on the consul. He gave us a visa for three months.

Everything was ready for our trip. But the money I had received from the underground six months earlier was running out. The money Hannah had brought with her was not enough for the trip. As we were trying to find a way to finance our trip, we unexpectedly ran into Hannah's parents on one of the main thoroughfares of Alexandria. They had come to Egypt to see us, but missed us in Cairo and followed us to Alexandria without our knowledge. They told us they were going on a trip to Marseilles. I immediately decided we would go with them, since it was common in Egypt for a couple to have the bride's parents accompany them on their honeymoon. They were happy to have us come along, and Hannah's father was glad to pay for our trip.

We passed the harbor inspection without a hitch. Everyone congratulated the newlyweds and the proud parents of the bride, and we sailed to Marseilles to begin our underground work in France aimed at London, the capital of the foreign occupier.

From Marseilles we took the train to Paris and checked into the Grand Lafayette Hotel, near the Cadet metro station. Not wasting any time, I started to set up LEHI's headquarters in Paris for Europe as well as the United States. My goal was to establish a center as important as the one back home, drawing on the resources of the Jews in the Western world, and perhaps also the equally great potential of Britain's enemies in the Middle East.

THIRTY-TWO

Second Front in Europe

When I arrived in France I had the addresses of several LEHI sympathizers, as well as the address of a writer named Knut, a hero of the French Resistance during World War Two. I contacted him and explained to him the objectives of our struggle. He told me he was an ardent supporter of LEHI, but was busy with his literary work and the Jewish Center he headed in Paris. He referred me to his stepdaughter, Betty Knut-Lazarus, a brave young woman who had also been active in the anti-Nazi underground in France and had a circle of friends supportive of the fight for a Jewish state. I met with Betty and she became an important contact. She put me in touch with people who soon began to organize secret cells of French Jewish students, and even some Christians, who were sympathetic toward our cause. Some of those people were ex-Resistance members, and they helped us obtain pistols, submachine guns and especially explosives and other materials for making bombs.

Next I began to organize an underground rear. The rear cosisted of Jews who had some economic base in Paris, such as real estate, factories, warehouses, etc. All those were needed for training, arms storage, labs, and support systems. The head of our group of friends was a French Jew named Schumacher, who owned a pants factory. His apartment, factory and warehouses became our base of operations in France.

We began to attract important sympathizers, including Sorbonne professors, the most famous of whom was Jean Paul Sartre, who supported us during our entire struggle. We got special help from members of the chemistry and bacteriology faculties, including scientists of the Pasteur Institute. Among our supporters were former pilots who had served in the Middle East, and were able to provide us with vital information on such secret matters as British installations in Iraq. One of our greatest supporters was a famous French Jewish physician, who lived in one of the richest suburbs of Paris. His palatial home was a regular hideout for our men who went on missions to London. Those supporters gave us some material support as well, but we did most of our fund-raising among larger groups of Jews and Christians who contributed generously. The money we raised financed our operations in Europe and was also used to buy arms for our people back home.

While preparing our base of operations, I also worked on establishing two other important institutions: our information and propaganda department, and our political department. The first was run by Betty, who was a talented writer and journalist and put us in touch with the editors of all the important newspapers in Paris as well as foreign correspondents, especially Americans.

Those editors and correspondents helped me publicize the work of LEHI, transmit orders of the day, and give interviews. The interviews were given under the veil of secrecy, with the interviewee, usually myself, sitting behind a screen hidden from the interviewer. One day, for instance, I met Moshe Perlman, a writer of the Paris-based American newspaper *The New York Herald Tribune*. We met at the George the Fifth Hotel in Paris, while the British delegation to the peace conference, headed by Foreign Minister Ernest Bevin, was staying in the upper floors of the hotel. The hotel was heavily guarded against Jewish terrorists, but Perlman was able to obtain a pass for me. During the interview I told Perlman that if LEHI had not given its promise not to violate France's neutrality, it would have blown up the hotel without any difficulty and reduced it to a heap of rubble, as had been done to the King David Hotel in Jerusalem. The proof lay in the fact that I was able to walk past all the guards and enter the hotel. Perlman published the interview the next day and the British were aghast. I found out later on from a reliable source that despite the good care British security forces took of him, Bevin would never go to bed without first checking under his bed to make sure someone had not left a bomb.

Negotiations with France

Our information department in Paris issued a monthly publication called *L'Endependence*, the organ of the Fighters for the Freedom of Israel in Europe which had wide circulation. In addition we would send propaganda material through the mail to public figures, newspapers and all the diplomatic corps. Through our center in Paris I hoped to cultivate relations with major countries who might help us with our quest for independence. My most important contact was with France itself, since France resented the fact that England had forced it out of its sphere of influence in the Near East. At that time we had a representative in Beirut named Gabriel Messeri, a senior LEHI commander, who met with Colonel Alexandre, De Gaulle's man in Beirut. The two discussed French cooperation with LEHI's struggle against the British, in the form of weapons, training and political support. The colonel told Museri he was about to be transferred to France and it would be desirable for a LEHI representative in France to get in touch with him in order to look further into the idea of French help to LEHI. Before I left for Egypt, I had spoken to Shamir about it and agreed to get in touch with Alexandre when I got to Paris.

It was easier said than done. I had no way of finding out where that person was. I finally decided to get in touch with the French Foreign Ministry. One morning I went to Quai d'Orcey and walked in with such self-assurance that the guard did not bother to ask me for an ID. I followed the sign to the Middle East section. I asked for the chief, and was shown into an office. The chief received me cordially and asked me who my liaison was. I now realized he thought I was a French agent who had instructions to see him. He did not ask for my name or where I came from. Instead, he waited to hear what I had to say. I strained to control myself and told him I was indeed from the Middle East, but I had come to see Colonel Alexandre. He told me Alexandre was now the governor of Bizerte, Tunisia, and would be back in Paris in a few months. If I cared to leave him my address, he would put me in touch with him. I refused, but asked for the colonel's address so I could communicate with him in writing.

I had written Alexandre twice, but did not get an answer. One month after my visit to the Foreign Ministry the concierge of my humble hotel informed me a veryimportant person had come to see me. I quickly put on my coat and tie and went downstairs. A tall, aristocratic-looking Frenchman stood there, with a stick, a monocle and a top hat. After he verified my identity he embraced me like an old friend. We chatted for a few minutes, and he told me he would put me in touch with certain French institutions in order to begin negotiations. He also explained how I could get in touch with him. Since he was staying in Paris only for a month, he hoped to get back to me in a week or two. We agreed that no negotiations would start until we had time to form our own delegation.

That same evening I informed our center by coded message about my meeting with Alexandre, and suggested they send a team to initiate official negotiations. A few days later Gabriel Messeri and Yaakov Yardor arrived, and I invited our man in Rome, Avraham Blas, to join us. We arranged a meeting with Alexandre on the second floor of Cafe Fleur in Saint Germain de-Pres.

Opposite us sat a French delegation made up of four men, headed by Andre Blumel, former official in Leon Blum's government. Blumel at that time was performing important missions for the French government. He was a Jew, a Zionist, a former president of the Zionist Federation of France. He believed that only by fighting the British we could achieve independence. For this reason he agreed to head the delegation. We could tell he was friendly to our cause. To the French, the basis for negotiations was the struggle against the Muslim Algerian insurgents, who at that time fought the French with increasing fury. They also wanted us to remember France after we got our independence and help her return to the Levant. We for our part asked the French for arms and for a secret base for war against London. We also wanted to openly train Jews from the DP camps in France, and open a radio station, called The Voice of Reborn Zion, which would broadcast around the world.

The French wrote down our demands during the first meeting. Blumel told us he was authorized to tell us in the name of the French government that the government was willing in principle to sign an agreement with LEHI, and only needed a few days to fully study the matter. Before we adjourned he gave me his business card and told me if I needed anything in the meantime he would be glad to help me. Later on I did need his help. In fact, he practically saved my life.

The second and third meetings took pace without Blumel and Alexandre (the latter had returned to his post in Bizerte). We met at a Latin Quarter restaurant with military experts and discussed the types and quantities of weapons we needed in order to train our men, as well as the training camps. We also talked about the type and power of the transmitter we needed for our radio station. The French agreed to let our men train in their officers' school in small-unit warfare. But they seemed most interested in the possibility of LEHI operations in Algeria. They argued that only an underground could beat another underground, albeit the Algerian one had become quite strong by then. The French military personnel listened to us in rapt attention as we spoke about underground warfare. They were unfamiliar with the subject, and did not know how to go about fighting an underground.

During those technical meetings we had the feelings we were nearing an agreement. But when we met for the fourth time, Blumel came and said that although everyone seemed satisfied with the technical meetings, and we could certainly have a most fruitful cooperation, there were certain difficulties. The French government had studied the matter, and decided that it could not act openly, since it might get into political trouble with the British. It was therefore looking into implementing the plan clandestinely. But even if it took a long time to put the agreement into effect, he, Blumel, hoped that LEHI got all the assistance it needed in its struggle against the British.

We continued to meet with Blumel alone at Cafe Fleur. The meetings helped us form an ongoing contact with the French government through a man who did wonders in that role, Dr. Shmuel Ariel. With the help of Madame Vidra, an outstanding woman who was a hero of the French underground and had great influence in the French government after the liberation of France, Dr. Ariel was able to persuade the government to help Jewish refugees under its jurisdiction, and to assist the activities of the Irgun and LEHI in France. Thanks to him we could, for instance, obtain French travel documents and move freely throughout Europe. He also persuaded the government to allow us to use Paris as our base of operations against London. Ariel met frequently with French security officers, and as a result of his meetings we were given a free hand on condition that our operations emanated not directly from France but from neighboring countries, in order not to implicate France in a diplomatic conflict with England.

Some limits were set on our activities. Thus, for example, when the King of England came to Paris for a visit, the British security agents asked their French counterparts to keep Shamir and myself away from the capital. Through Ariel, the French security service asked that the two of us go to a resort town on the Spanish border during the king's visit. Ariel also helped procure arms for the underground from the French arsenal. Thanks to his activities, the French allowed a large supply of weapons to be sent on the ship *Altalena* which was loaded at the French Riviera. Hundreds of French army trucks brought the materiel directly from the army depot to the ship to be used in the war for Israel's independence. I had the historical privilege of witnessing the loading of the *Altalena*, since LEHI also loaded weapons on that ship.

Bombs in London

My political advisor during my operations against London was Alexander Aaronsohn. His brother, Aaron Aaronsohn, headed Nili, the first Hebrew underground in the twentieth century. Nili helped the British remove the Turks and their German allies from the Land of Israel in World War One, and rumor had it Alexander Aaronsohn, using his family contacts with British intelligence, continued to serve the British for many years. In any case, before the end of the Mandate, when the struggle of the Hebrew underground reached its peak, Aaronsohn disavowed his loyalty to Great Britain and offered to help LEHI. He lived in Paris, and was convinced that in order to get rid of the British one had to strike them full-force in their own capital. He gave up all his other interests and devoted all his time to LEHI. Aaronsohn had excellent connections in the French capital. He helped me with funds, put his Terminus Hotel near the Saint Lazarre train station at my disposal, offered me his car and his chauffeur and even his apartments and villas. In short, he did not spare anything that could help our cause. But most important was his political counselling. He told us that we had to concentrate on attacking the British leadership, especially the government members, as well as the Parliament, the House of Lords, etc. He also urged us to attack public institutions in order to cause hardship to the British public. He gave us specific places to strike at, and told us how much force to use. After each operation he would provide me with first-hand information on the reaction of the British government and its institutions, and would advise me on how to get the most publicity out of an operation and increase its impact.

For our first operation in London I chose a young French citizen named Martinsky, who fought with the Resistance and joined De Gaulle's army before the liberation. He had lost a leg in the war and had an artificial limb. Despite all he had been through, he was an ardent follower of LEHI, a brave man who performed well under pressure. I chose him for the London operation because of his qualities, his artificial leg, and the fact that his French citizenship enabled him to travel to England without a visa.

I gave Martinsky a quick yet thorough training in order to prepare him for the operation in London. The objective was the British War Office. The method used was sending a package addressed to a well-known general, at that office. The general we had chosen was a former commander of the British occupational army in the Land of Israel. His section of the War Office was in charge of developing weapons. They received all sorts of packages, which contained many different items used in their work. I therefore chose a package that would not arouse any suspicion, was sure to reach its destination and do its job. I received my information, of course, from Aaronsohn, who was familiar with all the government offices. I didn't tell him what specifically I intended to do with the information. I decided to have Martinsky send the War Office a box with a Mills grenade with the safety fuse removed and the cap placed directly on the detonator, after it was filled with quick burning gunpowder. Thus, when the lever released the striking pin, it would strike the cap and ignite it, the cap in turn would ignite the gunpowder which would ignite the mercury fulminate inside the detonator and cause the explosion.

After the grenade was ready, I took it apart and hid it in Martinsky's artificial leg. At the London airport each person underwent a thorough check. Martinsky arrived at the airport wearing his World War Two French decorations. He passed the search without a hitch and when he arrived in London he went to the post office and received a registered letter.

In the envelope he found a key to a deposit compartment at the Victoria railway station. In the compartment he found official British wrappers and an envelope used for official British mailing. Martinsky assembled the grenade and wrapped it, then put it in the envelope. He put on the official label and the wax seal with the imprint of the British crown. On the label was the name and address of the general at the British War Office. On top it said "Personal and Confidential," to make sure no one besides the general would open it.

It was late afternoon, the time when British government offices brought their mail to the main post office near Trafalgar Square. We hoped the package would reach its destination only the next day, in order to give Martinsky time to return to Paris safely. Indeed, one hour after the package was mailed I was sitting with Martinsky in Paris, I shook his hand and we drank to the success of the operation, as I used to do back home.

The next day, around 11:00 a.m., the package exploded in the

British War Office. The general and other officials were seriously wounded, and considerable damage was caused to the building. By 12:00 we had sent a press release to embassies and newspapers in Paris and London disclosing the identity of the perpetrators. The British government was shocked and angered. It realized a second front had been established in the war for the liberation of the Land of Israel. The British knew it was only the first salvo and there was more to come. Scotland Yard was alerted immediately and all government offices were put under tight security. Each minister was assigned a full-time bodyguard and would not go anywhere without a detective escort car to protect him from the Jewish terrorists who had now reached London.

Czech Jew made bomb in Whitehall

Named by Yard

From Daily Mail Correspondent

PARIS, Thursday.

A CAREFULLY - GUARDED packet brought over to Paris by Inspector Jones, of Scotland Yard, has started a nation-wide hunt in France for the Jewish terrorist believed to have made the bomb found at the Colonial Office in London.

From the packet Inspector Jones drew a photograph of the suspect, a Jacob Levestein, 35-year-old Czech Jew, with his finger-prints and other information.

After a conference with French detective chiefs Inspector Jones hurried back to London.

The hunt for Levestein is complicated because he has not been in police hands before, and there is also a woman in the case—the unidentified dark-haired woman who planted the bomb

It seems possible that she smuggled the bomb into England from the Continent, where it was made by Levestein.

He may be hiding in the British or French zones of Germany, where search is also being made. Should he be found in France, he will be extradited immediately.

Levestein.

Whitehall bomb was operation of war, says Stern girl

NEWS CHRONICLE REPORTER

A WOMAN who identified herself as a spokesman for the "Stern Gang group of fighters for the liberty of Israel" telephoned the Paris office of the Associated Press last night and dictated this statement in French :

"On April 15 at 10.55 o'clock the British Colonial Ministry, centre of the fight against the Jews, was attacked by our fighters in London.

"In spite of the rigorous surveillance exercised by Scotland Yard our fighters succeeded in penetrating into the very heart of the Empire to carry out an operation of war.

"The Jewish war of liberation will go on wherever the British flag flies."

Stocking ruse

A young Jewess is suspected of placing a time bomb found in Dover House, Whitehall, part of the Colonial Office

This girl called at the building on Tuesday afternoon and asked in broken English if she could be shown a place where she might repair a ladder in her stocking

She was carrying a parcel.

Permission was given, and it is believed that she went to the cloakroom. There, at 6.30 a.m. yesterday, the bomb was found by Mrs. H. E Greenstock, 52-year-old cleaner

The building was immediately cleared and Scotland Yard officers were called in.

French type

The explosive was sent to the Home Office, where experts found it to be of a type made in France and never previously encountered in this country.

Its explosion was timed to coincide with the hanging of Dov Gruner and three other terrorists at Acre. But there was a fault. The bomb did not go off as planned.

A full description of the young Jewess was obtained from officials who spoke to her. She is believed to have come from the Continent, and Scotland Yard are satisfied that they know her identity.

The operation, like any other successful operation, gave new impetus to our people in Paris and London. After the explosion at the War Office I continued to plan additional attacks on government institutions in London. I sent Betty Knut to London. She entered the British Colonial Office with explosive charges, which she left in one of the bathrooms. The package was discovered and dismantled, but the psychological impact was strong. Betty returned safely to Paris. For a while, she went into hiding at one of our supporter's homes in the south of France.

Shortly after the placing of the bomb at the Colonial Office, a delegation from that office visited the Sorbonne in Paris. One of Jean Paul Sartre's students was assigned as the host of the British delegation. The student, Robert Mizrahi, happened to be a LEHI member. Following my instructions, Mizrahi was most attentive toward the British visitors. Before they left, several members of the delegation insisted on hosting Mizrahi in London. He thanked them and accepted the invitation. After he told me about it I proceeded to make plans for getting the most out of our member's visit to the British Colonial Office.

I learned from Mizrahi the Colonial Office had an exclusive club for the senior officials. It was one of the places he was going to visit while in London. I reached the conclusion that the most appropriate weapon on this visit would be an explosive coat, like the one I invented and used in 1939 in the bombing of the Rex Theater in Jerusalem. Mizrahi wrote to one of the officials he had befriended, and the latter responded with a cordial invitation.

We bought Mizrahi a heavy overcoat, British style, to make him feel at home in London. I took out the shoulder pads and filled the spaces with blasting gelatin, which had been improved during World War Two and was much more powerful now than back in 1939. I gave him my ordinary wrist watch, the kind I had modified back in those days and used with many explosive devices. I taught Mizrahi how to set the watch and connect it before he went to the club. I checked the whole system carefully and found it to be in good working order. The electric detonators worked well, as did the watch.

Upon arrival in England, Mizrahi was carefully searched. His coat was found to be well made by British standards. In London Mizrahi got in touch with his good friend at the Colonial Office, who was happy to see him and proceeded to introduce him to the other members of the delegation who had visited the Sorbonne. The friend took Mizrahi to visit the sights of London, as well as government institutions. Mizrahi was treated like an important guest, and was invited to lecture at the Colonial Office about English-French relations. When his week-long visit was about to end, he was invited to an early supper at the club (it had to be early because of the fear of Jewish terrorists). That day the staff only worked half a day, and many staff members stayed at the club after lunch for a game or a chat. The club was full of senior officials, and the timing for a terrorist bomb was most appropriate.

Mizrahi prepared the explosive coat. He checked the electric connections, the batteries and the detonators. He also checked the timer, and carefully calculated the time. He knew exactly how long the meal would last, and figured the time it would take him to reach the airport by cab. After he had gone over everything several times, he put on his coat and went to the club.

WHITEHALL BOMB: HUNT FOR WOMAN

KNOWN TO BE JEWISH TERRORIST AGENT

FINGERPRINT FOUND ON TIMING DEVICE

MINISTERS' DOUBLE GUARD: WATCH AT STATIONS

DAILY TELEGRAPH REPORTER

Scotland Yard was last night trying to trace a smartly dressed Jewess of foreign extraction, aged apparently about 30. She is known to have planted a time-bomb in the Colonial Office, Dover House, Whitehall.

Guards on Ministers have been doubled. Police have been reinforced at all Government buildings. Special watch is being kept at cloak rooms at London railway termini and at Tube stations.

The bomb was found in a cloak room at Dover House just before seven o'clock yesterday morning. Last night's action followed consultations between Special Branch detectives and high officials of the Paris Sûreté and the Military Intelligence in Palestine and London.

The detectives have found a smudged fingerprint inside the case of a watch attached to the bomb and have a detailed description of the woman supplied by a member of the Colonial Office staff who saw her.

He went up the stairs and before entering the hall he hung his coat in the coatroom adjacent to the hall. He disregarded good English manners by ignoring the coatman and reaching over the counter and hanging the coat himself. The coatman forgave him, as he muttered to himself, "What can you expect from a Frenchman?" After he hung up his coat he walked into the hall. Here he was greeted by his friends whom he thanked for their wonderful hospitality. After the meal he said goodbye to his hosts, who knew he was going back to France that same afternoon. As good Englishmen who respect their guest's wishes, they did not ask him to stay longer. He thanked them again and departed. No one noticed he had forgotten his coat.

PACKED LONDON CLUB BLOWS UP: BOMB FEAR

SCOTLAND YARD called in a Home Office explosives expert after a suggestion that a bomb caused an explosion which last night wrecked part of a crowded Colonial men's club near St. Martin-in-the-Fields Church, London.

A fire officer thought a butterfly bomb was the cause.

Three coloured Servicemen were taken to hospital. Two were detained, one badly hurt.

Broken window frames and doors hurtled into St. Martin's-lane. Plaster and glass-splinters sprinkled on passers-by.

Ambulances and fire engines rushed to the club, in St. Martin's place. A first-aid unit treated casualties.

Part of the lane was cordoned off as police and firemen with torches searched the building. A second explosion was feared.

A senior fire officer ruled out a gas-leak as the cause—"there was no smell."

The Home Office expert left after fifteen minutes. "It was too dark inside. I shall have to see the building in daylight to make any conclusion."

Mr. S. E. Weller, Colonial Office Welfare Department, was sitting in his first-floor office when the explosion blew the door on to his head.

"I was choked with dust, but I managed to scramble out of the debris," he said.

Coloured airmen and seamen were playing draughts. Carlton Welsh, a Jamaican, said:

"The room shook, lights went out and I felt the debris falling all round me. I got out by climbing down a fire escape."

Two men were stopped from jumping out of a window.

Mizrahi walked out briskly and flagged a cab. He did not want to miss the plane to Paris. According to his calculation, the bomb had to go off while the plane was in the air. Indeed, as soon as the wheels left the runway the coat exploded in the Colonial Office. The damage was extensive. Several officials were killed and dozens wounded. As Mizrahi sat in front of me in Paris we had already heard the report on the BBC evening news. Mizrahi's face glowed as he filled me in on all the details.

The execution was perfect. I learned an important lesson. No security measures can stop sophisticated, imaginative planning. In any solid wall one could find a crack through which one could slip in and carry out an attack.

We immediately contacted the press and the radio stations in France and England as well as all the embassies in the French capital. In our communique we said that the operation was only a prelude, and we would continue to strike at the British capital, its leadership and institutions until the British left our land.

Letter Bombs

One week after the attack on the Colonial Office in London, I had another idea how to punish the British leadership. I came to the conclusion the best way to do it was through letter bombs. I was going to send an official letter addressed to a government member, with enough explosives to kill him. In 1947 I invented the letter bomb.

To make that bomb I needed special tools and skills. I could have used a sophisticated lab, but I had to make do without one. The elements I used were the following: High quality blasting gelatin, 9000-10,000 yards per second, powerful enough to kill at least one person. It weighed between 0.5-1 pound, and was shaped like a candle. It could be flattened and put inside an envelope, and remained soft so no one could suspect there was anything inside besides paper. I obtained fresh material that was easy to work with and did not emit poisonous gas that endangered the worker. As a safety measure, I used direct current detonators.

I would test the detonators with a voltometer, and use Eveready batteries, which were small and flat and could be easily hidden inside an envelope. To ensure the explosion, I used two detonators as well as two batteries, which I always checked beforehand.

The most important component was the firing device. When the envelope was opened this device connected the circuit from the batteries to the detonators and caused the explosion. I invented a rudimentary mechanism which remained open inside the envelope and would close as soon as the envelope was opened. All the components were attached to a thin sheet of cardboard so we could easily insert them into the envelope. The explosive charges were also attached to the cardboard. Inside the charges we attached the detonators. We then attached the batteries to the cardboard and underneath them we tied the firing device, with the spring pointing to the bottom of the envelope. When the envelope was opened the spring was released, the circuit was closed and the envelope exploded.

It was a most delicate operation. In order not to cause an explosion prior to putting the device into the envelope we would disconnect the detonators and put in their place a small electric bulb that could be lit by the batteries. We put the device into the envelope with disconnected detonators and a lit bulb. If the device was properly installed in the envelope, the bulb would go off, since the circuit inside the envelope was open. Now we had to seal the envelope, making sure the firing device remained disconnected. One of us would hold the envelope while the other took out the lightbulb and connected the detonators to the electric current. We sealed the envelope which now became a deadly trap.

We would use gray official British envelopes with the government heading. It was the best cover, since British officials expected to get mail

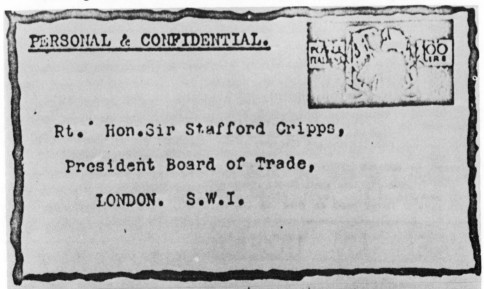

PERSONAL & CONFIDENTIAL.

Rt. Hon. Sir Stafford Cripps,

President Board of Trade,

LONDON. S.W.I.

Letter bomb to Sir Stafford . . . Postage 100 lire—about 2s. 3d.

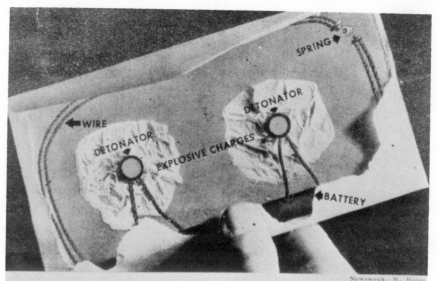

Letter from Turin: Palestine terrorists aim at top-ranking British officials

from their embassies around the world. The outer envelope had the address, while the inner one had the name of the minister and the words Personal and Confidential. We expected the secretary to open the first one, and let the boss open the second one.

It was a tedious job finding out the exact names and addresses of our targets. We had to obtain official government publications for that purpose. We also used the British press, especially the London *Times*. We got assistance from the British Institute for Foreign Studies, Paris branch. Thus we collected some seventy names and addresses.

In order to fill seventy envelopes we needed a large quantity of explosives and detonators. We could not obtain them in Paris, and had to contact a mine administrator in the Marseilles area through one of our members. The administrator agreed to loan us from his mines the explosives and detonators we needed. I had no choice at that time but to take my wife who was in her last month of pregnancy on a 12-hour train journey to Marseilles to pick up the material and bring it back to Paris. From Marseilles we travelled to the mines, where I took a suitcase full of explosives while Hannah took another one filled with detonators. The mine administrator was a French Jew who took great interest in the Jewish war for national liberation. He asked us many questions and gave us his blessing. We thanked him for his help and parted as good friends. When we got back to the train station I suddenly remembered I had forgotten something at the hotel where we had stayed. I left Hannah at the station with the two explosive suitcases and rushed to the hotel. When I came back she told me that while I was gone the customs officials came by and began to search for smuggled goods. Marseilles, of course, had always been an international smuggling center. Fortunately, they skipped Hannah, since they probably did not suspect a pregnant woman. Thus our oldest daughter, Irit, unbeknownst to her, helped her parents with their underground work.

As I had mentioned before, we had decided not to compromise French neutrality by operating on French soil. While we assembled the bombs and trained our people in France, we did our best not to operate directly out of France. We wanted to avoid using French stamps on the envelopes, so we decided to mail them from neighboring countries. For the most part we used Italy, since we had experience in slipping across the French-Italian border. Our experts in that area were Herzl Amiqam who had come to us illegally from Italy, and Zimka Randel who had served in the Jewish Brigade and joined LEHI in Europe. I assigned Zimka the task of taking the envelopes to Italy.

He took most of the envelopes, about sixty of them, put them in a knapsack and crossed the border like an alpinist. He reached Turin, where he mailed the letters, from different post offices, his heart pounding at each mailing. The post office person would attach the stamps and then apply a powerful cancellation pounding with his rubber stamp. Fortunately, there was no firing device in the upper right corner of the envelope. Each pounding, however, if not well directed, could have caused an explosion.

The post office in Turin must have thought Zimka was a British official, and saw to it that the letters were sent right away. But the good fortune Zimka had encountered in Italy evaded me when I went to Belgium.

THIRTY-THREE

Arrest in Belgium

Before I took the train to Belgium I met my aid, Amiqam, near the Arc de Triomphe. I gave him instructions on how to run the office in my absence. As we strolled about we bought chestnuts and cherries from street vendors and did not have to stop for lunch. As I was spitting the pits I told Herzl I had to go to Brussels that evening with Betty Knut and Rosenberger, and I did not have a good feeling. It was one of the few times I had such a feeling. In Belgium I was going to bomb a British destroyer, and act against the British Embassy and the Western Europe British Command, which was headquartered in the Belgian capital at that time. In addition, I intended to mail letter bombs from there to London. Those were major, complicated operations, and I did not trust anyone except myself to set the bombs and personally supervise the operations. I also wanted to meet with our Belgian cell which I had recently formed, since I knew they were suffering from inaction.

Betty Knut had to carry on her person the charges for the British destroyer. She and Rosenberger had double-bottom suitcases in which they would carry the letter bombs. The destroyer in question was none other than the *Chevron*, which we had failed to bomb in Egypt after she had been engaged in hunting Jewish immigrants in the eastern Mediterranean.

After I said goodbye to Herzl I met Betty and Rosenberger and we went to my office. The charges were carefully concealed under Betty's clothes. We had learned from our experience that on the express train bound for Belgium the customs officials did not frisk the passengers. We had high hopes for that operation, since we knew it would make a great impression around the world and might help the British to make up their minds to leave our land and let our people become free. But disaster awaited us from the outset. First, we missed the express train. We had to take the *Rapide* train, which was thoroughly searched by customs officials. I must confess that I knew the difference between the two trains and I should have postponed the trip until the next day. But this time I was lax, either because of carelessness or haste. I did not think logically and I insisted on sticking to my timetable.

When we reached the Belgian border the passengers had to get off the train, including the three of us. Our suitcases had to go through the routine customs check. As the train crowd was marching into the station, one woman customs official suddenly called Betty to come over for an inspection. It must have been a new procedure which was introduced after my last trip to that country. When they told her to come over I knew they would find out what she was carrying, so I took her suitcase and walked with it into the customs hall. Rosenberger and I passed the inspection without any problems, and we sat at the snack bar on the Belgian side of the border, sipping coffee and trying to decide what to do about Betty's imminent arrest. At that moment Betty showed up, and turned directly to me.

Betty was indeed caught carrying the charges, but she said she was smuggling it in for money, and intended to return to France. The official reassured her she would be able to resume her trip once the contraband was confiscated. In the meantime he told her to wait on the Belgian side, since he needed an authorization from the local police chief to let her continue her trip. Betty was fooled by the official's friendly reassurance.

I was about to yell at Betty for her carelessness in walking over toward me when a Belgian official tapped my shoulder and said politely, "Would you please come with me." Betty quickly realized the damage she had caused the underground, but it was too late. I had no choice but to go along with him, as other customs officials were looking on, ready to come to his aid. He also asked me about Rosenberger, but I made a motion with my hand as if to say, he has nothing to do with it. Rosenberger played along, pretending to be a stranger we had met on the train.

After I was taken in, Rosenberger took his suitcase with the letter bombs and boarded the train, leaving Betty's suitcase behind. The suitcase aroused suspicion and was taken in for inspection. Betty's personal belongings were in it, and the false bottom was soon discovered. They began to cut the bottom with a knife. I told Betty I was going to step on her foot as a signal for her to get up and tell them not to open the envelopes, since there was no point in any of them being harmed and in us being accused of murder.

Betty and I were extremely tense. The officials were experienced professionals. They carefully opened the false bottom and discovered the letter bombs neatly arranged side by side. The chief of customs took one envelope and read the address: Mr. Shaw, the Secretary General of the British Administration in Palestine. I was about to step on Betty's foot, but it was not necessary. One envelope for some odd reason had an electric wire protruding at one end. When the official saw it his eyes almost popped out as he began to shout: "Bomb! Bomb!"

He quickly put down the envelope on the table and all the customs staff began to move away from the envelopes. They hid behind the doors

LETTER BOMB PLOT. Jacob Elias, a Stateless Jew of Russian extraction, and Gilberte Lazarus, a French Jewess, who have been remanded after being charged in Belgium. It was alleged that the woman had concealed letter bombs in her luggage when passing the frontier.

and began to swear at us. I felt greatly relieved, since I no longer had to worry about any of them getting hurt. Now they would bring a bomb expert and dismantle the envelopes. One official, however, yelled at me: "Too bad Hitler did not kill all of you." I told him exactly what I thought of him.

The customs officials now realized how dangerous we were, and they called for reinforcement. Suddenly I saw gun barrels pointed at us from every door and window. We sat there for about an hour, surrounded by those guns, when police in armored cars came and sealed off the customs house. They walked in and turned to us. They handcuffed each one of us and took us away separately. The next time I saw Betty was in the courthouse.

I was taken to the Mons police station. Previously, when I was first searched by customs, they felt something in my outer chest pocket and asked me what it was. I told them it was a watch. This caused them a great deal of consternation. When the Scotland Yard representative came to Belgium later on to ask for my extradition, he commented after he read the report that my timepiece was most likely an explosive watch, and asked the Belgians to do all they could to find that watch. They turned the customs house upside down and even searched the sewer, but could not find the watch. I did throw it in the sewer after I was arrested, when they let me go into the bathroom. Fortunately they did not find it, and could not accuse me of trying to commit an act of sabotage in Belgium.

When we arrived in the town of Mons, I was taken in for a thorough investigation at the local police station. I was brought in under a heavy guard. Three respectable-looking gentlemen were sitting there, who turned out to be the district police commander, the district head detective, and the customs chief. A stenographer was sitting at the end of the table, ready to take down my statement. They had also brought an interpreter. I told them very firmly: "I don't know, I haven't seen, I haven't heard. I have come to Belgium for a visit. I met the lady on the train, as any man would meet a nice woman, and that was the extent of our relation."

They kept questioning me but I refused to add anything. After half an hour they gave up. The stenographer did not even use her writing instruments. They were angry and at one point they turned red. But they had no choice but to send me to jail. In Belgium, as in the rest of Europe, the first questioning is done by the police. After the arrestee is put in jail, the investigation is continued by a judge who decides whether to put the suspect on trial or to free him.

When I entered my cell it was late in the evening. I fell asleep right away. The next morning I was awakened by a knock on the door. A small window opened and I was served tea, soup, bread and jelly. I ate with great appetite and started to survey my surroundings. The cell was about five by eight feet, barely large enough for the bed. The bed could be folded into a table, and there was a chair in the corner. There was a small window near the ceiling with three layers of bars. In the door there was a peephole for the warden to look in. They used that cell to keep prisoners up to five years, as if that were the period of time for someone to be left alone and repent. After five years the prisoner was transferred to a larger cell with other inmates, and could work in the prison shops. I found out later on that some prisoners in Belgium who were kept in that solitary confinement for five years had lost their sanity.

During the first few days of my stay in jail I was treated cordially. I saw the prison director who told me my offense was not so serious and I should be able to be let off with a fine or a token jail term. I was not too closely guarded, and was even allowed to take walks with other inmates in the courtyard, which meant that I was not too dangerous. But after a few days things changed. I was taken to the prison office and was made to wait with my face to the wall, which was the procedure used with inmates who waited for an appointment. After I stood in this position for a few moments the door opened and someone addressed me by my old name, Levstein, which I had since Hebraized to Eliav. I instinctively turned my head, when I heard: "Aha, Mr. Levstein, we have finally caught you. Now you can no longer hide behind the name Elias, which is written on your travel document."

The person who called me by my old name invited me into the room. I went in and saw a very distinguished group of men. The three who had originally questioned me were there. They were joined by the chief of the Belgian police, the commander of the Belgian secret police, someone from the Belgian justice ministry, and, among them, appearing rather expansive, a typical English gentleman in a striped suit. By his clothes, physical stature and haircut, I could tell right away what his profession was. He had a picture spread in front of him, and kept glancing at it and at me, back and forth. I realized I was sitting before a Scotland Yard person who had all he needed to know about me, having received my file from the British police back in my homeland. He passed the pictures around, and everyone agreed on the resemblance between one picture in particular and myself.

They took me into the investigation room where a secretary sat behind a typewriter. As soon as I sat down they began to fire questions at me. First they wanted to establish my identity. "Surely," one of them said, "your name is Levstein. You have escaped from the central prison in Jerusalem and now you are the LEHI commander in Europe, and you are the one responsible for mailing the letter bombs. You have sent Betty Knut with explosive charges concealed on her person to blow up the destroyer *Chevron* which was visiting Belgium, and you must have planned to bomb the British Embassy in Brussels." They added: "We know everything, so you may as well confess so we may reduce your sentence."

Without batting an eyelash I said to them: "I have nothing to do with the name Levstein. I don't know where you got it from. My name is Elias. I am a survivor of the concentration camps. I have nothing to do with LEHI. Therefore, I have no connection to any of the things you are accusing me of. I am innocent, and I demand that you release me immediately."

They questioned me for about an hour. I stuck to my guns: my name is Elias. I have nothing against Belgium. I only came on a visit. My words angered the British agent. He showed something in the book he was holding to the Belgian head detective. The latter jumped up and took my right arm. He looked at my elbow and saw a scar. He pointed at it and shouted: "Of course you are Levstein. You have a scar."

This scar had been recorded by the CID. It was a result of a grenade wound I suffered in one of our operations.

The Belgian detective shouted again: "You don't admit you are Levstein?" I told him again I was Elias and knew nothing about Levstein. I was so angry I stood up and said that to judge from the looks and manner of the person sitting opposite me I could tell he was an Englishman, and I did not think it was proper for the Belgians to have a British official at my investigation, and therefore I would not answer any questions. I could not understand why the Belgians would want to question me in his presence.

The investigators lost their patience. They began to shout at the wardens to take me away. When I walked out I was surrounded and watched like the most dangerous person in the world. They took me to the prison lab and gave me "special cosmetics," as we used to call it, befitting a dangerous prisoner. They photographed me from all sides, fingerprinted me again, took blood and hair samples, and checked me from head to foot for special marks. They took me back to my cell where the light was left on now day and night. They installed a lamp over my head to light my face, and did not allow me to cover my head, which was a real torture. The guard would peek in every hour to make sure I had not evaporated. A sign was affixed to my jail door which read: "Very dangerous prisoner, special security arrangements." The other inmates nicknamed me the Dynamite Man. I was limited in my walks and could only go to an enclosed yard.

After my arrest it was not difficult for Scotland Yard to realize that LEHI had launched a letter bomb attack on important people and institutions in the British capital. Scotland Yard sent instructions to all concerned not to open any envelopes before they underwent an inspection. The letters sent by our man from Turin, Italy, were discovered, as well as the ones that Rosenberger had managed to bring into Belgium and mail.

Our letters did not explode, but they served their purpose. The British were afraid of additional attacks. They posted guards at all the government buildings, and gave each member of government special protective measures, such as bodyguards and an escort police car, as well as guards at the minister's private residence. In the meantime, the British began to pressure the Belgian authorities to extradite me. They argued that they had found my fingerprints on the bomb at the Colonial Office which did not explode. In addition, it was clear to them I was the one who had assembled the letter bombs that had been sent to England.

My friends in Paris came to my rescue, especially Herzl Amiqam, who did not spare any effort to foil the British designs. My friendship with Andre Blumel proved most useful. When he found out about my arrest he came to my aid. He was even able to secure a large contribution from Guy de Rothschild, who gave willingly, on humanitarian grounds.

After he mailed the letters from Belgium, Rosenberger returned immediately to Paris and told Amiqam what had happened at the border. Herzl assumed, of course, that the British would discover my identity and do everything they could to have me extradited. He did everything he could to have my jail term shortened, so I could return to active duty. While Herzl was active on the outside, I was undergoing a jail experience which was no different from anything in the past. After Betty and I were captured the entire European press was filled with the news. The papers kept writing about letter bombs, about our arrest, the time bomb Betty

had put in the British Colonial Office, and of course the LEHI organization, its aims, its tactics and its ideology. Inside the prison I was given a
special status because of the security arrangements the prison had provided in my honor. Even the guards gave me special treatment, despite
my classification as "dangerous."

One day I received a kosher gourmet food package. The guard told
me it had been sent by a Jewish family from Mons. The family, named
Mandelbaum, said they were willing to send me anything I needed. It
was my first contact with my fellow Jews. I was not alone. Even in the
Mons prison I continued my mission and my fight. I asked for a rabbi,
and one was sent over. When I spoke to the prison director, I made it a
point to tell him about the Jews' war for national liberation.

One day I asked to see the prison director about a personal matter.
After he called me into his office I told him the conditions in the jail were
inhuman, and unless they were changed I would declare a hunger strike.
He told me he was only doing what he was being instructed to do. I
suggested to him he should not become personally implicated in this
problem. He might have concluded my friends on the outside would not
forgive him for it. He seemed to take my grievance seriously, and said he
would see what he could do. I waited for a week but there was no change.
I decided to take stronger measures. I announced that if within a week all
the special restrictions imposed on me were not removed, I would start
my hunger strike. I also wrote to the Queen Mother of Belgium, since
one of her charitable activities was helping prisoners. Two days before
my hunger strike was to start the director told me my petition was
accepted. The light over my head would be removed, although some
indirect lighting would be kept during the night. The warden would stop
bothering me by opening the peephole every hour, although they would
continue to watch me.

Before he left the director told me: "You know that Belgium is not
an interested party in the conflict between England and the Jewish
people. However, Belgium cannot allow action against the British on
Belgian soil, since the British are welcome guests in Belgium." Since I
continued to insist at that point that I had nothing to do with the letter
bombs or the charges found on Betty, I told him it was none of my
business. He did not say anything, but before he left he shook my hand
and smiled.

After the police investigation in which the Scotland Yard agent took
part, my case was handed over to the investigating judge, who had to

decide if there was cause for putting me on trial, and gather the evidence against me. The judge would summon me once a week, then every other week, for a questioning session on the reasons for my visit to Belgium. Did I intend to bomb the British Embassy in Brussels or perhaps the British destroyer *Chevron* during its visit to Belgium, or did I plan to put bombs in British cargo at the Antwerp harbor? As I listened to his questions I used to say to myself, I wish I had done at least some of the things you are mentioning. To him I said: "I know nothing about it, I have no idea what you are talking about." He also asked me about my friends in Brussels. I did visit Brussels before my arrest, and the police had found out in which hotel I was staying. They tried to listen in on my phone calls, but the hotel I stayed in had direct dialing and they were not able to monitor my calls. This fact made the judge quite unhappy.

During those sessions I had two surprise visits. The first was Andre Blumel, the well-known French leader and attorney, who had represented the French government in the negotiations with LEHI. This time he had brought with him two lawyers. One was the son of Kreton Devier, former justice minister of Belgium, and the other was my prospective defense attorney. Devier was going to defend Betty. They came to discuss my line of defense in court. I had gotten a message by then from the LEHI center back home and was instructed to lay my cards on the table in the courtroom and speak openly about the aims of LEHI's fight. Kreton and Blumel agreed with the line of defense. Blumel informed me France had requested my extradition, since the accusation of transporting explosive charges from France meant that my crime began in that country. Once I was sent back to France, Blumel would see to it that I was released.

The second unexpected visitor was my wife, Hannah, and my newly born daughter, Irit, who was then four months old. When I had left for Belgium Irit was only one month old. From the moment I was put in jail I did not stop for a moment worrying about my wife and daughter, and I suffered constantly. I was overjoyed to see Hannah, smiling at me, looking well, with a baby in her arms looking at me with bright eyes. Hannah told me all was well with her and the baby, and the only thing she had been worrying about was that I might be turned over to the British.

Hannah had brought me the decision of the LEHI center to allow me to appear before my captors in Belgium as a LEHI member and take my stand in the courtroom not as the accused but as the accuser. When I met again with the judge I finally told him I was a LEHI member and I gave him a long lecture about our ideology and the aims of our war in the Land of Israel. He listened with interest and recorded my statement, visibly happy to be able finally to write down that I had come to Belgium in order to perform the terrorist acts dictated by our ideology. I had to disappoint him again. I told him I had only come to Belgium to engage in propaganda. I said that in our country and in England we resorted to hostilities, but not in Belgium, since we did not wish to violate the neutrality of that lovely country, which had suffered so much under German occupation.

When he asked me for the names of LEHI members in Belgium my patience ended, and I asked him testily: "Did you collaborate with the German occupiers?" As I had expected, he was shaken to his core. He stood up and said: "Sir, I was a member of the Belgian underground during the German occupation. I fought against the Germans and I was even arrested, and only survived by sheer chance. I ask you not to insult me." This was exactly what I had hoped he would say. I told him that I admired his anti-German activities, which were proper for a Belgian who had national honor. I asked him: "Do you think I ought to betray my friends and give you a list of LEHI members in Belgium, so I can be accused of betraying my people?" He remained silent. After a while I could see a smile in his eyes. He said: "You win. You are right. I won't question you any further. I have no choice but to put you on trial, in the hope that the Belgian court will listen to your plea and will pass a just sentence."

Two weeks later I was brought before a Belgian court in the town of Mons on charges of smuggling explosives into Belgium in order to commit terrorist acts against the British in that country. I prepared thoroughly for that trial. I wrote my speeches carefully and memorized them. I saw my trial as another opportunity to fight our British enemy.

When the guards came to take me to court at 8 o'clock in the morning, I waited for them wearing a suit and tie, my face clean shaven and my hair neatly combed. A closed carriage waited for me outside, drawn by two Belgian horses. I was asked to climb into the back of it, where four armed policemen waited for me. Suddenly one of the Belgian gendarmes, in his Napoleonic uniform, looked at me with a sly smile and said, "Shmah Israel." He must have been a Belgian Jew who remembered two Jewish words of prayer.

The courthouse was surrounded by police, and as soon as I stepped down from the carriage I was surrounded by reporters and camerapersons who snapped my picture over and over again. In the courtroom I was assailed by the reporters who, over the objections of the police, tried to ask me questions. I spoke freely, although I was being careful not to say anything in all that excitement which might be misinterpreted.

It was a district court with three judges. The defendants were Betty Knut and myself. At the opening of the trial I denied the charges against me which referred to letter bombs and explosives intended for the British destroyer and British objectives in the Belgian capital. But I admitted I was a member of the LEHI underground. In a long discourse I explained why I was a LEHI member and what the goals of our struggle for national liberation were. I was surprised to find out that the presiding judge did not stop me and even nodded sympathetically. Betty's attorney and mine spoke next, and brought examples from the struggle of other nations for national liberation, mainly the fight of the Belgian underground against the German occupier. After both sides were heard, the judges went out to reach a verdict. The prosecutor asked for five years in prison, based on a Belgian law dating back to 1882. But from his own words, and more so from the judges' reactions, I could tell his case had little to do with present legal reality. The defense did not try too hard to refute him. After an hour-long consultation, the judges returned and announced the sentence. Betty was given one year in jail, and I was given eight months. Since I had already served four, I felt I was very close to becoming a free man.

After the trial I was able to communicate with the press. I told the reporters from now on LEHI would intensify its activities in Europe, and the main target was London. We had to force the British to reach the right conclusion and leave our land. As I walked out of the courtroom, a middle-aged man stood up and shook my hand. He said in Hebrew: "Be strong and of good courage. I am Mandelbaum." He was the man who had sent me kosher food packages while I was in jail.

When I returned to the jail the inmates were more friendly, as was the director. The name Dynamite Man was forgotten, and I was allowed to take more walks in the courtyard. Before long I was told I would be sent back to France after my release, as Blumel had promised me. One week before my release I received the good news that the Queen Mother had granted Betty clemency and she would be released after eight months as well.

On the day of my release I was driven to the French border. Here I was met by French detectives with a warrant for my arrest. They handcuffed me and even tied me to the chair. As I was trying to make sense out of my new predicament, the door opened and my wife, Hannah, flew into my arms. She told me I would be set free in a few days. All the French were doing was going through some formalities. She seemed very happy. After she left the room I was taken under heavy guard to the police station on the French side of the border, ostensibly to keep me there until it was decided what to do with me. I was taken to see the local chief of police, who looked stern as he said to me: "I know all about you. You cannot hide anything from me. Tell me, *entre nous*, did you really kill Englishmen?" I instinctively denied it. He had expected me to deny it and said: "Of course you deny it, I didn't expect you not to. I am not investigating you, you see. We are friends. As for your denial, if it is true, you are not worth anything in my eyes. One should kill the British wherever one can find them. They are pathological liars, and this is how they have ruled the whole world. I saw it myself. I served in Lebanon and in Syria in De Gaulle's Free France army. We spilled our blood helping the British in the Levant, and after they took over Lebanon and Syria they threw us to the dogs. This is why I support your struggle, and if you sent letter bombs to London and are responsible for the explosions in the British government offices, I admire you." He took out a bottle of wine and we drank to each other's health. He became excited and said: "Let us drink to your war of liberation, let us drink to your continued attacks on the British capital."

After he finished he embraced me and told me for the time being he had no choice but to put me in jail, but I should soon be released. He instructed one of his men to help me with my suitcase. I was taken into town, where I was shown into the jail, and put into a large cell full of criminals, murderers and rapists. I made myself at home, but three days later I was summoned to the prison office and told I was free. I was also given an official permission to remain in France. At the office I saw my friend, the chief of police. He wished me well and reminded me not to forget to kill Englishmen.

THIRTY-FOUR

The End of the Mission

On the train taking me to Paris I was flying high. I could not wait to see my wife and my baby daughter, whom I had barely held in my arms. As the train reached the station in north Paris and the passengers were getting off, I thought I was dreaming. I saw Hannah getting off another train. I dropped my suitcase and flew into her arms. She was so happy she almost burst into tears. We stood in the middle of the station hugging each other, unaware of anyone or anything around us.

For one day I enjoyed the bliss of a loving wife and a darling daughter. The next day I was back to work with our LEHI staff in Paris, discussing ways to renew our activities against the British. It seemed to me that I had exhausted the conventional terrorist tactics, and I began to look for new ideas.

But the decision of the United Nations to partition the Land of Israel and establish a Jewish state and the British announcement of their intention to evacuate our land changed everything. Our dream was being fulfilled, and it was no longer necessary to punish London.

At that point the LEHI center ordered a cessation of all action against the British abroad, and ordered its members to concentrate on the imminent battle against the Arab forces who were preparing to massacre the Hebrew Yishuv as soon as the British left. I decided to terminate my mission to Europe and return home earlier than I had originally planned.

My last mission before returning home was political. LEHI activities abroad gave the organization a reputation of a force fighting British imperialism. It was only natural that we gained the sympathy of the USSR and its communist allies. I decided to make contact with the Soviet Embassy in Paris. We had kept them on our mailing list and they received all our publications. One day I went with Betty Knut to the Soviet Embassy and we were received by a man who introduced himself as the first secretary of the embassy. He was probably their head of the secret police. We gave him a summary of our objectives. He showed particular interest in our anti-imperialist activities in the Middle East. We asked for political support and weapons, and for the opportunity to give Jews military training in the Soviet Union before they left for Israel. It was, in a way, Yair's 40,000 Plan. We decided on a way of communicating with him in case we got an answer from Moscow. The answer was slow in coming.

When I found out that Molotov, the Soviet foreign minister, was coming to Paris, I suggested to Betty Knut, who was his niece, to try and pay him a family visit, so she could use the occasion to explain to him what we were fighting for and what we needed. Betty did meet with Molotov and spoke to him about our organization. He listened without

Haj Amin al-Husseini confers with Hitler.

committing himself. Quite possibly, our contacts with the Soviets in Paris might have played a part in the Soviet Union's support of the UN resolution on the establishment of a Jewish state and of Czechoslovakia's decision to send arms to the new state, which were crucial to us in our War of Independence.

As I was about to leave Europe and enlist in our new army, I found out that the Grand Mufti of Jerusalem, Haj Amin al-Husseini, the arch-enemy of the Jews in the Middle East, had escaped from Germany and took refuge near Paris.

Al-Husseini headed the Arab marauders in the Land of Israel from the very beginning. During World War Two he went to Germany and assisted Hitler in the genocide of European Jewry. Now he came to Paris to save his own life. I ordered my men to follow him and find out a way to

The author (right) during Israel's War of Independence in 1948, with comrades Herzl Amiqam and Dov (the Blond) Granek.

kill him. They found out the best way to do it was by hiding a bomb in his car. I prepared a powerful bomb which would not have left a trace of him. Before we planted the bomb we found out he had disappeared.

On May 15, 1948 I returned to Israel with my little family by direct flight. That week I came out of the underground. After twelve years of clandestine fighting I enlisted in the Defense Army of Israel as second-in-command of the 89th Regiment, 8th Brigade, under Yitzhak Sadeh's command. I saw action in Lod, Ramleh, Metzudat Yoav and the battles of the Negev which ended in El Arish.

The author (pointing) as Golani regiment commander, explains the condition of the battlefield to Prime Minister Ben-Gurion and Chief of Staff Yigal Yadin.

Index